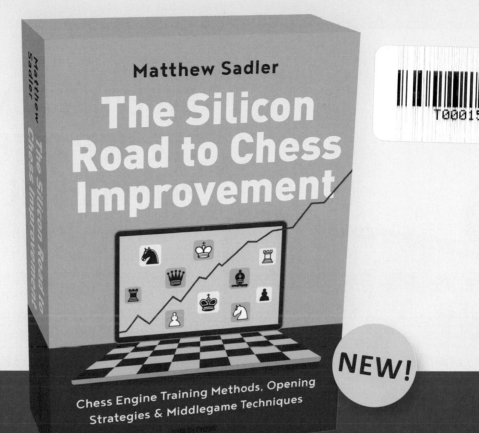

2021#7
NEW IN CHESS

Contents

'Block out time in your schedule to relax and think'

CONTRIBUTORS TO THIS ISSUE

James Altucher, Magnus Carlsen, Maria Emelianova, Jorden van Foreest, Anish Giri, Nils Grandelius, John Henderson, Ilya Levitov, Dylan Loeb McClain, Peter Heine Nielsen, Maxim Notkin, Judit Polgar, Matthew Sadler, Han Schut, David Smerdon, Jonathan Speelman, Jan Timman, Jonathan Tisdall, Thomas Willemze

SUBSCRIPTIONS: p. 96 COLOPHON: p. 9

Getting Blitzed

The word on the rue is there's a new chess-themed bar and restaurant in Paris: Blitz Society, located at 4 Rue du Sabot in the fashionable Saint-Germain-des-Prés district.

Blitz Society opened on October 15 with a promising premiss for hostelry-goers, their marketing slogan being 'Eat. Drink. Mate'. One of the four owners is the Swiss national youth coach FM Vincent Riff, who also runs the nearby chess school Palamède Echecs.

We did like the vibe coming from the pre-opening shots of Blitz Society – particularly the iconic photo of a deep-thinking Misha Tal overlooking a table in the bar. Certainly, the 8th World Chess Champion was no stranger himself to both blitz and the occasional libation or three!

Blitz with Mikhail Tal. Sounds good.

The Fat Slags Gambit

From tiny beginnings, the profane and surreal *Viz* magazine (a brilliant hybrid of punk fanzine and kids' comic) went on to sell a million copies in the United Kingdom – and made characters such as the Fat Slags, Spoilt Bastard and Roger Mellie household names. Now it turns its attention to Chess and the success of *The Queen's Gambit*, though with the frequently foul-mouthed comic's very own twist. The latest issue, 309, October 2021, has a wickedly satirical 5-page Chess Special, the reading of which surely would be enough to see a Swiss-based chess historian being rushed to his nearest intensive care unit, as it goes about its business with a toilet humour brand of anarchy and fakery.

The inviting cover of the Chess Special of *Viz* magazine.

It starts with a chess-themed front cover and the teaser 'chess-mad laundry worker takes Netflix to cleaners', a not-too subtle reference to just about everyone claiming to be the inspiration for Beth Harmon's backstory, not to mention the makers of *TQG* being sued by the five-time Women's World Champion Nona Gaprindashvili (see page 74).

But our favourite was the 'Where is it Now?' feature on Deep Blue, the IBM supercomputer that went from a high of challenging and then beating Garry Kasparov, to the nadir of working in low-budget porn movies – *Electric Deep Blue* and *Deep Blue Throat* – before being bought by a Silicon Valley startup and broke up for spare parts, only for its cooling fan and power cables to be salvaged and now on display in the World Chess Hall of Fame in St. Louis.

The Big Deal

It's always nice to hear of more sponsors coming forward to support the game. Still, FIDE made the news for all the wrong reasons in late September with a controversial new deal – hailed as the largest corporate sponsorship ever for the women's game – by partnering with the breast enlargement company Motiva (Establishment Labs).

The game's governing body faced a growing backlash from angry female players who claimed it to be 'gross' and 'misogynistic'. Speaking to *The New York Times*, IM Jennifer Shahade, the women's program director at the U.S. Chess Federation, didn't believe that the company should sponsor women's chess. 'It's not like breast implants are categorically bad, it's just another example of the ways in which women's looks are often given more attention than their moves and minds.'

Some titled players though welcomed the deal, such as IM Sheila Barth Stanford. 'We desperately need a sponsor,' the Norwegian said to *The Guardian*. 'We play for less money than the men, which makes it more difficult to bet on chess. I hope it makes it easier for women to play professionally.'

In a statement, FIDE's managing director, Dana Reizniece-Ozola, highlighted the benefits of breast reconstruction for cancer survivors who undergo mastectomies. 'At FIDE, we value Establishment Labs' commitment to women's health and well-being. The company supports expanded access to breast reconstruction and has been a pioneer in offering technologies that can improve the outcomes for these women.'

Jennifer Shahade believes the interest in women's chess should be about moves and minds.

She also added: 'FIDE is not encouraging plastic surgery, but if an adult freely makes this choice, our organisation endorses Motiva, a company that has demonstrated its strong commitment towards women.'

Just for Laughs

'He who laughs last, laughs the longest,' so goes the old idiom. But for Magnus Carlsen, he who laughs last could well turn out to be the winner, because through September and into October, that's the challenge of a crazy new Norwegian TV reality show he's appearing in.

The World Champion is a contestant in VGTV's 'Ikke lov å le på hytta' (in English, 'Not allowed to laugh in

Funny that Magnus Carlsen (right) looks surprised. He should have seen himself!

the cottage'), as twelve of Norway's funniest comedians, artists, sport personalities and influencers are stuck together in a cabin, with only one house rule: You cannot laugh.

In the seven-part, pre-recorded weekly series (clips can be found on YouTube with sub-titles), Carlsen is challenged to roast the other participants, play characters and tell jokes where the objective of the contest is to get everyone else to laugh. The one who manages this, and at the same time avoids cracking up from the other contestant's jokes, wins the prize.

And the reason for Carlsen's blonde wig and garish outfit in one of the shots released for the series, is his parody of Oslo après-ski prince and beat-master DJ Dan, as he teamed up with another contestant for a skit on recently ousted Prime Minister Erna Solberg, who had just lost the country's General Election as the first episode aired.

Carlsen advised friends and colleagues not to watch the reality show, as it is 'just awkward' for him. But his good friend Norwegian GM Jon Ludvig Hammer showed no mercy, quipping: 'That's got to be the best reason for me to watch the show!'

Torre! Torre! Torre!

'There are heroes who never were' is the intriguing tagline for the new Mexican documentary *Torre x Torre* (Artegios, 105 minutes) on the enigma that was Carlos Torre Repetto, now available to rent or stream anytime on Vimeo, Google Play, Apple TV and many other digital platforms.

Using rare archive footage, photographs and interviews, it tells the sad story of Torre, who at 21, following a series of impressive performances through 1924-26, was considered world champion material. But tragedy struck when Torre suffered a nervous breakdown in New York City and was forced to return home to Mérida. He never played competitive chess again and died impoverished in 1978, just a year after FIDE retrospectively bestowed the Grandmaster title on him.

Carlos Torre, a star that faded suddenly.

The documentary is directed by Juan Obergón and Roberto Garza, and includes new material and insight from Gabriel Velasco, the author of *The Life and Times of Carlos Torre*.

Fighting Chess

It was a fitting end to an epic trilogy, and hailed to be one of the greatest fights in history, as Tyson Fury knocked out Deontay Wilder in the 11th round of what proved to be a tumultuous contest to retain his WBC heavyweight title in Las Vegas. But spare a thought for the guy who 'coulda been a contender', as the saying goes.

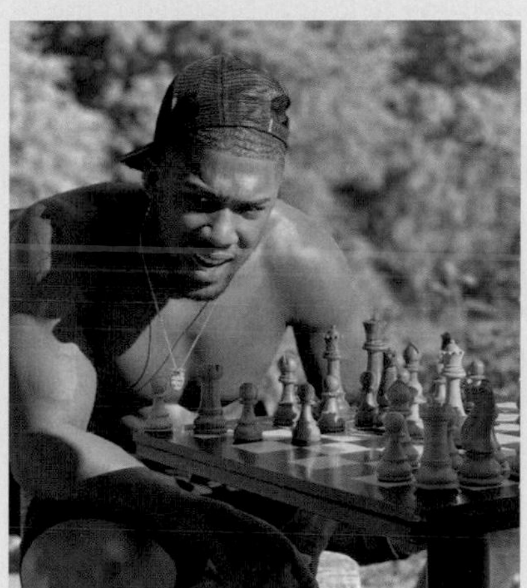

Anthony Joshua is hoping that mental strength will be the secret weapon to upset Tyson Fury.

That's Anthony Joshua, the now former WBA, WBO and IBF heavyweight king who was originally scheduled to take on Fury back in the summer, in what was expected to be the first part of their unification double-header. But AJ's plans were put in check when the 'Gypsy King' was ordered to fight Wilder for a third time.

When the Fury fight was cancelled in May, the British superstar went on a social media blitz to plot his next move – and that involved stripping down to his shorts, not to take to the ring, but to play topless chess, claiming he would instead be honing his mental and strategic skills. ■

Your Move

The Golmayo's

In New In Chess 2021/6, in NIC's Café, the story was told of father and son Heidenfeld, who were both national chess champions, and the reader was invited to come up with other examples. While reading the article, I immediately thought of the Golmayo family. The father, Celso Golmayo Zúpide (1820-1898), was a Spanish attorney who spent most of his life in Cuba. After beating Sicre in 1862, he remained the unofficial Cuban champion almost until his death in 1898. In this period, he took part in the famous 1867 Paris tournament, where he placed 7th in a strong field that featured some of the 19th century greats like Kolisch, Winawer and Steinitz. He also helped turn Cuba into a chess mecca, which resulted in frequent visits by distinguished masters and in the organization of several international contests, including the two Steinitz-Chigorin World Championship matches in 1889 and 1892. As champion of the host island, Celso Golmayo played many of the visitors, losing interesting matches to Steinitz, Blackburne, Mackenzie and Lasker.

Celso had two sons, who both became prominent chess players. Celso junior, or 'Celsito' (1879-1924), won the Cuban championship in 1897, ahead of Juan Corzo and his younger brother Manuel (1883-1973). The triumph of an 18-year-old boy, and the good showing of 14-year-old Manuel, caused quite a stir in Cuban chess circles, somehow anticipating the rise of Capablanca a few years later.

When Cuba became independent, in 1898, Celso Jr and Manuel moved to Spain. The first Spanish Chess Championship, organized to celebrate the crowning of King Alfonso XIII in 1902, saw the triumph of Manuel Golmayo. He remained Spanish champion for nearly 30 years until he lost his title to Ramón Rey Ardid in 1930. Similar to his father in Cuba, Manuel was a pivotal figure in the Spanish chess scene of the early 20th century. In 1922 he lost a 2-game match against Alexander Alekhine, who was touring Spain, but managed to draw the second game with a study-like finish. He ended fourth in the 1928 Amateur World Championship in The Hague won by Euwe, and finished sixth in the 1929 Barcelona tournament where Tartakower gave birth to the Catalan Opening.

The Golmayo family, father and two sons, dominated chess life in Cuba and Spain for nearly 70 years. Not a record, perhaps, but no mean achievement either.

Fernando Luis
Zaragoza, Spain

Limiting the damage

I always enjoy Max Notkin's tactics column 'Maximize Your Tactics', and I am always impressed how compact the analysis of the 9 tactics is on one page! However, in New In Chess 2021/6, on page 78 in the 5th position taken from the game Barsegyan-Cuenca, Barcelona 2021, I think he missed a better defensive move for White:

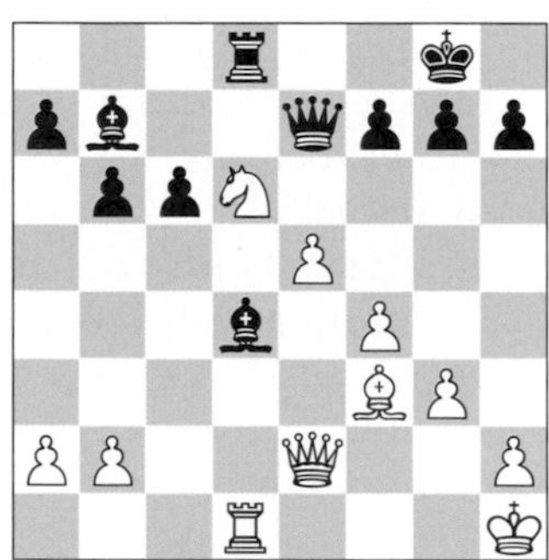

Barsegyan-Cuenca
Barcelona 2021

24...♖xd6! Eliminating the strong white knight. **25.exd6 ♕xe2 26.♗xe2** And White resigned, as after 26...c5+ he is checkmated.

After 24...♖xd6 White also has 25.♕e4!? (instead of 25.exd6, as given by Notkin), after which both Black's rook on d6 and bishop on d4 are attacked. After this move I believe White can limit the damage in the end to being one pawn down in a possibly tenable rook (bishop) endgame: 25...♗xe5(!) 26.♖e1!,

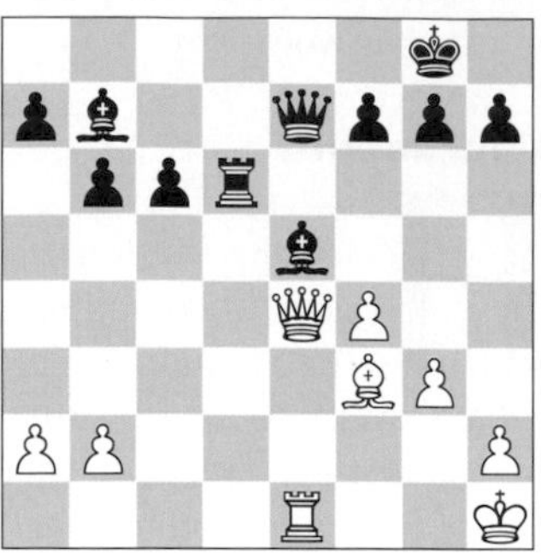

and now for example 26...♖d7 27.♕xe5 ♕xe5 28.♖xe5 ♔f8 (29.♖e8 mate was threatened) 29.♖e2 c5 30.♗xb7 ♖xb7 31.a4.

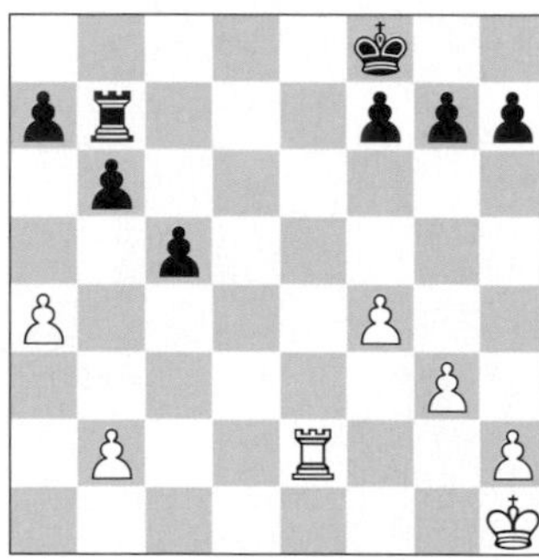

I have to admit I didn't use an engine and I am looking forward to Max Notkin's counter-analysis.

Boudewijn van Beckhoven
Amsterdam, The Netherlands

Postscript Max Notkin:

Kudos to Mr. van Beckhoven for spotting this smart resource! True, it doesn't change the general assessment as in the final position of his analysis White is lost after, say, 31...♖e7 32.♖d2 ♖e4. And even without the weakening a2-a4, Black will win by gradually bringing the king to the queenside and creating a passed pawn there. Besides, Black has other good options to emerge with at least a sound extra pawn, e.g. 26...♖e6 27.fxe5 f6 or 26...♖d5 27.fxe5 c5 threatening ...♖d1!. Nonetheless, 25.♕e4 (first choice of the engines)

Letter of the Month

The case for Chess15 (rather than 960)

With the aim of avoiding ever-expanding opening theory, Chess 960 has grown to be the most popular alternative to classical chess. However, is this the best solution?

The following idea of reducing Chess960 to Chess15 was prompted by Vladimir Kramnik's recent suggestion of a no-castling version of chess. While no doubt interesting to play, it merely defers the problem, as it too is only one layer of complexity and is just as vulnerable to eventually being played out. (Actually, it is slightly less complex than chess, as castling will be removed from some nodes of the analysis tree.)

This made me realize precisely the opposite: To best preserve the character of classical chess, castling must be retained as it is. Not changing the way the pieces move is fundamental to retaining the nature of the game. Ill-fated have been attempts to add pieces and increase the size of the board (such as that suggested by Capablanca and others).

In order to achieve this the kings and rooks need to all be on their same initial squares as in classical chess. The remainder of the pieces are then randomized in the starting positions, which are the same for Black and White. There are 30 permutations of these positions. With the opposite-coloured bishops' constraint that reduces to 16. Less one for the classical chess initial position gives Chess15.

Chess15 allows the retention of conventional castling and only allows permutations of the initial position with the same board and pieces that have all the pieces move in the same way. The 15 layers of complexity are enough to make memorizing opening theory impractical while retaining as much of the character of the classical game as possible. Only in future centuries, when Chess15 is played out, should we consider expanding to a larger subset of the 960.

Paul van Rensburg
Cape Town, South Africa

Write and win!
If your letter to the editor gets selected as 'Letter of the Month', you will receive a book by Jan Timman signed by the author.

Write your letter to:
New In Chess, P.O. Box 1093
1810 KB Alkmaar, The Netherlands
or e-mail: editors@newinchess.com
Letters may be edited or abridged

is critical and the most challenging move, after which Black has to find the only tactical way to claim an advantage. Therefore, this line should have been indicated in my notes.

Tennis and chess

In the profile of tennis star Daniil Medvedev in New in Chess 2021/5, it is stated that tennis uses a version of the Elo rating system. Nothing could be further from the truth; tennis rankings are determined solely by how far one goes in a tournament and how prestigious the tournament is, with no account taken of the strength of the opposition, and hence is philosophically worlds apart from Professor Elo's system.

Andrew Mendelson
Dublin, Ireland

Postscript John Henderson:

Thank you for your letter. While the ratings in chess and tennis differ, the Association of Tennis Professionals (ATP) – the world governing body for men's tennis – in 1972, after the success of the Elo list in chess, formally computerised tennis rankings. The ATP also based their world rankings on an interpretation of Prof Arpad Elo's system, and acknowledged as such, the list often being referred to in publications as the 'Elo list', 'Elo indicator' or 'Elo top ten', such as in a recent article on the Tennis Signal website entitled 'Daniil Medvedev's Leading Elo Indicator'.

Ripped off

I was disappointed that Mr Timman (see New In Chess 2021/5) seems to think that by writing a low-quality book of the match, Ray Keene was somehow justified in breaking the terms of his contract with Kortchnoi in 1978. The quality of the book is irrelevant. A contract is a contract. The other damning implication of Timman's words is that anyone who bought the book was clearly ripped off.

Paul Pritchard
Harrogate, UK

COLOPHON

PUBLISHER: Remmelt Otten
EDITOR-IN-CHIEF:
Dirk Jan ten Geuzendam
HONORARY EDITOR: Jan Timman
CONTRIBUTING EDITOR: Anish Giri
EDITORS: Peter Boel, René Olthof
PRODUCTION: Joop de Groot
TRANSLATOR: Piet Verhagen
SALES AND ADVERTISING: Edwin van Haastert
PHOTOS AND ILLUSTRATIONS IN THIS ISSUE:
Boris Dolmatovsky, Maria Emelianova, Lars Hedlund, Eteri Kublashvili, Lennart Ootes, Berend Vonk
COVER PHOTO: Eteri Kublashvili
COVER DESIGN: Hélène Bergmans

NEW IN CHESS
P.O. BOX 1093
1810 KB ALKMAAR
THE NETHERLANDS

PHONE: 00-31-(0)72-51 27 137
SUBSCRIPTIONS: nic@newinchess.com
EDITORS: editors@newinchess.com

WWW.NEWINCHESS.COM

Great Chess Coming

What are Ian Nepomniachtchi's chances against Magnus Carlsen?

For a third time, Magnus Carlsen will face a prodigious talent born in 1990, the same year as he himself appeared on earth, in a World Championship match. **ILYA LEVITOV** weighs the chances of the Champ and his Challenger, Ian Nepomniachtchi, whom the author has come to appreciate as 'an educated, sharp, and incredibly gifted person'.

'Some players are very strong in tournaments, but not dangerous in matches. In a tournament, you can sometimes win thanks to a rapid onslaught, pressure, whereas in a match, something can be achieved only by objective knowledge, maximum patience, care and work.' (Georg Marco, *Wiener Schachzeitung* 1909)

The summer of 2010 in Moscow was hell on earth. The temperatures got slowly but surely over 40 degrees, burning peatlands were covering the city in a caustic fog and people were afraid to leave home, fearing they would stifle. What on earth could force me to stay in town at that moment? Chess. I had just begun my work, precisely at that time, as Executive Director of the Russian Chess Federation. Heading to the old building on 14 Gogolevsky Boulevard and upon finding no air-conditioning there, I understood I was up for a long and tough fight in order to save this endgame.

My first visitor was a young and talented player... Ian Nepomniachtchi. As I remember now, he came wearing a jersey on which was written 'Russia', and asked for help in the preparation for an upcoming competition. I didn't know him until that moment, and communication between us was extremely difficult. I didn't understand 90% of what he said – not only does Ian play quickly, he expresses his thoughts at the exact same pace. At that moment I thought to myself that, in fact, the lack of air-conditioning was not going to be my main issue anymore...

A couple of months later we flew over to Taganrog together, where Ian had to play a simul. In the plane something struck me: he opened a classical Russian novel and dove into it for a couple of hours. Once I started to understand what he was saying, Ian bred in me a deep and lasting feeling of affection, which was only reinforced with time. He is an educated, sharp, incredibly gifted person, with an intricate personality (I have a liking for such people).

Not only does Ian play quickly, he expresses his thoughts at the exact same pace

Over the years we got a tad closer, in fact, as much as it is possible with a top-level chess player. I saw him fall apart, when it seemed that this bright young man would remain in the category of the 'up-and-coming players'. I saw him surge also, when he began giving the impression that he could beat anyone at any given moment.

Little by little, Ian began to get rid of his weaknesses. Gradually, step by step, he moved towards becoming a stable player, a feature he had always been missing, and by 2019 he was already there. A strong motivation for self-fulfilment emerged – time goes by, enough joking around, time had come to go for it. A team was gathered, goals were set, new problems emerged, everything was all of a sudden in its right place. Ian's winning performance at the Candidates Tournament is the product of his work on himself – the hardest work there is, not only for chess players.

Playing football with Magnus

I do not recall whether it was in 2012 or in 2013 that Ian called me and said 'Do you want to play football with Magnus Carlsen who's here on a training camp?' Don't ask me

Their last game before the match was the Armageddon game in the final round of Norway Chess. Having won the Armageddon game in Round 4, Magnus Carlsen again defeated Ian Nepomniachtchi, this time with the black pieces.

twice, nor my chess boss at the time, Arkady Dvorkovich. It was very interesting to me to see Magnus in a live environment and have a chance to get to know him better. His style at football struck me – I never saw in anyone such a willingness to beat an opponent. During the whole match, he passed the ball to his teammates two or three times, and time and time again he tried to dribble people he didn't manage to dribble. He broke his neck here and there, but kept going forward anyway. It was a rather curious scene to witness, a rather strange one. At the same time, by the way, Ian scored the decisive goal of the match... After that we had dinner, and I saw in front of me a person with whom I couldn't establish contact. Magnus was in his own world, immerged in his thoughts, and wouldn't react immediately to anyone talking to him. A great chess player, to put it bluntly.

Half a year ago, I interviewed Magnus on my YouTube channel, and was absolutely amazed. Quick-witted, talkative and very alert. Ten years had passed, and he was unrecognizable. He now streams on YouTube from a jacuzzi, jabs at Anish Giri, gives funny interviews, jokes on Twitter and so on, and so forth. I cannot believe that this came to him easily, I am almost sure it took him quite some work on himself to not only become the face of contemporary chess, but also the grand leader of an industry called Play Magnus.

A formidable champion

It seems absolutely logical and right to me that precisely these two opponents are to face up in a match.

Magnus Carlsen is a formidable champion, who will already play his fifth(!) World Championship match. A chess player who has absolutely been dominating chess for more than ten years already, with no desire to stop here. It is clear that Carlsen is firmly determined to take away from Kasparov the spot of Greatest Of All Time.

Ian Nepomniachtchi is a natural talent, who has learnt about everything you could possibly do in chess. He shows fantastic preparation, is by no means afraid of getting himself into the most complex of fights and can bother anyone in any equal endgame. He overall possesses all the modern top-player arsenal. On top of which he plays incredibly quickly and always poses problems to his opponents. His style of play

It is clear that Carlsen is firmly determined to take away from Kasparov the spot of Greatest Of All Time

MARIA EMELIANOVA

Both the Champion and the Challenger are fanatical football players.

was very acutely described by Alexander Grischuk: 'You can beat Ian in a game, but you will not enjoy the process whatsoever.'

The ability to change oneself, evolve and rise above oneself is always what struck me the most with chess players. I remember how difficult it was in 2016 for Magnus against Sergey Karjakin in the World Championship match in New York. How he worried during the games, how nothing went his way, how he escaped from the press-conferences... Nevertheless, the Champion managed to overcome his moments of weakness and in the end got the better of his remarkably well-prepared opponent.

That is a different story for Ian – he is such a man, after all, but he learnt patience, how to play dry positions, how to make draws, and how to patiently wait in order to take his chance.

I can assure you that this will be a match for the ages. We, the chess fans, did deserve that.

Incredible marathon

In 2016, no one could talk to Sergey Karjakin for a few months. His wife Galiya kept his phone, and she examined the requests he received – whether they were worth bothering Sergey for or not, whether they were distracting him from his preparation to the match. Chess players used to disappear for a couple of months prior to a world title match, and one could only guess in which state of form they were. Naturally, Ian followed this secular tradition and almost dropped off from the face of the earth. He successfully warmed up in a blitz tournament in Moscow, then played rather poorly in Stavanger, and disappeared.

In contrast, what Magnus has been doing for the last months is nothing but puzzling. This is either wisdom for which he shall get rewarded a Nobel Prize, or sheer nonsense that shall lead to the loss of his title. Beginning from the end of June and for three months onwards, the World Champion played 27 classical games, 14 rapid over-the-board games at the World Cup and 120 games(!) of rapid chess online. And we are not even counting the blitz games. In fact, Magnus played chess for three months without stopping.

What Magnus has been doing for the last months is nothing but puzzling

What is the result of this incredible marathon that the World Champion went through? Without a doubt, he got in shape. The oversights and blunders that stained his games in the World Cup in July slowly faded away. His level of play during the second half of Stavanger did remind us of the best moments of Carlsen's fantastic career.

The question yet to answer is whether this form of his remains, and whether he will not lack the invested energy in the second half of the match in Dubai. We are used to Magnus's sturdiness, we know that he does not get tired, and always keeps his freshness somehow. But all of that may come to an end at some point, and even a sportsman like Carlsen can falter after what was not a marathon, but a chess 'Iron Man'.

The effects of losing

I came to the conclusion that this match will be a complete clash of styles. As we know from previous tournaments, Magnus is a slow starter, he often finds himself trailing after four or five rounds, after which, considering his unbelievable physical condition and motivation, he is capable of winning five games out of six. By contrast, Ian can begin all guns blazing, winning game after game, but often does not hold his own in the long run, and starts dropping points during the second half.

Losing has different effects on them: it helps Magnus become stronger, whereas Ian often collapses. We saw this precise picture in Stavanger this year – which was the last time these two faced off.

The World Champion is the embodiment of the sportsman, being always in top physical shape, capable of playing for seven hours a day, every day at the same level. Ian, as it were, is not in ideal physical shape, and that may be the reason why he has problems at the end of tournaments. Carlsen always blames himself when he loses, or blames his play, whereas Ian often blames his opponents (for instance, Nakamura in their match in the 2015 World Cup), fate, the weather, and a hundred more things.

First match ever

Giving a proper forecast for a match is a most ungrateful task. The World Championship matches have their own laws, the majority of which no one knows. How come Kasparov

Ian Nepomniachtchi and Ilya Levitov at the Levitov Chess Week in Amsterdam two years ago.

did not manage to win a single time in the first 31 games of his unlimited match against Karpov in 1984-1985, and then went on to not win a single game in his match against Vladimir Kramnik in 2000? How come Kramnik himself lost 3 out of his first 6 games against Anand in Bonn? And, more importantly, why did Carlsen win only one classical game out of 24 in his matches versus Karjakin and Caruana?

Foreseeing what will happen during the match is almost impossible for one additional reason, namely, that Ian Nepomniachtchi has never played matches! Back in the day, the Candidates consisted of matches, which gave the players much-needed experience, but these do not exist anymore. A player must learn by doing during the match itself, taking the pressure, coping with his nerves in a situation where the whole world is watching. Magnus already has a gigantic experience in matches, he played four of them. I see the first part of the match as extremely dangerous for Ian, in this respect.

Of course, the games they played together give food for thought, but I would not overstate the meaning of the 4-1 score in Ian's favour in classical games, nor would I exaggerate the significance of Magnus's lead in their online rapid encounters. Ian won two games in their early youth, and his finest victory against Magnus dates back from 2011, with the black pieces, in Wijk aan Zee. By today's standards, ten years ago equals the Stone Age. Magnus can boast a win in Croatia in 2019, which he got after a big blunder from Ian.

Overall, one can notice from their games that Ian is not inferior to the World Champion, and even demonstrates in a way that he can take the upper hand. And above all, he is not afraid of Carlsen. He goes for full-blooded battles and plays for the win with both colours.

I am sure that Ian's preparation will allow him to play on equal terms with Carlsen, yet the question remains whether he can hold the distance, especially considering the atrocious schedule they were gifted by FIDE. For the first time in the history of chess the players will have to play three games within three days in a row. In a match where there is no possibility to take a breather against weaker opponents, this schedule is manageable if everything goes well. If it does not, you do not have time to either fix an opening or properly rest and collect yourself. It seems to me that this is the crux of this match, i.e. how Nepomniachtchi shall handle a couple of 6-hour games in a row, where one imprecision can cost a full point against an opponent who does not know what 'fatigue' is.

For the first time in the history of chess the players will have to play three games within three days in a row

All in all, we are in for an unforgettable show. The third chess player from the great 1990 generation (Carlsen, Karjakin, Nepomniachtchi, MVL) is up to play the first World Championship match of his career. I will of course root for Ian, but, alongside with that, I am eagerly waiting for really *great* chess, the chess that we missed so much during the pandemic and the countless online tournaments. ■

From 2010 to 2014, Ilya Levitov was the Executive Director of the Russian Chess Federation, organizing many prominent events, including the World Chess Championship Match in 2012. Together with Evgeny Bareev, he wrote From London to Elista (2007), an acclaimed account of Vladimir Kramnik's World Championship matches. He shares his passion for chess on his YouTube channel Levitov Chess.

World Championship: The Tale of the Tape

The wait is almost over. After being postponed because of the pandemic, the World Championship begins November 24 in Dubai and Ian Nepomniachtchi will finally have the chance to try to wrest the crown from Magnus Carlsen, his long-time rival, but also close friend.

Nepomniachtchi faces an uphill struggle, even though he has a good record against Carlsen in classical, or slow, games.

Nepomniachtchi has risen to a career best No. 4 in the world rankings, but Carlsen has the clear edge in rating (classical and rapid) and match experience.

According to an analysis of the possible results based on 1,000 simulations, which was posted on Chess.com in September, Carlsen has a 69 percent change of winning the match during the classical segment.

The good news for Nepomniachtchi is that, if the match is not decided during that first phase and it goes to tiebreakers, according to another 1,000 simulations for the rapid and blitz segments, his chances improve.

There is another factor that may help Nepomniachtchi: He worked with Carlsen when he was preparing for his 2016 match against Sergey Karjakin, so he knows how Carlsen trains and prepares, which gives him valuable insight.

DYLAN LOEB McCLAIN

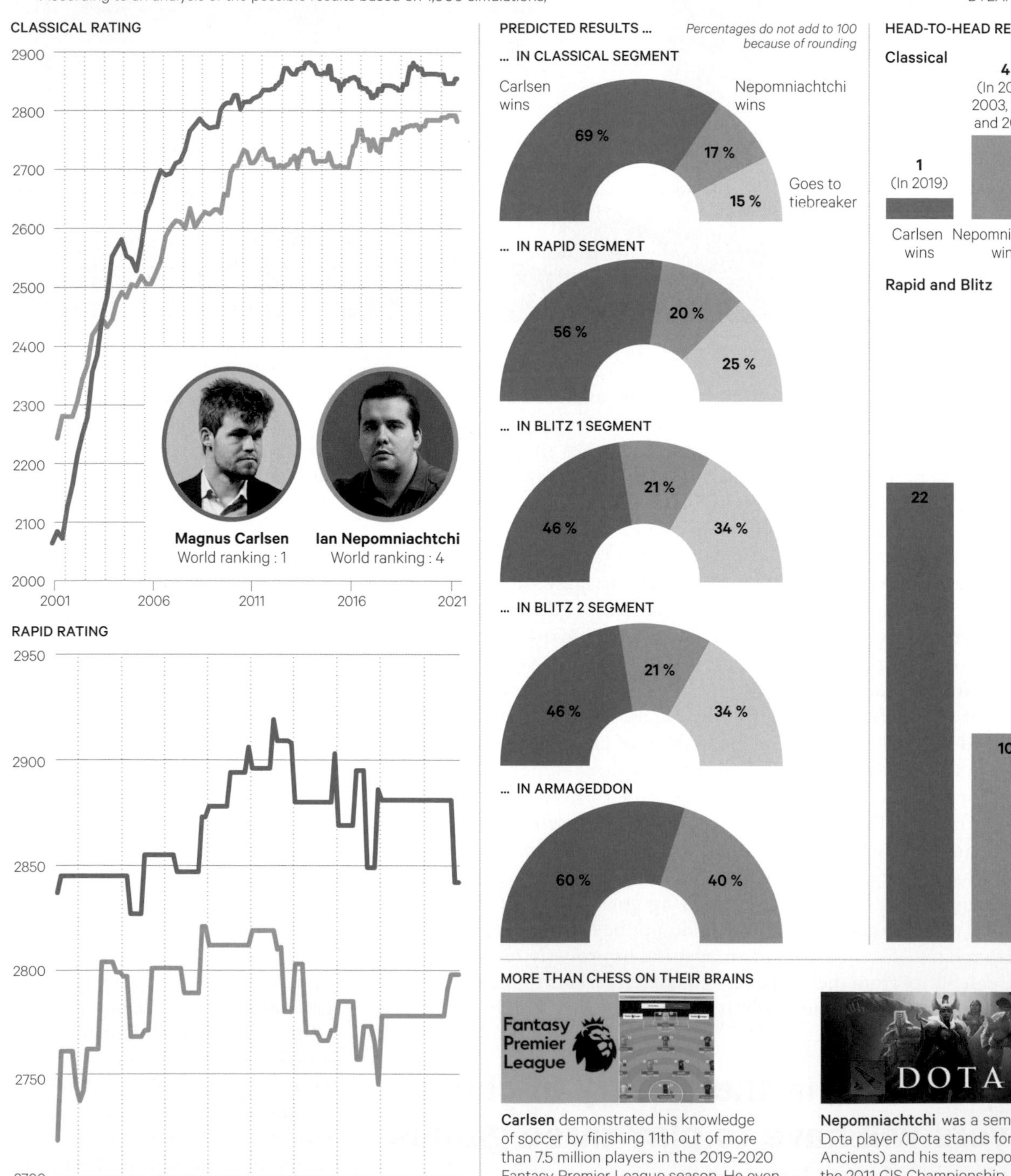

MORE THAN CHESS ON THEIR BRAINS

Carlsen demonstrated his knowledge of soccer by finishing 11th out of more than 7.5 million players in the 2019-2020 Fantasy Premier League season. He even led the standings in December 2019.

Nepomniachtchi was a semi-professional Dota player (Dota stands for Defense of the Ancients) and his team reportedly won the 2011 CIS Championship, which includes Russia and other former Soviet republics.

Ian Nepomniachtchi: 'It took me quite some time to realize that work is a vital part of any progress'

As the world title match is approaching rapidly, Ian Nepomniachtchi only has time for chess, training and chess. Nevertheless, **MARIA EMELIANOVA** managed to have a long talk with the Challenger as he was driving home from his training camp to feed and play with his dog Snow and his cat Richie. An exclusive interview about childhood memories, coaches, Dota 2, Magnus, cats and dogs, and more.

A long car ride from his training camp in an undisclosed place to his home in Moscow proved to be the chink in the armour of Ian Nepomniachtchi's tight schedule. He had agreed to give an interview, but the first big question was: when? The answer proved to be this car ride. While Snow and Richie were in eager anticipation of their boss's arrival, Ian took his time to answer my questions. As I complimented him on his heroic act to interrupt his training to feed his pets, he shrugged. That was only normal, and he noted that Moscow is not that big when there are no traffic jams.

Moscow has been Ian's home for many years now, but he was born in Bryansk, a city nestled between Belarus and Ukraine, some 350 kilometres from Moscow. My first question is how he remembers his childhood years in Bryansk.

'I think that after some time has passed, you think your childhood was surely the best part of your life. You basically remember only the positive moments, and these memories always warm my heart. I was a pretty normal kid, and I used to spend a lot of time in the courtyard, especially in summer – playing hide-and-seek, table tennis with bricks in the middle instead of a net... the same as in many courtyards across Mother Russia. When someone had a ball, we played football, but it was pretty limited because they normally would say, don't kick it too hard! The balls were not of high quality then.

'Of course we had no computers or other electronic devices, so I was very happy when I could play some Dandy or Sega. Many parents these days try to keep their children busy with dancing or singing classes, or some sports like hockey or gymnastics. For me chess was the only hobby that wasn't in school. That started quite early on. When I was five, I finally went to the chess club, where I met my first chess coach Valentin Evdokimenko.'

You did well in school and graduated from high school with a gold medal...

'Yes, I was among the best pupils, but I was surely not the best. I wasn't too bright in subjects like biology and chemistry. My favourite subjects were Russian language and literature, and I even participated in some school Olympiads. I think when I was 14 or 15, there was a choice to go to the Russian Chess Club Cup in Sochi or to the National Russian Language Olympiad, and I actually picked the second option. But it was quite disappointing. Out of 100 candidates all over Russia, 20 would qualify to the second round, and I finished in 20th place, and then for some reason they decided to cut this limit down to 16, and I was out, which was quite disappointing. The next year I made my debut at the Russian Club Cup, playing for Tomsk 400.

'Back then I didn't play that much, maybe four or five tournaments a year that required me to leave the city. I would miss probably two or sometimes three months in total (of school). And it was relatively easy for me to catch up with Russian language and literature, because my uncle is a very good teacher, an honorary teacher of Russia, so we could basically do this at home. I come from a teachers' dynasty; my mother taught me maths.'

You went to a university that supported chess players...

'I actually had a choice to go to one of the best universities in Russia, MSU. My grandfather and my uncle got accepted at MSU and graduated from it, and when I was in 10th grade we visited it and had a meeting at the philosophical faculty. They were quite happy to see me, and the university has a good chess tradition. For example, Petrosian got his PhD here. But studying there would mean that I would be focused on my studies much more than when I decided to go to the Russian State Social University. I chose to study journalism, but I had a wide range of options. Most importantly, back then the university was very friendly towards chess players, because of Alexander Kostiev. He was

'My mindset was "you need to play well and you need to enjoy", otherwise there's little sense in playing'

MARIA EMELIANOVA/CHESS.COM

Vladimir Potkin and Ian Nepomniachtchi in Ivory Coast for the Abidjan Rapid & Blitz. The two former European Champions have been working together for the past 14 years.

the dean of one of the faculties and he was building a good university chess team.'

Is it safe to say you never really considered getting a regular job and always were going to be a chess professional?
'It was kind of a decision I took when I turned 16. When I was thinking about which major to study, I looked for something that would be easy to combine with my chess. Now it is difficult to imagine a professional chess player with a regular job, but for example Botvinnik was a scientist and Tal was a very famous sports journalist. Of course, the situation has changed a lot in the past 20 or 30 years, and now you no longer can sit on two chairs.'

MARIA EMELIANOVA/CHESS.COM

Ian Nepomniachtchi and Magnus Carlsen having fun at the 2015 World Rapid & Blitz in Berlin. Cracking jokes will probably not be on the menu in Dubai.

You had a lot of great coaches throughout your chess career. Could you name a few that left the most lasting imprint?
'It is hard to overestimate the experience that I got from my collaboration with Valery Zilbershtein. He was really successful at creating the right mindset. It sounds very simple, but in order to get results you need to play well. A lot of young talented players are in a hurry to complete some norms or to win medals in youth championships, but in my case the mindset was "you need to play well and you need to enjoy", otherwise there's little sense in playing.

'Of course, there were also a lot of really useful tips chess-wise, daily routines during a tournament, tips I am still using even now. It's really sad that he passed away so early, when I was 14 or 15. It was a great shock to me. But I am very thankful for all the time he dedicated to me and for all the knowledge and wisdom he shared.

'In general I am lucky with the people that surround me, including the coaches. I was very lucky to work with Vladimir Potkin for the last 14 years. This has been quite a fruitful period for both of us, as many like to say. For example, I became European Champion (in 2010) and Vladimir became European Champion a year later.

'Also it's worth mentioning Sergey Yanovsky, who was the first grandmaster I ever worked with. He was the coach of the Russian youth team, so he was also helping us with visas and booking flights. Later, when he saw promise in me, he worked with me for some years and we have kept our friendship till this day.'

What memories do you have of winning the U10 and U12 European Youth Championships and then the U12 World Youth Championship in 2002?
'The first trip was very nice. It was my first time so far away from home, in Kallithea, Greece. I was most impressed with the restaurant, the buffet... so much food, especially sweets. All three times I won the European Championships, I won with a round to spare. The first time was nice and memorable, but the next two years, I wouldn't call it routine, but it wasn't nearly as close to the same emotions. I wasn't so successful at the Russian Championships, because I normally shared first place with other guys like Ildar Khairullin or Egor Krivoborodov, and I never came first because of the tiebreaks. So that's why I normally played only the European Championships and not the World Championships. We didn't have so much money and no sponsorship, so I couldn't go to both and had to pick one. And only if I won the European Championship did we have a reason to find more money and go to the World Youth. My first try in Oropesa del Mar in 2001 wasn't successful. I finished 8th, but the year after I shared first place with Magnus, but with a better tie-break.'

Did you already have ambitions to be the World Champion one day?
'Frankly speaking, I never really thought about this. I had this mindset of just playing well and improving. And it doesn't really matter how fast it comes, but sooner or later I will become an International Master, then a Grandmaster and then we'll just see what happens. Maybe this was somewhat harmful for my career, this idea that it didn't really matter whether it happened slowly or fast. Of course I was ambitious, but I wasn't working hard enough. Sooner or later it would come, so I was waiting. It took me quite some time to realize that work is a vital part of any progress.

'I guess it was when I was 25 or 26 that I found out I actually had no big achievements apart from playing well for the Russian team. But even after I understood this, it still took me some time to start working more. Maybe I am just a very slow dude.'

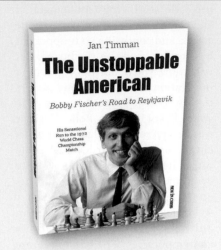

How did it change? Did you start working with more people?
'It's not so much about hiring extra coaches, but about changing your mindset and dedicating more time to chess. Spending less time on hobbies and games or hanging around and having fun. Overall, becoming more professional chess-wise.'

Speaking of games, you were very good at Dota 2. Did you ever consider a professional Esports career?
'Yes, absolutely. I can't say I was really super-successful at Dota, but at some point I was a really decent player. Maybe because I spent lots of time, like 10 hours a day, when I was 20, 21, mastering the game. But back then there was literally zero money in Esports. Ironically, the year I won something I decided to quit Dota, because there was no sports organization, no professional team. At that time, I was in the top 15 in the FIDE rating list and I thought, enough is enough; I only will play for fun. That was exactly the year Valve announced their first international tournament with a one-million dollar prize fund. That was completely shocking. But I can't say I would definitely have made it to a team, but I had decent chances.'

Do you still play online games?
'Very, very seldom, because I am a person who doesn't like to lose in any game, and I also got used to playing well, at least in this particular game. Now for obvious reasons, because I only play once or twice a month, I am playing worse and worse. The game changed and I changed and got older, and I have less relevant experience and general in-game reaction. I am still trying to do things my way and it doesn't work, so you lose and get angry and frustrated, and it's the wrong way to spend your time, you know. Spend a few hours, get angry, then spend even more hours and get even angrier. I also play FIFA on my PlayStation sometimes, but also just once a month. Sometimes Hearthstone, but the only reason I play it is because it can be installed on my phone, unlike the other games.'

Who are your favourite chess players?
'One of the first books I studied was *Alexander Alekhine's Best Games*. I had quite patriotic feelings when as a seven-year-old I read about the first-ever Russian World Chess Champion. But starting from a more or less serious age, 10 or 11 years old, I started trying to learn as much as possible from any player. And I have the same attitude right now. Of course I try to learn from the best, but I think almost any strong grandmaster can share some wisdom. Not necessarily by teaching you, but by playing a chess game. And you study this game and understand something new.'

'I try to learn from the best, but I think almost any strong grandmaster can share some wisdom'

Was your style inspired by any player in particular, perhaps Mikhail Tal?
'Of course Tal's games are the most picturesque ones since the 19th century, the romantic era of chess. I think very few players could emulate

this style, sacrificing a lot of material and playing for beauty, playing for the attack, and confusing your opponent by creating chaos on the board. But you know, you're normally grabbing inspiration from very strong players if you're trying to become one yourself. For instance, Robert Fischer was never a role model for me, but his chess was at a stellar level when he was at his best. If we try to evaluate or compare a chess player and his contemporaries, I guess Fischer was much better, perhaps even on a different level, compared to his contemporaries. The gap was more serious than in any other epoch. We can't really compare him to the times of Tal or Morphy. He was far ahead with his chess level, and he's the one we should be thankful for in terms of changing chess to a professional sport with serious prize money.'

You are going to play for the world title against Magnus. Does it feel kind of inevitable to be playing a match against him, given your history and being the same age?
'Well, I know some people like to think that way, but I think that the winner of the Candidates is playing the reigning World Champion. In general, that's how it goes. It's quite interesting that we're meeting each other 19 years after we played our first game, but I guess that for example Anand and Gelfand, when they played their match, also had a big history of playing each other before. It just means we are players of the same generation, born in the same year – I guess that's it. For people who like to see this as something special or supernatural, that's of course another point of view that should be respected.'

People also like to mention that the two of you are on good terms, and that at some point you helped him as his second.
'Well, I helped him during the London tournament in 2012, but that was the only time. There were a few occasions that we worked together in 2011 and 2013, but that was not about being a second, just about trying to improve. Magnus likes working with different people, and I believe he has lots of training sessions with many top players, so I don't think it's something special to speak about. It's too much to say it was a special cooperation.'

Did working with him back then provide you with insights that might be useful in the match?
'I don't know, I honestly don't know, but if this was the case I would probably not tell you.'

Magnus's overall record is impressive. Are there any achievements, other than being World Champion, that stand out for you?
'I guess holding all the (world) titles is quite impressive – classic, rapid and blitz. But overall I think he's a very stable player, who even on the worst days still fights until the last chance, and that's why he normally – speaking about winning percentages – seems to score higher than other players. He's probably the most stable compared to the other guys. I don't know if it's a good idea to give an example, but for example Caruana playing Wijk aan Zee before he won the Candidates, scored something like -3, which is a very poor result for a player of his calibre, but this year he scored +3. In Magnus's case that range wouldn't be so wide. His level is very constant, and even when in bad form, his play isn't dropping too low. On top of that he's a very good sportsman and absolutely hates losing in any game.'

'There were a few occasions that Magnus and I worked together, but it's too much to say it was a special cooperation'

Speaking of your own victories, do you have any favourites?
'I don't like thinking about these questions, so I always say it's yet to come. But now, of course, I can mention the Candidates career-wise. While I obviously didn't show the best chess of my life, it was my best result. And it wasn't about showing the best chess, but about scoring more points than the other players.'

You are working harder these days than you did before. On average, how many hours would you say you work on chess every day?
'I don't know, the last 20 months I've worked really hard, starting with the first Candidates leg last year. Also it became impossible to spend time on most of my hobbies. I couldn't play football or go to the cinema because of the Covid situation. And spending less time on small pleasures meant spending more time on chess, because what else are you going to do? But it's much more than it used to be. Before, I could work a lot one day, and then another day, I would play a couple of blitz games online and that was it. Now it's quite a different story.'

The two previous World Championship matches were decided in rapid games. What are your thoughts on the current match format?
'Well, it was quite a normal thing, I guess. Kramnik versus Topalov was settled in rapid, and Anand versus Topalov was close to rapid, because Topalov only lost the last game. Anand versus Gelfand was also decided in rapid. I think only the two matches between Anand and Carlsen were different. You see 12 draws [as in the Carlsen-Caruana

match – ME], and it seems slightly shocking and unexpected, but chess is a well-balanced game and, I try to avoid the word drawish, but with deeper theory, over time it wouldn't take too much to predict that more draws would occur.'

So more classical games simply means more draws?
'Not necessarily. It could just be a coincidence, but in general a draw is a normal result. Twelve in a row is of course some kind of a deviation from what we expect, but nothing is impossible to imagine. For example, when we speak of Karpov against Kasparov, their first match was stopped when the score was 5-3 [only wins were counted – ME]. When the score was 5-0, Kasparov started winning at some point, but there were 40 draws, 17 of them in a row. So maybe 12 draws in a row is unusual, but it isn't the first time in chess history that this has occurred.'

SNEZHANA FOMICHEVA

Ian Nepomniachtchi adores his cat Richie ('Very talkative; he hates being alone and always needs company') and his sheepdog Snow.

Your result in Norway Chess wasn't what you might have hoped for. Because you had to hide some of your prep?
'That wasn't the only reason, and I wouldn't want to take credit away from the other guys. What affected me the most was the visa issue and having no rest day as a result, which I think also affected Sergey Karjakin [as they played their postponed round-one game on the free day – ME]. But in general I don't think this result was a catastrophe. It's sad to finish on a minus score, but it's also really hard to recall a tournament where two players – especially at the end of the tournament – each scored four wins in a row. Sometimes it's a matter of luck, or your opponent's bad form, but you can't take this outstanding result away from them.'

How did you see the games you played against Magnus in Norway Chess?
'Of course in some way it was different to play Magnus compared to the other guys, but in general the points of these games will not be counted for the match, so they were just two games against a very strong opponent. Of course it's better to win than to lose, but I wouldn't be too happy if I performed too well in this tournament. As it is, I wasn't too disappointed with my result. It's not the end of the world, and overall the tournament is part of my preparation.'

Chess players travel a lot. Do you ever get homesick?
'Well, I thought I really wanted to spend more time at home. Especially in 2019, from April to the end of the year I only had a maximum of 14 days in a row that I could spend at home, out of a total of 60 days. I read a similar complaint in an interview with MVL – a lot of guys felt the same. So at the start of 2020 I thought, okay, just the Candidates and then I will have some rest. And as they say, you should be careful what you wish for. After this I was stuck at home for a year, as we all were. But in general, I don't know about now, but previously coming back home and doing nothing for a few days was my favourite part.'

You're not taking something with you that makes you feel like at home?
'No, I am like a turtle, I bring my home with me. Just my luggage and my laptop.'

You might want to take your animals with you, but that's not possible. You have a cat and a dog. But are you a cat or a dog person?
'Neither, I guess. When I was a kid, we had a dog, a Scottish shepherd, a very smart and nice doggie. I really miss him. Now we have a Bengal cat called Richard or Richie. Very talkative; he hates being alone and always needs company. And the dog we have is pretty much the same. He is slightly over a year old, an old-English sheepdog named Snow. But I can't say that I know how to evaluate, how I spread my love between them.' ■

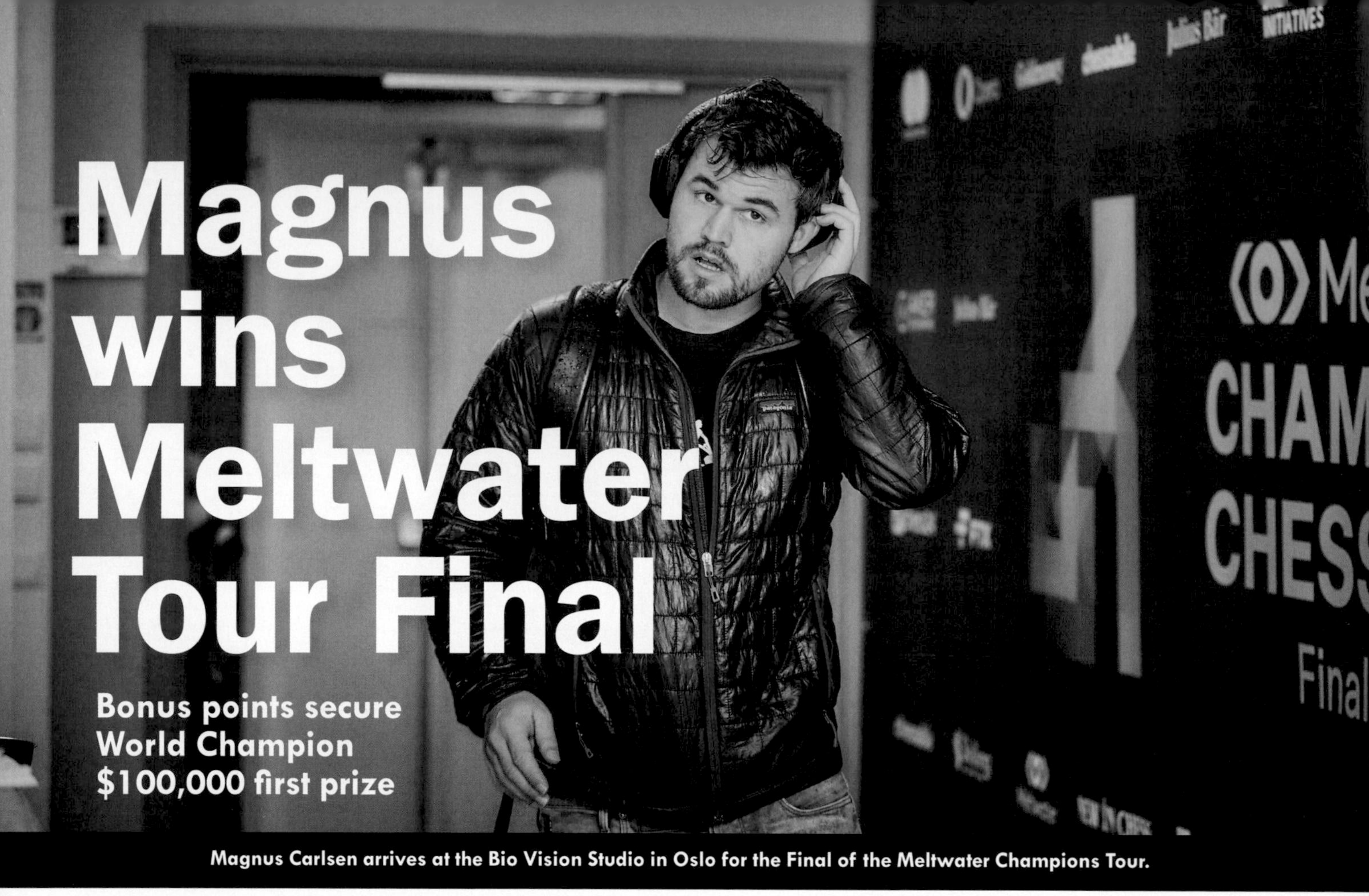

Magnus wins Meltwater Tour Final

Bonus points secure World Champion $100,000 first prize

Magnus Carlsen arrives at the Bio Vision Studio in Oslo for the Final of the Meltwater Champions Tour.

The World Champion alternated brilliancies with lesser moments, but the bonus points that he had started with proved to be a comfortable cushion. At the end of the Final of the Meltwater Champions Tour, Magnus Carlsen could rightly call himself the best online player in the world in 2021. **JONATHAN TISDALL** reports.

The Meltwater Champions Chess Tour has been a success by almost any yardstick. Perhaps the best one, still, is by measuring an event's reach beyond the game's traditional boundaries. Front-page reports in outlets as grand as CNN and Eurosport are a clear indication of the Tour's impact.

The 2021 season of ten top-flight rapid knockout events was the follow-on of the pilot Magnus Chess Tour in 2020, which kept spectators and elite players busy online during the bleakest times of the Covid pandemic. The format evolved constantly and was more or less fixed by the time this year's Tour unfolded, with a series of gruelling events where a field of established players and upcoming young talents were whittled down in qualifying round-robins, followed by a quarterfinal KO stage.

Tour Director Arne Horvei explained to me some of the behind-the-scenes dynamics of the event's evolution, where a range of Play Magnus Group staff consistently brainstormed how to keep improving the tour on the fly. 'There are a lot of creative and smart people involved, who see things from different angles and they all participate with suggestions about how to take it further, who to invite, how to execute the qualifiers, and all inputs are considered. Next season we will have one tour under the belt, have more knowledge and experience about everything, and hopefully get things sorted out faster.'

The 2021 tour attracted a series of commercial partners – Skilling, Airthings, Opera, FTX, Goldmoney,

Breakthrough, Aker BioMarine, MPL – and most recently announced, Mastercard. The tour prize fund allowed 44 players from 18 countries to make an appearance, and provided USD 1.6 million in rewards. A side event was spawned, the Julius Bär Challengers Chess Tour, a youngsters battlefield that provided wildcard spots in the qualifier stages. The climax of the year-long contest was the Tour Final... and this was confusing.

The climax of the year-long contest was the Tour Final ... and this was confusing

It's complicated...

This final tournament with a $300,000 prize fund was originally scheduled to be an in-person event in San Francisco, but when this proved logistically impossible it became a hybrid event with three players playing from Oslo – Carlsen, Giri and Duda – and the others playing online. The idea of the Final was to provide a crowning clash to round off the entire series, and this desire to be both a separate and a unifying event provided some unique challenges.

In order to maintain the importance of the preceding tournaments and provide a strong sense of an overall Tour champion, the field was made up primarily of the top of the Tour leader board, and these players started the final with bonus points representing their season success. The 10-player field was completed with three wild-card players, one of whom was a late replacement for world title challenger Ian Nepomniachtchi, who had conflicting prior engagements at home in Russia.

Arne said the bonus point system was inspired by the professional golf tour, where the point spread is based on the standings and performances of the season, and was adopted because the focus was meant to be on the totality more than a grand final. 'The concept of this season of the tour was to decide who is the best online player in the world over a *full* season. We were also open about not deciding the format of next year's final before testing it out in real life', he said.

The potential drawback was having a favourite with a clear head start, and there was general agreement that this ended up creating a sense of anticlimax. Why this was, can be easily gleaned from the number of bonus points the players started the Final with. Carlsen started with 16.5 points, So 12.5, Aronian 8, Radjabov 6, Giri 5.5, Nakamura 4, Artemiev 3.5, MVL 2.5, Mamedyarov 0.5 and Duda 0.

For the first time the tournament was a round-robin instead of a knockout, with 3 points for a rapid match win over four games, 2 points for winning a tie-broken duel, and one point for losing a tiebreak.

The score table focused on the points won here plus tour bonus, and it was fairly clear before the start that first place could only be wrested from leader Magnus Carlsen by his main and constant rival this year, Wesley So. When Wesley struggled with both the chase and his form, the drama at the top evaporated fairly early – despite some truly remarkable events just behind the pre-tournament leaders.

Arne revealed that the Group would definitely be reconsidering the format of the final after this first run, and that changes would be made to try to ensure it becomes an exciting event for *everyone*. 'We haven't done our official internal review yet, so it is too early to say how big the changes will be', he said.

To be fair, I think this will be a very tricky equation to solve. There was quite a bit of redemption possible with the scoring system, and it could have easily been as exciting at the top as it was for 2nd-4th. With a little tweaking and a bit of luck they could strike gold.

An abundance of action

With so much going on, I would imagine that people experienced the final in very different ways. With no knockouts, the sheer number of games never diminished, and there were many places to shift your focus. I have to confess that I didn't get a real sense of overview of the actual final in isolation until I created a crosstable by hand, filling in the 0-1-2-3s and then digesting the results (I recommend this!). Here is my personal review of the event and talking points.

Although both Magnus and Wesley opened the event well, stage one of the tournament revealed signs that overtaking a World Champion with a four-point head start was an unnerving task. Especially with Magnus in truly violent mood. Have a look at the following brilliant miniature.

Meltwater Champions Chess Tour Final 2021

			Elo rapid	1	2	3	4	5	6	7	8	9	10	final	prev rounds	CCT total
1	Magnus Carlsen	RUS	2747	*	0	0	3	3	0	2	2	3	2	15	16.5	31.5
2	Teimour Radjabov	USA	2836	3	*	3	3	1	1	1	3	3	3	21	6	27
3	Levon Aronian	ARM	2761	3	0	*	3	0	3	3	1	0	3	16	8	24
4	Wesley So	NOR	2842	0	0	0	*	1	3	2	0	2	3	11	12.5	23.5
5	Hikaru Nakamura	RUS	2755	0	2	3	2	*	2	1	2	3	2	17	4	21
6	Vladislav Artemiev	POL	2801	3	2	0	0	1	*	3	2	0	3	14	3.5	17.5
7	Anish Giri	USA	2766	1	2	0	1	2	0	*	3	0	0	9	5.5	14.5
8	Maxime Vachier-Lagrave	FRA	2773	1	0	2	3	1	1	0	*	3	0	11	2.5	13.5
9	Jan-Krzysztof Duda	NED	2767	0	0	3	1	0	3	3	0	*	2	12	0	12
10	Shakhriyar Mamedyarov	AZE	2727	1	0	0	0	1	0	3	3	1	*	9	0.5	9.5

A round is 4 rapid games. 3 points for winning, 0 for losing.
If 2-2, Armageddon decides: 2 points for winning, 1 for losing.

NOTES BY
Peter Heine Nielsen

Magnus Carlsen
Jan-Krzysztof Duda
Meltwater CCT Final 2021 (1.1)
Queen's Gambit Declined, Semi-Tarrasch

1.d4 ♘f6 2.c4 e6 3.♘c3 d5 4.cxd5 ♘xd5 5.♘f3 c5 6.e3 cxd4 7.exd4 ♘xc3!? 8.bxc3 ♕c7!

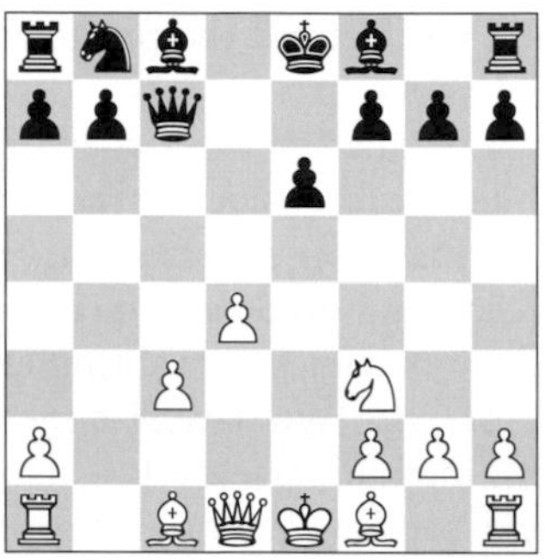

This move was one of the key points when Vladimir Kramnik made the Semi-Tarrasch part of his repertoire, soon to be copied by a lot of other players. Black has changed the structure from isolated pawn to hanging pawns, and immediately attacks c3, in order to prevent White from developing freely, since 9.♗d3?? ♕xc3+ now wins a piece for Black.

9.♗d2 is the obvious move, but also is purely defensive and White never managed to develop his initiative fully after that move. Therefore Magnus tries a more ambitious concept, not caring that it costs a pawn.

9.♖b1!? ♘d7

In case of the immediate 9...♕xc3+, 10.♗d2 gives White a huge lead in development. ♗d3 or ♗b5+ is next, followed by castling. But Black does not bite that easily, and instead makes a sensible developing move, again leaving White with the question of how to progress without having to play the passive ♗d2.

10.♗d3!

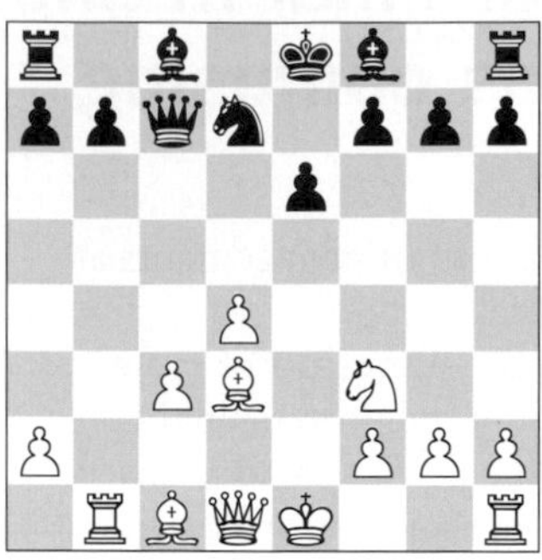

This is the point of Magnus's concept. As castling is a threat, when Black's ...♕c7 could be seen as a failure, Duda is almost forced to accept the gift.

10...♕xc3+

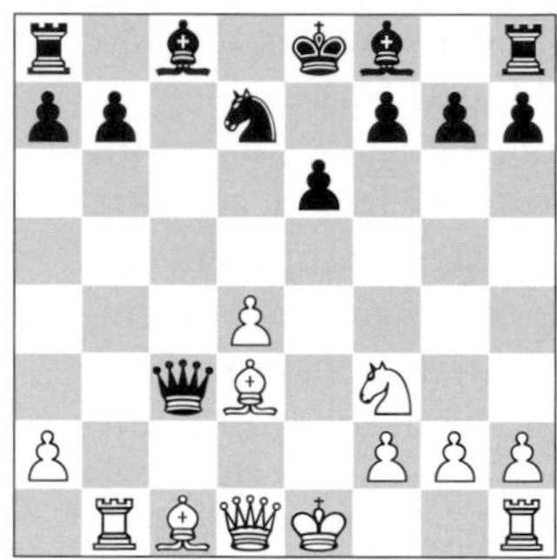

11.♔f1

Forced, as 11.♗d2 obviously loses to 11...♕xd3. At first it looks close to insanity. White has not only lost a pawn, but also the right to castle, meaning his rooks will not manage to connect and his king will be stuck at f1. And as Ulf Andersson once joked: losing an isolated pawn means you have no weaknesses anymore, but losing a hanging pawn is really bad.... Which means that Magnus is also now left with a weak isolated pawn on d4. Were this a game of a beginner, we would rightly point out all these deficits, but since this is the World Champion, we will point to the fact that his rooks will not trip over each other, but have attacking potential on their respective flanks; that the king is safe on f1; and that his lead in development may make it possible to launch a 'blitz-attack' against Black's undeveloped position!

11...♗e7 12.h4!

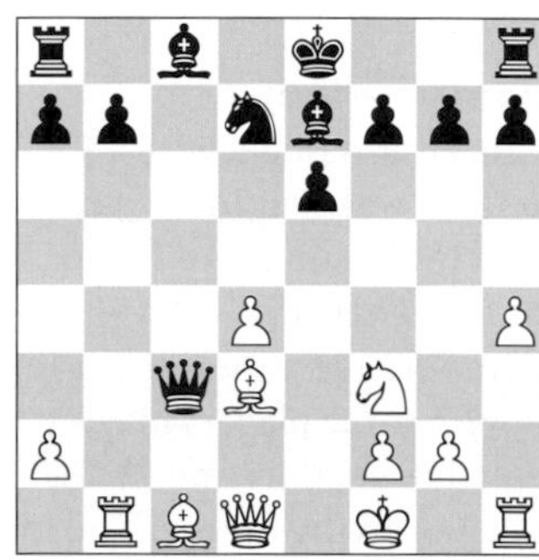

The rook now will appear on h3, and either the bishop or the knight, depending on the circumstances, can land on g5. White's king will be perfectly safe on g1, but it doesn't even need to waste time to get there, as f1 is safe, too. White's pieces all have obvious destinations, whereas things are more complicated for Black. For a start, where to place the king? Duda does the natural thing and castles.

12...0-0 13.♖h3!

Activating the rook and heading for g3. And as it threatens 14.♗xh7+ ♔xh7 15.♘g5+, winning the queen on c3, Black has to retreat, giving even more momentum to White's attack.

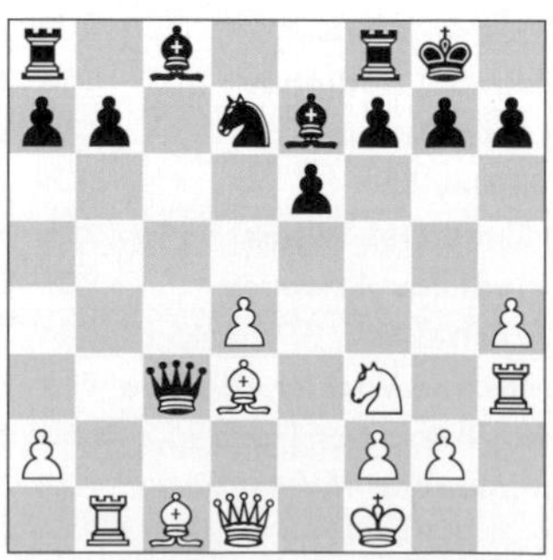

Were this a game of a beginner, we would rightly point out all these deficits, but since this is the World Champion...

As he was the only player who started the Final with zero points, Jan-Krzysztof Duda felt absolutely free to stick to his thrill-seeking adventurous style.

13...♘f6?
Logical but losing. Retreating would have been best after all, and after 13...♕c7 Black can still put up a fight.
14.♘e5! ♕a5

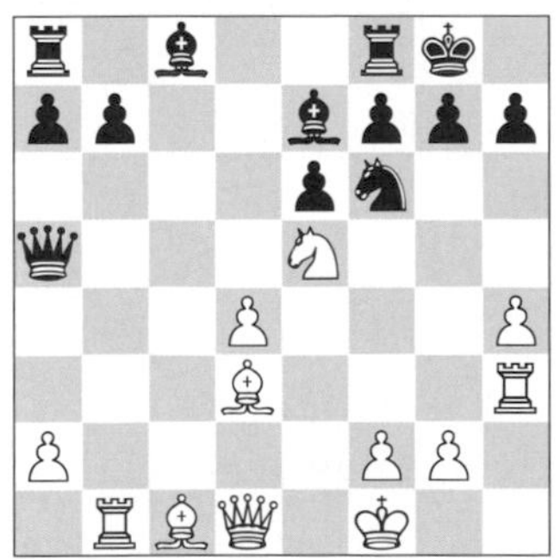

15.♖g3
A good move, but 15.♗h6 was even flashier, and also winning. The main point is that 15...gxh6 16.♕c1! leaves Black completely helpless against the threat of ♕xh6, followed by ♖g3 and mate on g7, as the knight needs to protect against mate on h7, and the rook against ♘xf7. But what Magnus played is both logical and strong.
15...♔h8 16.♗g5 h6
Allowing a beautiful finish; but so would 16...♕d8, as after 17.♗xf6 ♗xf6 (17....gxf6 18.♕g4! mates next move!) 18.♕h5 h6 there is 19.♖g6!!, with mate to follow shortly.
17.♗xh6! gxh6 18.♕f3!

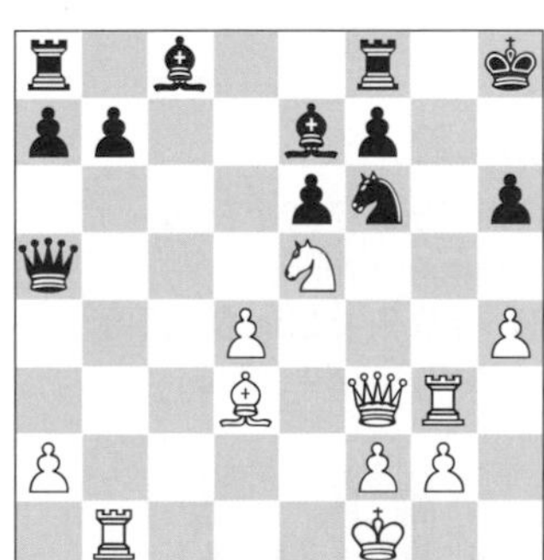

Duda now thought for a few minutes, and resigned! Justifiably so. The computer suggests 18...♕d2 19.♖d1 ♕xd3+ as Black's best option, but that would obviously win trivially for White.
At first it might seem surprising that things are that bad for Black, but White has 19.♕f4, threatening mate on h6. 18...♕d8 19.♕f4 ♘g8 looks like the logical way to defend, but 20.♕xf7!!

ANALYSIS DIAGRAM

ends the game immediately, and in style! Magnus, and Modern Chess at its best.

Swashbuckling streak

One running theme of the event was a swashbuckling streak from Magnus, which began already in this first match vs. Duda. He seemed to have entertaining very much on his mind. He sealed this contest with a crowd-pleasing duel of anti-materialism, and would repeatedly sacrifice his queen over the next week.

Jan-Krzysztof Duda
Magnus Carlsen
Meltwater CCT Final 2021 (1.2)

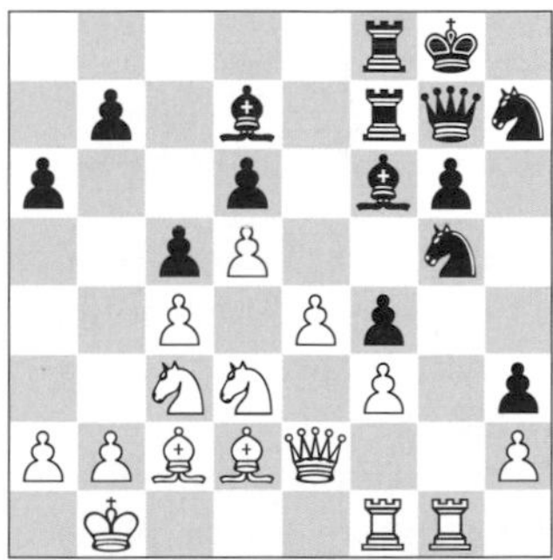
position after 25...♗f6

Although Duda would assess his performance in this game as a sequence of tactical errors, to the more forgiving observer it also gives a sense of his taste for adventure and sacrifice...
26.♗xf4!
This obviously expands the activity of just about every bit of material east of the c-file.
26...♗xc3

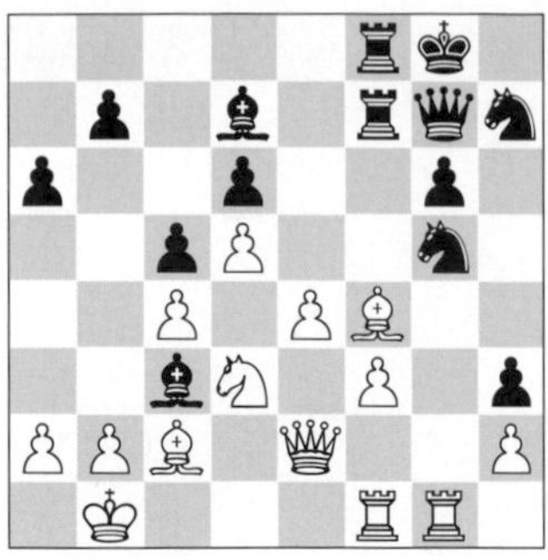

27.♗xd6 Instead, 27.♗xg5 ♘xg5 (no good either is 27...♗d4 28.♗e3 g5 29.f4) 28.♖xg5 was simple and strong, when Black will presumably complicate by flicking in ...b5 while also trying to prevent total catastrophe on the g-file. Instead, Duda embarks on a long contest of ignoring standard material considerations.

27...♗d4 28.f4 28.♗xf8 was good, though 28...♖xf8 29.♖g3 b5 generates a mess. **28...♗xg1**

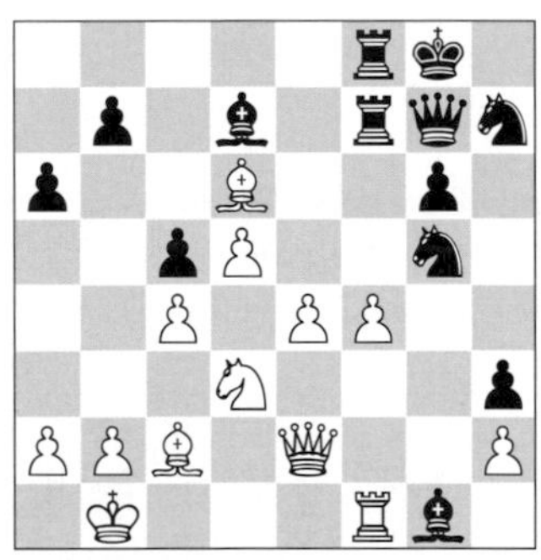

29.♗e5 29.♖xg1 ♕d4 presumably didn't impress White, though your engine will disagree.

29...♘f6

29...♖xf4!! was the inhuman solution, settling for an extra piece after 30.♗xf4 (or 30.♖xf4 ♕e7) 30...♗d4.

30.fxg5

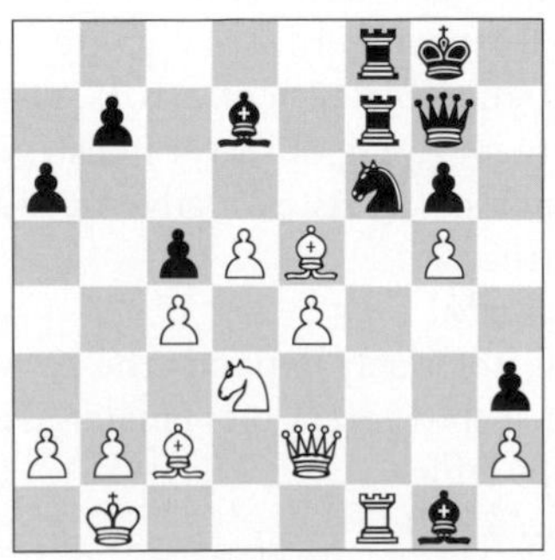

30...♘g4! White was probably envisioning decisive compensation for a sacrificed exchange after something like 30...♗d4 31.♗xf6 ♗xf6 32.gxf6 ♖xf6 33.♖e1 but Black defends with a corresponding disdain for worldly goods.

31.♗f6 ♗xh2! 32.e5 ♘xf6 33.exf6 ♗d6! 34.♘f4 ♖xf6! 34...♕h7 35.♘xg6 and the ensuing compensatory chaos should favour ... White.

35.gxf6 ♖xf6

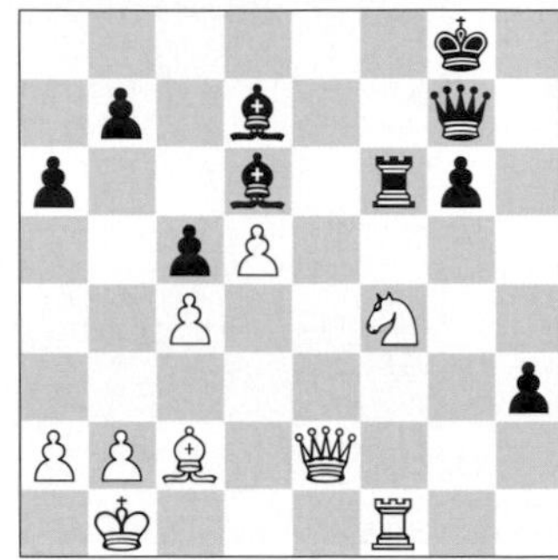

The rabid anti-materialism interlude is over, Black settling for just an extra pawn and a safe, lethal advantage.

36.♘e6 ♖xf1+ 37.♕xf1 ♕h6 38.♕f6 h2 39.♗e4 h1♕+ 40.♗xh1 ♕xh1+ 41.♔c2 ♕e4+

White resigned.

Anish Giri
Magnus Carlsen
Meltwater CCT Final 2021 (6.5)
Sicilian Defence, Rossolimo Variation

1.e4 c5 2.♘f3 ♘c6 3.♗b5 e6 4.0-0 ♘ge7 5.d4 cxd4 6.♘xd4 ♕b6

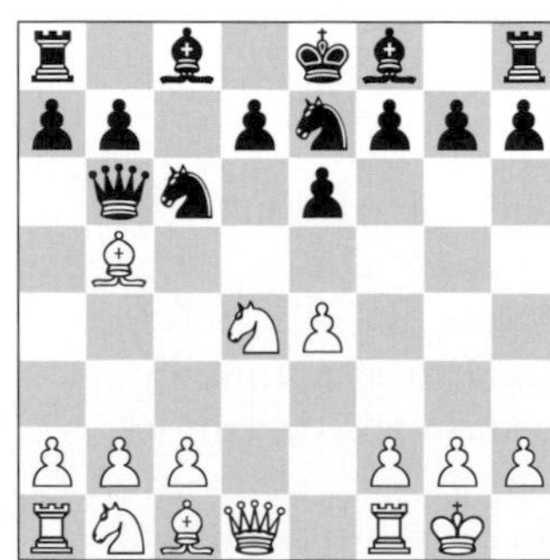

Anish came to this blitz tiebreak game armed with an extremely sharp and interesting idea. After:

7.♗e3!? ♘xd4 8.a4

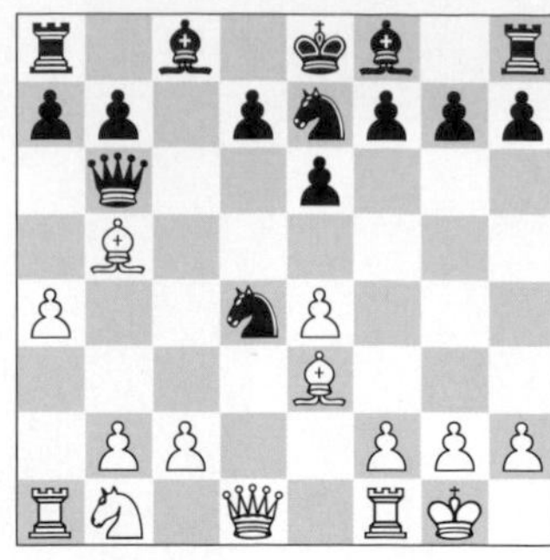

Black 'should' play the defensively materialistic:

8...♘xb5!? After 8...e5 9.c3 a6 White has a variety of fascinating attacking possibilities, and was doubtless armed with them. Magnus opted for the countersurprise.

9.♗xb6 axb6 With three minor pieces but some interim dangers for the queen. This bold and quick-witted decision paid off, with some hair-raising complications, eventually resulting in the minors emerging rampant. Fantastic entertainment value, and at blitz tempo.

10.♘d2?! ♘d6 11.e5 ♘df5 12.♘e4 ♘c6 13.g4 ♘h4 14.f4 h5 15.h3 hxg4 16.hxg4 d5 17.exd6 ♖a5 18.c4 f5

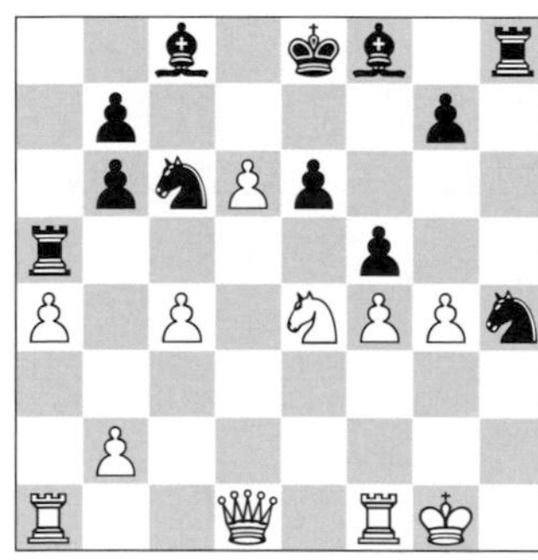

19.b4! ♘xb4 20.d7+ ♗xd7 21.♘d6+ ♗xd6 22.♕xd6 ♘c6

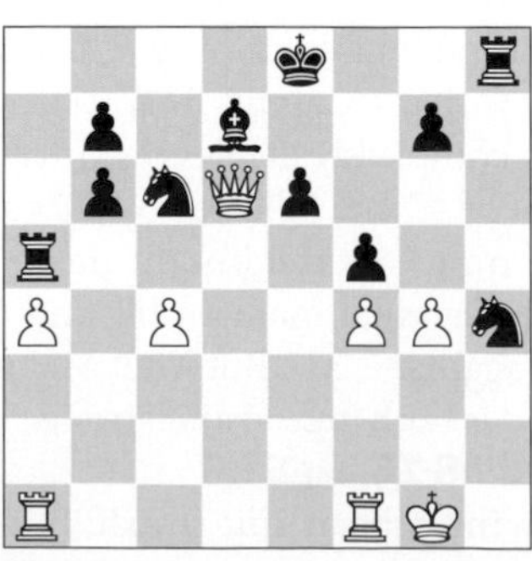

After all four rapid games had ended in draws, Magnus Carlsen decided his match against Anish Giri in his favour in a spectacular blitz tiebreaker.

23.♖ad1?
The fatal error. Magnus was worried about 23.♕c7!, which keeps the black king glued to the centre, and poses difficult problems to solve at any speed.
23...♗c8! 24.g5
Since Black can meet 24.♕c7 with the very belated 24...0-0! he has achieved stability and king safety, and the minor pieces gradually romp.
24...♘g6 25.♖f2 ♔f7 26.♕c7+ ♘ce7 27.♖d8 ♖xd8 28.♕xd8 ♖xa4 29.♕c7 e5 30.fxe5 ♗e6 31.♕xb7 ♖xc4 32.♕xb6 ♘xe5 33.♖e2 ♖c6 34.♕e3 ♘5g6 35.♔h2 ♗c4 36.♖b2 ♖e6 37.♕f3 ♖e4 38.♖b7 ♗e6 39.♔g1 ♖g4+ 40.♔h2 ♖xg5 41.♖b6 ♗d5 42.♕e3 ♖g2+ 43.♔h3 ♖g4 44.♔h2 f4

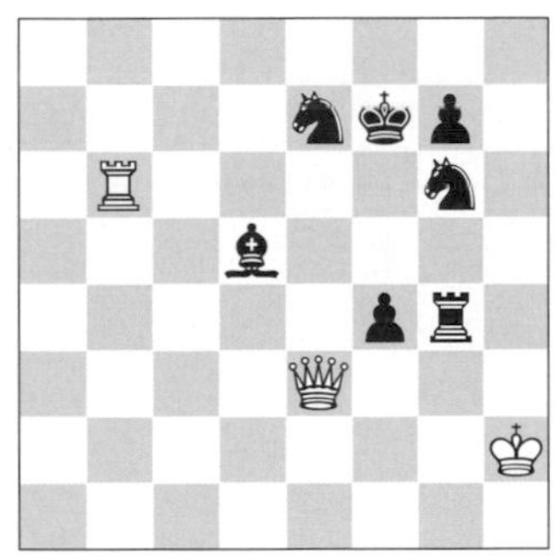

45.♕d4 ♖g5 46.♖d6 f3 47.♖d7 ♖f5 48.♕g4 ♗e6 49.♖d1 ♘e5 50.♕h4 f2 51.♔g2 ♗d5+ 52.♔f1 ♗c4+ 53.♔g2 f1♕+
White resigned.

Enter Teimour Radjabov

Wesley So stumbled in the second round vs. Maxime Vachier-Lagrave, which already started my mind wandering to consider other, smaller dramas. One thing that caught my eye was Teimour Radjabov's odd trio of opening tie-break defeats. The first was after a hard-fought quartet of rapid games, and the decider was a nice advertisement for Vlad Artemiev's skill set. Quickly scanning all the action, one could understandably be taken aback by how abruptly he converted optically gentle pressure.

Vladislav Artemiev
Teimour Radjabov
Meltwater CCT Final 2021 (1.5)

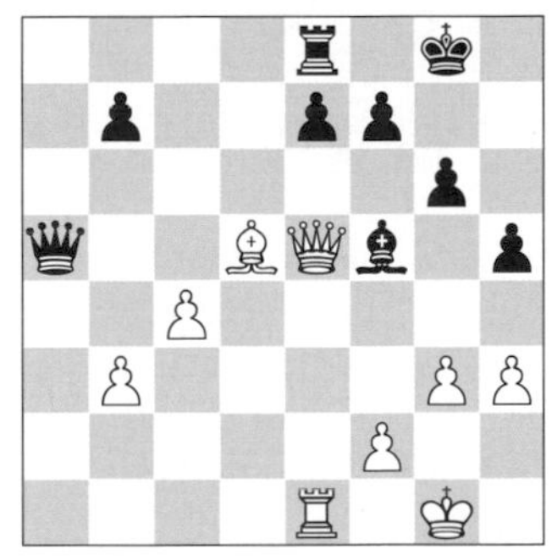

position after 28.♕xe5

The finish of this game made a striking impression on me, not least because of the duel between Artemiev's wily creativity and Radjabov's generally impenetrable defence. The speed and violence of what happens from here is shocking.
28...♕b4?!
This looks incredibly natural, eyeing all the relevant squares and creating counterplay against b3, but 28...b6 29.♔g2 e6 was better, striving to trade queens. White now has a startlingly dangerous attack.
29.♔g2! ♕xb3 29...e6 30.♗f3 ♗c2 31.♖e3 leaves White poised to pry open the kingside. **30.g4!**

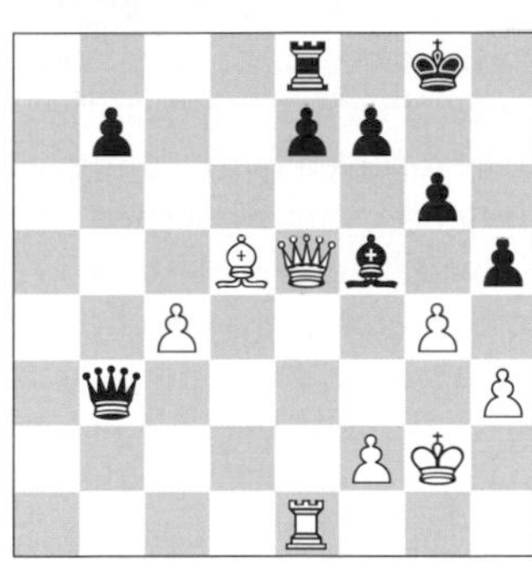

30...♗c8 30...hxg4 31.hxg4 ♗xg4 32.♖h1 ♗h5 33.♖xh5 gxh5 34.♕g5+ ♔f8 35.♕h6+ ♔g8 36.♕g6+.
31.♖e3! ♕d1 32.♖f3

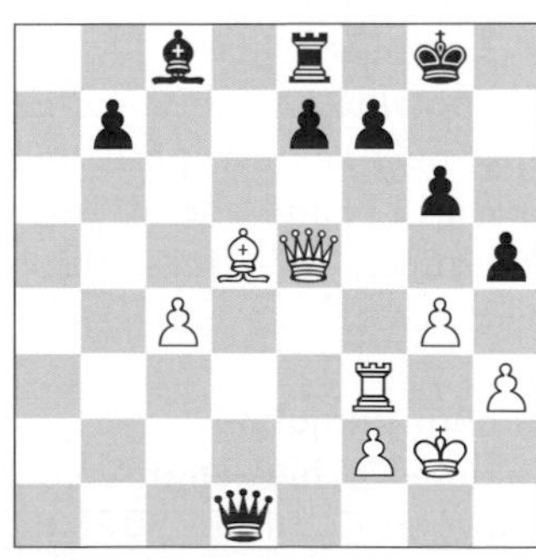

And Black's kingside crumbles.
32...e6 33.gxh5 gxh5 34.♕g5+ ♔f8 35.♕f6 Black resigned.

A perfect solution

In Round 2 'Radja' took part in an exercise that often featured over the course of the tour, and which would arguably later torpedo So's title hopes – choosing to go straight to tiebreaks with a series of short rapid game draws vs. Hikaru Nakamura. I'm probably naive, but I have never understood the benefits of taking on Naka at a faster time control than necessary. (For the spectators this meant that they could safely ignore their rapid games as they featured repetitions of well-known opening draws. One 19-move draw in the Queen's Gambit these same players had already played against each other in two previous legs; this time they showed their expertise in this drawing mechanism by playing it with both colours – ed.)

In Round 3, Radjabov was tie-broken by Anish Giri, despite having taken the lead in the rapid section. Teimour is so hard to beat that one could be forgiven for thinking he was heading for a cursed event – instead he 'solved' the event – by winning *all* of his remaining matches in the rapid segment, for a perfect finish of 18/18, and was the only player not to lose in 'regular time'. If that isn't a convincing argument for striving to avoid tiebreaks, what is?

Given the constant focus on the overall tour standings, this spectacular feat became the real story of the final, and catapulted the Azeri GM from fourth to second, obliterating So's 6.5 point head start.

Two notable Radjabov moments: a supremely smooth performance against MVL, and one of Carlsen's set of queen sacrifices, this one 'unnecessary':

Teimour Radjabov
Maxime Vachier-Lagrave
Meltwater CCT Final 2021 (9.2)
Queen's Gambit Declined, Ragozin Variation

1.♘f3 ♘f6 2.c4 e6 3.d4 d5 4.♘c3 ♗b4 5.cxd5 exd5 6.♗f4 ♘e4 7.♖c1 c6 8.e3 ♘d7 9.♗d3 ♘df6 10.0-0 ♗g4

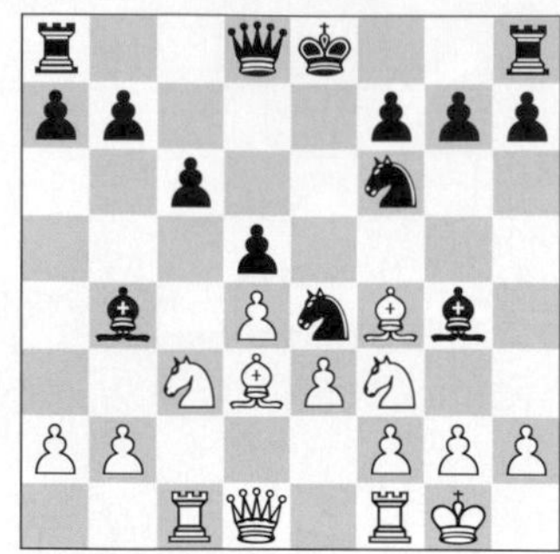

11.♕c2! A nice move that brands Black's last as a waste of time if he doesn't capture on f3.

11...♗xf3 12.gxf3 ♘xc3 13.bxc3 ♗d6 14.♗g3

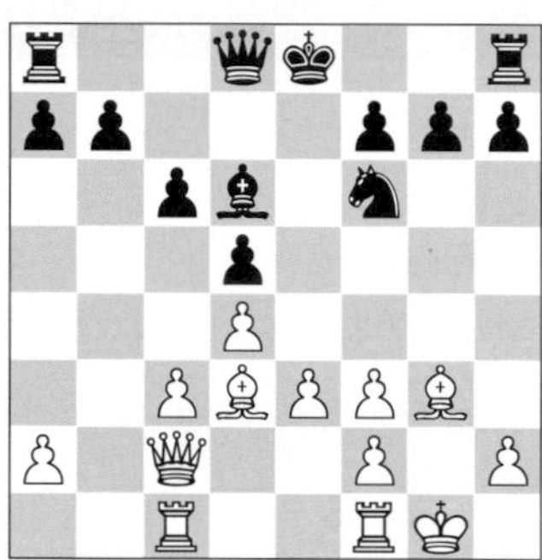

14...♘h5 14...h5!? doesn't solve Black's problems but does refuse to complete White's desired structural transformation. 15.♗h4!? or 15.c4!? intending 15...h4 16.♗e5 should both also favour White.

15.c4 dxc4 16.♕xc4 ♘xg3 17.hxg3

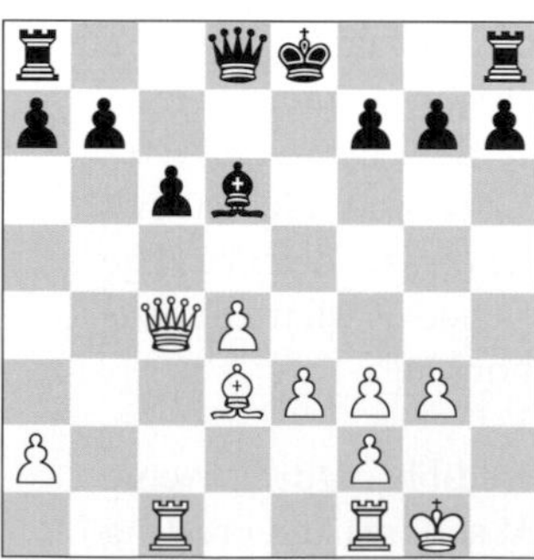

White's lovely pawn mass and ownership of the relevant open files makes this incredibly unpleasant for Black, and Radjabov increases the pressure with fearsome precision.

17...0-0 18.♔g2 g6 19.♖h1 ♔g7 20.d5 c5 21.♕c3+ f6

Forced due to the possibility of ♖xh7.

22.f4 ♕e7 23.a4! ♖ac8 24.♕c4 f5 25.♖b1 ♖c7

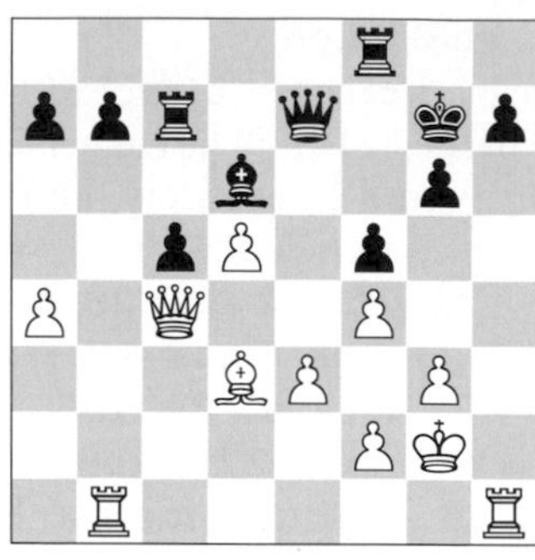

26.e4! fxe4 27.♖he1 ♕f6 28.♖xe4 ♖e7 29.♖e6 ♖xe6 30.dxe6 b6 31.a5! ♖e8 32.axb6 axb6 33.♖xb6 ♕xe6

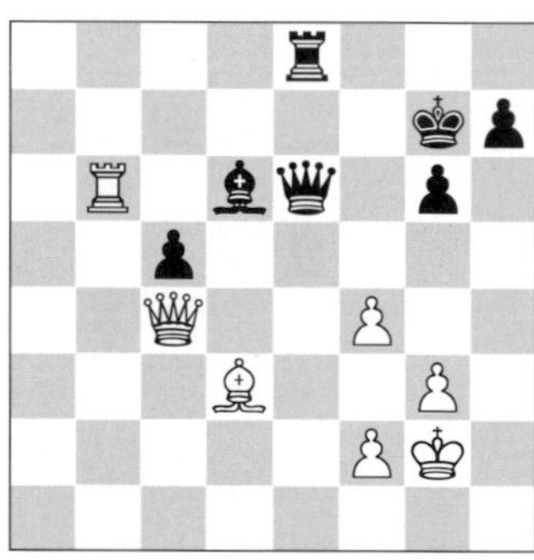

The simplifications have methodically opened lines and given White deadly access to the king.

34.♕c3+ ♔h6 35.♗c4 ♕e7 36.f5!

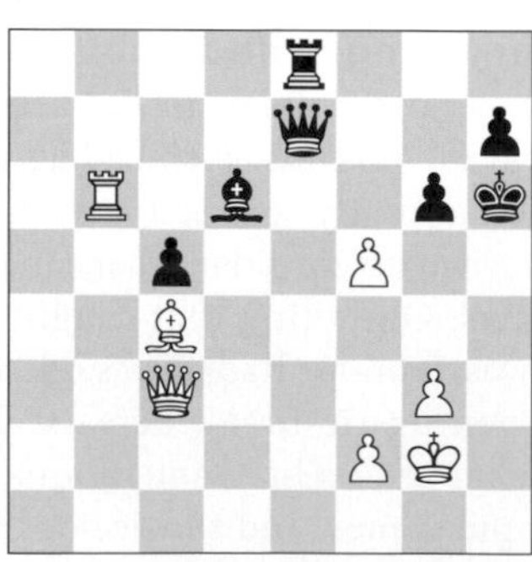

36...♗e5 36...♖d8 was the only way to parry ♕d2+ and fight on.

37.♕e3+ ♔g7 37...♕g5 38.♕xg5+ ♔xg5 39.f4+ ♗xf4 40.gxf4+ ♔xf4

41.f6. **38.♗b5**

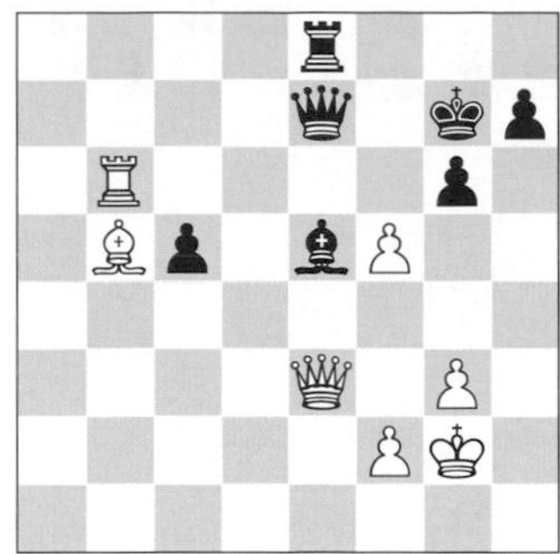

Making ♖e6 a deadly threat, since White can now answer a check on b7 with ♗c6. **38...♖c8 39.♗a6** Preventing the check on b7 and leaving Black defenceless against the threats on c8 and e6. A textbook exploitation of the advantages White gained from the opening. Black resigned.

Magnus Carlsen
Teimour Radjabov
Meltwater CCT Final 2021 (7.3)

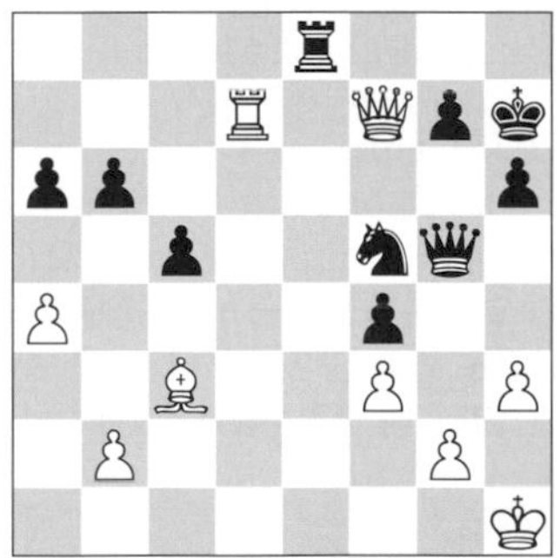

position after 36.♕f7

This is what Magnus referred to as his 'own goal' vs. Radjabov. Whether this fragment was coloured by the knowledge that Wesley So's ongoing debacle vs. Levon Aronian would clinch overall tour victory for Magnus, or was just an example of his occasional excessive determination, is hard to say.
36...♖e7 37.♕xf5+
37.♖xe7 ♘xe7 38.♕c4 gives White full value for the pawn but no more.
37...♕xf5 38.♖xe7
This isn't bad, but even Magnus seemed a bit puzzled afterwards about why it had attracted him.
38...♕g5

Playing from Moscow, Teimour Radjabov collected more points than anyone else and shot up to second place in the final standings.

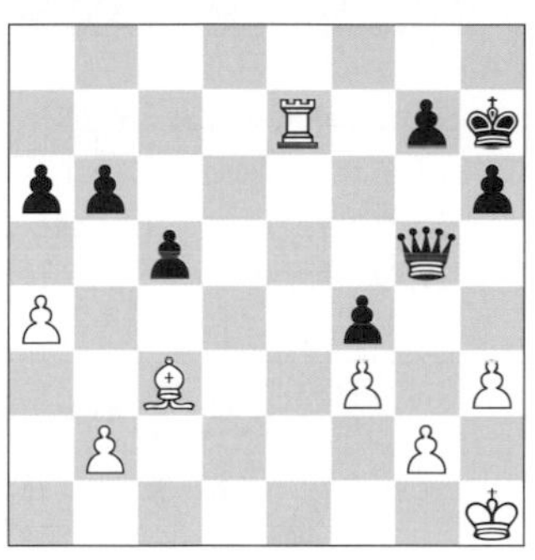

39.♖a7? This is an error though. White is aiming to immobilize the queenside pawns when he would have no worries, but this allows them to run. 39.♖b7 was OK for White.
39...b5! 40.axb5 axb5 41.♖a5 c4 42.♖a7 ♔g8 43.♖b7 g6

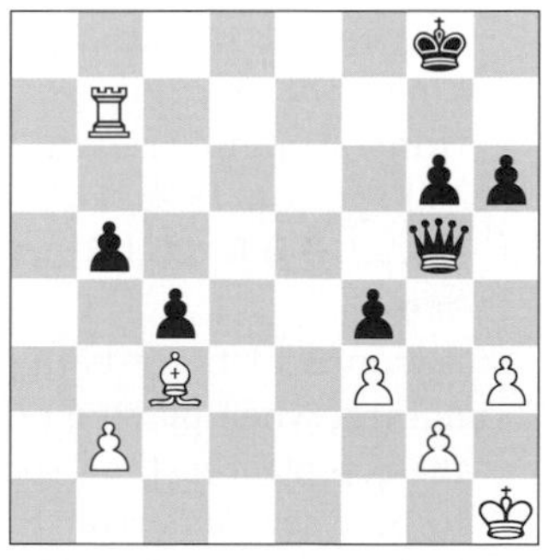

And Black converted his material advantage (0-1, 74).

Levon Aronian also leap-frogged So, his steady third-place performance including 3-point wins over Magnus and Wesley. If you haven't extracted the final results from the tour results, you might be surprised to learn that Hikaru came second, and Magnus fourth...

Non-games, and extra games

As mentioned, So's decision in Round 4 to burn all four rapid games in quick draws vs. Nakamura looked like the psychological if not mathematical turning point of the event. Like Radjabov, So paid the price of duelling with Hikaru at blitz, and had to settle for a single point. With a bit more ambition and steel the day could have been so much different, as Magnus stumbled and lost his first rapid match, to Artemiev. Perhaps Wesley's choice to guarantee himself a point rather than push for three hinted he was thinking more about safeguarding second place than overhauling Carlsen in first? From here on in, Wesley's resolve and form seemed to desert him.

From here on in, Wesley So's resolve and form seemed to desert him

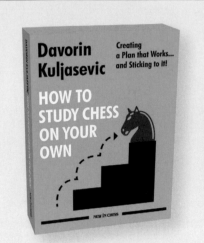

Wesley So
Hikaru Nakamura
Meltwater CCT Final 2021 (4.6)
1.e4 e5 2.♘f3 ♘c6 3.d4 exd4 4.♘xd4 ♘f6 5.♘xc6 bxc6 6.e5 ♕e7 7.♕e2 ♘d5 8.h4 a5 9.c4 ♘b6 10.♘d2 g6 11.h5 ♗g7 12.♘f3

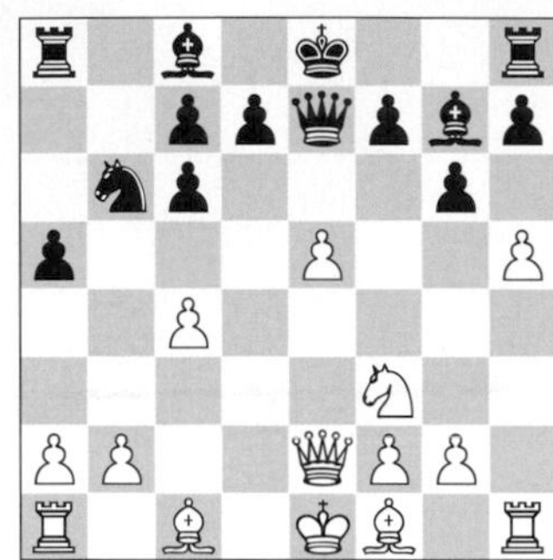

12...♕b4+ 13.♔d1!?
13.♗d2 ♕xb2 14.♖c1 0-0 (14...♗a6 15.♕e4) 15.hxg6 fxg6 16.♕e4 d5 17.♕h4 was also exciting.

13...♗a6!?
Our engine friends say that White's king is the more exposed after something straightforward like 13...0-0 14.hxg6 fxg6 15.♕e4 d5 16.♕h4 h5.
14.b3 0-0-0 15.h6 ♗f8 16.♘g5 ♕e7
Apropos of there being very little natural when playing positions like these, protecting the f7-pawn appears to be a serious error. Black should lash out with 16...d5 and invest the exchange in line-opening. The biggest danger for Black in this kind of position is long-term burial of the minor pieces on the queenside.
17.♖h3 d5 18.exd6

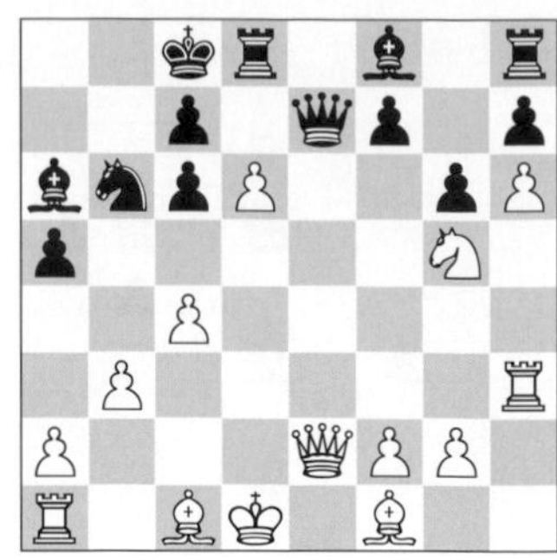

18...♕d7!? Cute. Nakamura wants to keep the queens on and this odd shuffle actually coordinates his kingside piece development. **19.♔c2 ♗xd6 20.♖d3 ♖he8 21.♕f3 f5**

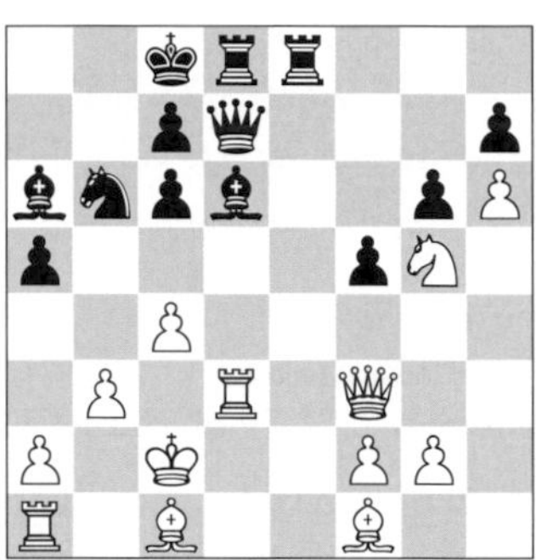

22.♗e3?! This feels less natural than either 22.♗f4 or 22.♗b2, when White is getting the upper hand. **22...c5 23.♗e2 ♕e7 24.♕h3 ♔b8 25.g3 ♗c8 26.♕h1??** 26.f4 had to be played. **26...f4 27.gxf4 ♗xf4**

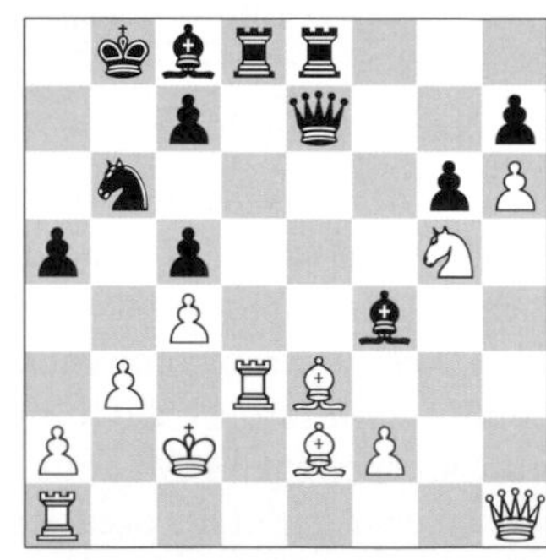

All of White's developed pieces are suddenly horribly misplaced. Something like 28.♘e4 (28.♗xf4 ♕xe2+ 29.♖d2 ♗f5+ 30.♔c1 ♖xd2 31.♗xd2 ♕d3 32.♕d1 ♖e2) 28...♖xd3 29.♗xd3 ♗xe3 30.fxe3 ♗b7 wins by suddenly pinning the ♘e4 from a different direction. White resigned.

One of the wildest matches was the clash between Jan-Krzysztof Duda and Shakhriyar Mamedyarov, two daredevils who fully lived up to their reputation.

While bloodless games of various sorts have been a recurring point of contention during the Tour, at least for many viewers venting on social media, the day's non-event rapid match caused perhaps the only furore of the tournament, when Nakamura was spotted taking part in a big blitz event on Chess.com during the day's 'play'. Hikaru later said that Tour spectators 'got their money's worth' in the tie-break vs. So, and that he needed his fix of daily chess – and he does seem to stream chess action at least 24 hours a day.

I asked the Tour director if this simultaneous display had ruffled feathers within the organization. Arne Horvei's carefully considered reply covered a lot of ground: 'We've had some situations in the course of the season where we have learned that contracts and regulations for next season need to be a little bit more specified on certain elements.'

Strategic thinking

On the thorny subject of safe draws, I noticed a variety of such decisions, including the semi-peaceful pair followed by two fights in the all-Azeri duel between Mamedyarov and Radjabov, and an unusual single burned White by Anish Giri in his match with MVL. I asked Anish if there was a more detailed explanation than just the apparent desire to get a game closer to victory when leading – one would think that there is some risk in donating a white to this end.

Anish explained that his decision was indeed just to get closer, but revealed some nuances regarding repertoire strategy: 'Yes, with MVL I was one up at that point and the ideas that I had against his openings that I prepared for that day with White, were involving some risks. And at the same time I felt confident to hold the next Black game.'

'I can only speak for myself. For others I would think a lot of it comes from having no issues with Black and no (good, risk free) ideas with White – Radja for example had a solid Black opening repertoire and a very predictable dull White.'

That's entertainment

Judging from the pre-final bonus points, MVL and Mamedyarov were the original wild cards, and Jan-Krzysztof Duda was Nepo's stand-in. For me, the man who produced the most sit-back-and-just-smile moments was Mamedyarov, whose meagre bonus allotment gave him little incentive other than to just have fun, and he served it up for the spectators as well. Duda literally had no bonus start, and he let loose as well. Their match was video game levels of mayhem.

Jan-Krzysztof Duda
Shakhriyar Mamedyarov
Meltwater CCT Final 2021 (3.3)

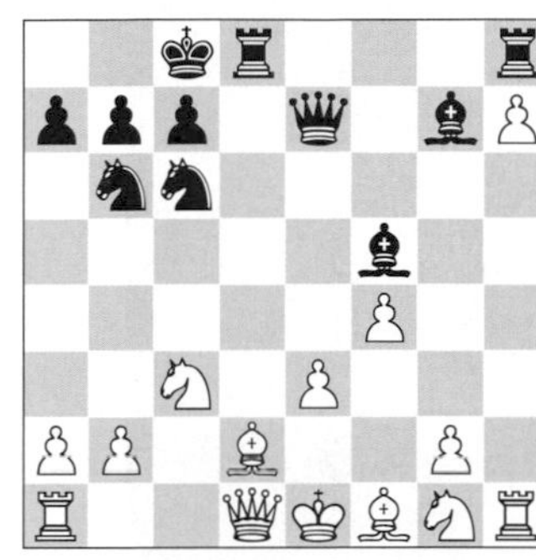

position after 13...0-0-0

This position occurred in what would be the first draw in this insanely violent match. I don't know what shocks me more about this position – that White survived it (½-½, 40), or that my engine is currently generating a series of lines assessed as 0.00...

Jan-Krzysztof Duda
Shakhriyar Mamedyarov
Meltwater CCT Final 2021 (3.5)

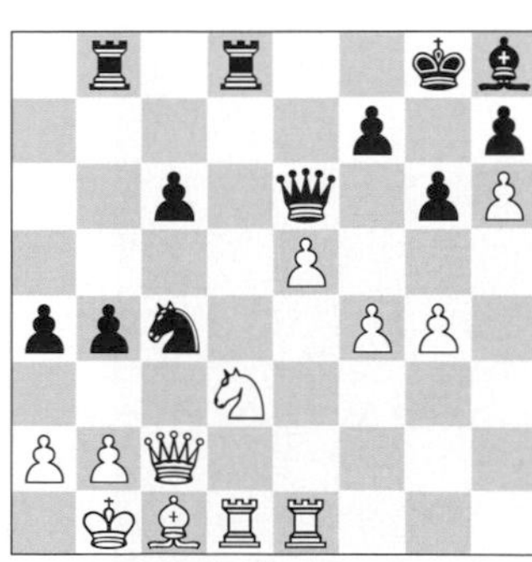

position after 27.f4

I never feel comfortable annotating blitz games played by people of extreme skill. They should really be simply experienced at speed, and with

There are supremely humbling examples of what magic the modern elite can produce with extremely limited time to think

the full sense of how mind-boggling the complications are they are trying to navigate, and how bewildering it is just trying to watch. Anyway, this is a typical brawl from this duel of two aggressive entertainers. The only difference between this and their other punch-ups is that they had even less time to figure things out here.

27...b3 28.axb3

White has no choice because after 28.♕c3 ♘a3+! promotes the a-pawn!

28...axb3 29.♕c3

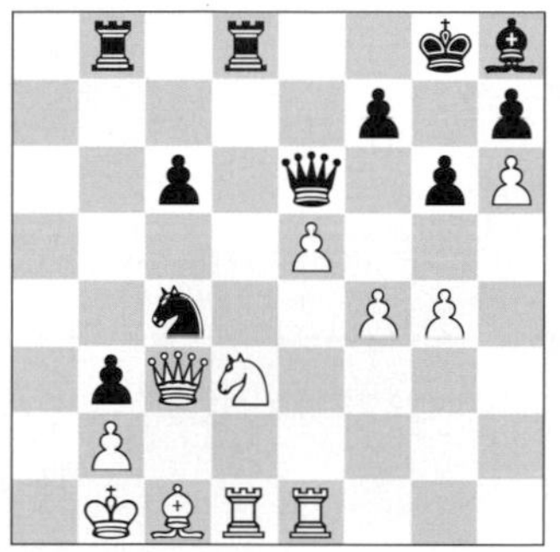

29...♘b6 Black should rush to exploit the pawn on b3 with 29...♕d5.

30.f5 ♕d5 31.♘c5

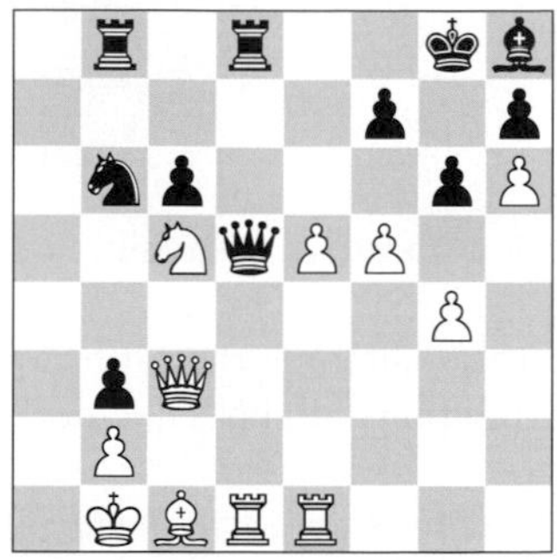

31...♕g2 31...♕xd1 32.♖xd1 ♖xd1 33.f6 should leave Black's kingside a fatal liability. **32.♕xb3**

32.♖xd8+ ♖xd8 33.♕xb3.

32...♘d5 33.♕c2

White worries about accidents on d1 and forgets the g4-pawn.

He should have played 33.♕c4.

33...♕xg4 34.f6

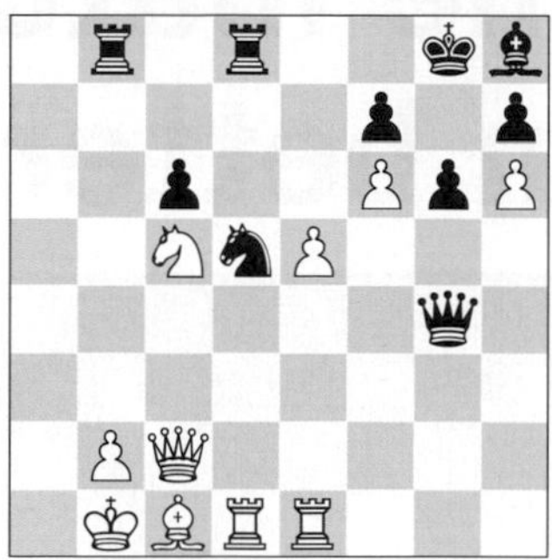

34...♕b4 34...♘c3+! would have won the exchange, but White would still have practical chances thanks to the ♗h8. **35.♘e4** Addressing the c3 issue, but 35.♘a6 was strong. **35...♖a8 36.♗d2 ♕b5 37.♗c3 ♕a6**

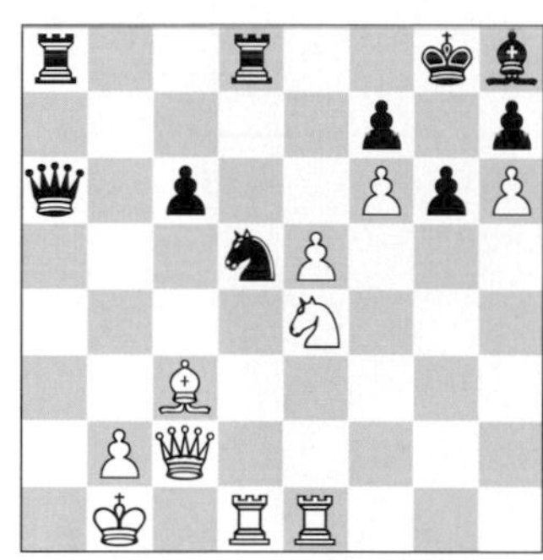

Now the a-file causes enough trouble to weigh up for his serious kingside congestion. Unfortunately for Black, he has spotted a wicked tactic in the blitz melee.

38.♔c1 ♘e3 On a good day this would win nicely. Black should have settled for 38...♕a1+ 39.♕b1 ♕a7 but is tempted by his tactical vision.

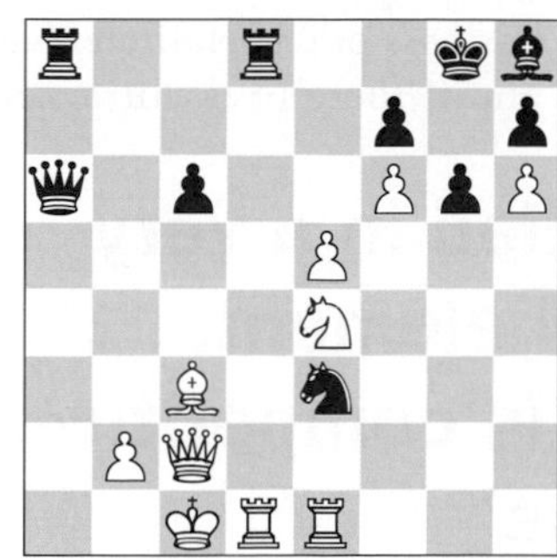

39.♖xd8+ ♖xd8 40.♖xe3 ♕a1+ 41.♕b1 ♖d1+ 42.♔xd1 ♕xb1+ 43.♔d2

Black cannot arrange king safety.

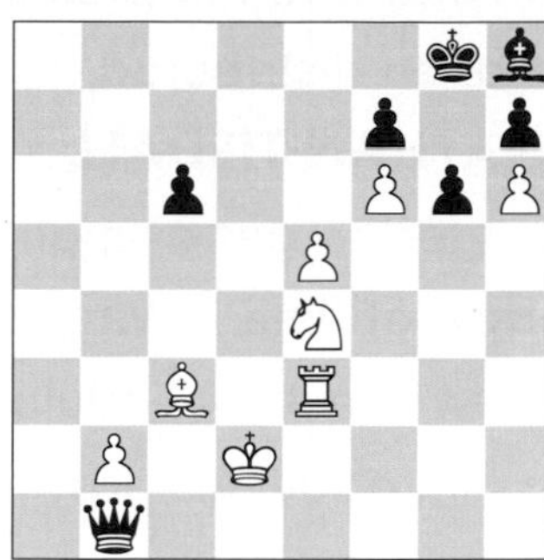

43...♕h1 43...♔f8 runs into 44.♖d3 ♔e8 45.♘d6+.

44.♖d3 ♕xh6+ 45.♔c2 ♗g7 46.♖d8+ ♗f8 47.♗b4

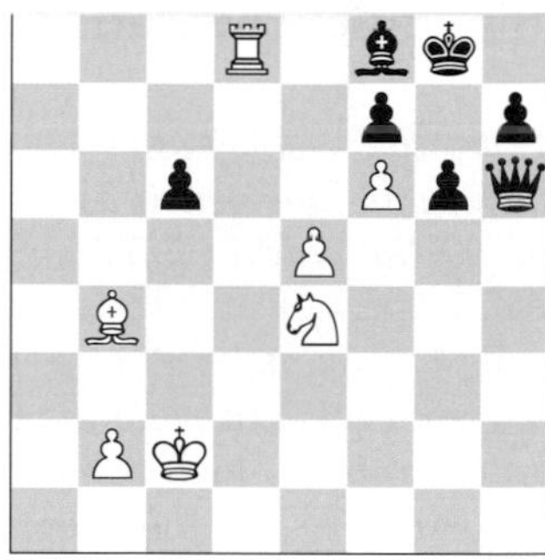

Heartbreak for Black. But play through Shakh's efforts from the event, he was a force of nature, and another highlight duel was his 7-game all White wins vs. Carlsen. ('I was lucky I had four whites' – Magnus)

There is so much here – over 200 games instead of the 45 a classical event would produce, and many more on my lists of intriguing or educational moments. Sure, some things go very wrong at high speed, but there are also supremely humbling examples of what magic or power the modern elite can produce with even extremely limited time to think.

What started as a lifeline during isolated times is growing into a fixture that aims to keep all of the newly curious as well as the long converted hooked on the game.

Magnus Carlsen: 'My biggest advantage in the match is that I am better at chess'

After the Meltwater Champions Tour had come to an end and the prizes had been distributed, **JONATHAN TISDALL** managed to get a small window of time in Magnus Carlsen's hectic schedule to quiz him about his post-tour impressions and the upcoming match. As usual, the Champ shoots from the hip and never pulls a punch on the topics covered.

LENNART OOTES

What are your feelings after winning the Tour, and how was it as preparation for the World Championship match?
'Overall, I think playing in the Tour was a great experience and in terms of preparation – just constantly playing games against tough opposition, even in rapid, is useful. So I'm looking forward to next year's Tour as well. Obviously I feel like there's a lot of things I can do better.'

Did it feel like you came fourth, or won the Tour?
'I think it felt like I won the Tour to be fair. I was kind of tired most of the Final and after it was clear that Wesley wasn't really catching me I couldn't really find the energy to play for the best result.'

You joked on Twitter about the result of the event being stacked in your favour. What do you think about the format looking back on it now?
'I think there are a lot of factors that should be in play in such an event if you have a year-long tour and you want to find the best player. Then the top finishers need to have some sort of an advantage – but I think we failed in a very crucial element, which is competitive intrigue. I think that's the most important thing. We are in the business of entertainment after all, and if there's very little doubt about the outcome then it becomes an exhibition and that's not ideal.'

'We failed in a very crucial element, which is competitive intrigue'

There's a problem when the favourite has the head start...
'I think people would have looked at it a bit differently if I was the one trying to catch up.'

But there were a lot of big changes in the standings...
'There certainly were, but just not for first place. I think for next season we'll have to think of something else

there, and there are many possible solutions or alterations. But I don't think it worked. It certainly worked in terms of the intrigue for second or third place, then it had a perfect dramatic conclusion, but first place is what most people will care about.'

'Rapid chess fits both the realities of top level chess, and the realities of entertainment, better'

Radjabov's result was insane.
'Yeah. He had a slow start and then just took off, yes, he was great. I do feel that my own result against him was a bit of an own goal, but overall he was amazing.'

The Tour concept is billed as finding the best online player in the world. Do you feel like you have a new world title now?
'No, because I don't feel that I was convincing enough.'

You can't do more than win the tour though...?
'I guess I can always play better. I felt that this season I was first among equals, which of course is OK, but it's not what I aspire to.'

How online is it really? This could easily translate into an OTB format.
'Yes, and I think that we are looking at the possibility of having some of the tournaments over the board already next year. As well as OTB tournaments there is the possibility of having these tournaments where everybody is in the same place, like a sports arena. I thought it was pretty exciting having just a few players in Oslo now, (Anish Giri and Jan-Krzysztof Duda were physically present in the Norway studio – JT) so hopefully we can do that as well.'

What about the aspects of things like mouse slips and pre-moves, contrasted with not knocking pieces over in Armageddon.
'It is a bit easier online but overall I don't think it makes a massive difference. If you're not used to playing online now, you're never going to be. At this point it is mainly a bit easier to organize it online, it is just more practical.'

It seems like a way of popularizing your preferred format for absolute elite events, more games, faster games – rather than classical and draws. Do you see it as an alternative to classical, or even more?
'I do feel overall that rapid chess should take more and more of the calendar for top events. As you said, classical is getting harder and harder to get anywhere in the opening, so more games and less time means more decisive games. I think it fits both the realities of top level chess, and the realities of entertainment, better.'

Looking ahead to the title match, how do you assess Ian Nepomniachtchi as a challenger – most people see him as a different and dangerous player, and a contrast to those you faced before, and to your own style.
'A very interesting challenger definitely, and as you said, different. But I do think we are going to see a little bit of a different version of him than we have in the past, probably a bit more solid. Apart from that I think he's an interesting opponent but I don't mind facing him compared to a Caruana or Ding.'

Do you feel a different pressure, or less pressure compared to facing Caruana? I thought London might have been special since both title and number one spot were on the line.
'I would say it's a bit of both, in some ways there is more pressure, in some ways less. Caruana was equal in terms of rating and had had better results than me recently, while Ian had an incredible Candidates but otherwise hasn't shown the consistency to be over 2800. So it probably feels more that this is someone who is very strong that I should probably beat, while last time it felt like more of an equal match. We'll see.'

Are you prioritizing physical fitness this time? It will be a longer match, do you think that will be a factor?
'Yes, that will be very important. Maybe for him more than me. I've usually been able to last these matches pretty well, while he's had a tendency to kind of fade at the end of tournaments. I will definitely be trying to be as fit as I have been in years.'

Do you think that your previous match experience is maybe your biggest advantage?
'No, my biggest advantage is that I am better at chess.'

'I think we are going to see a little bit of a different version of Nepomniachtchi than we have in the past, probably a bit more solid'

There was a recent video from Chess24 about your troubled relationship with the title – that you regularly contemplate not defending the title?
'I've said that every time.'

How do you make that decision, what's the equation?
'I guess I will talk about that after the match, either way.' ■

Fast forward Van Foreest

Dutch grandmaster sets a cracking pace in Malmö

The Tepe Sigeman tournament once again proved to be the flagship of Swedish chess with a fine mix of experience and up-and-coming talents. Jorden van Foreest showed great form and took first place with a round to spare. NILS GRANDELIUS reports.

The 2021 edition of the Tepe Sigeman tournament was the 10th time that I took part, but needless to say it was by far the strangest one. The tournament had originally been scheduled to take place in May 2020, was postponed several times due to Covid, and was finally played almost a year and a half after the original date. When the starting field was announced at the time, it made headlines due to the participation of Anatoly Karpov. Unfortunately, after all the postponements, the former World Champion, who celebrated his 70th birthday last May, was forced to cancel his participation. But the organizers haven't given up the idea of having Karpov taking part in the 2022 edition...

As for the rest of the field, it was also changed, of course, but it ended up being a typical clash between experience and youth, with three previous winners and three players born in 2004. However, the clash between experience and youth wasn't resolved clearly, there being a 40-year (!) difference between two of the players sharing second to fourth place.

In the end, the young-but-not-so-young Jorden van Foreest (22) turned out to be outstanding enough to win the tournament, with a round to spare, even. In his winner's speech, the Dutchman mentioned that he had never had so much time to prepare as for this tournament, with almost two years between getting the invitation and sitting down to play.

Delving deeper

What struck me the most during the event, though, was the eagerness everyone exuded to be back at the board playing classical chess. This resulted in a lot of fighting chess and many interesting games, but perhaps the main difference with the shorter time-controls was the emphasis on endgames. In a rapid or blitz game you rarely have more than seconds trying to navigate complicated endgames, whereas in a classical game you can really delve deeply into the mysteries of the position.

As for my own performance, it was a rather modest affair. I have always enjoyed playing in my former home town of Malmö, and the tournament was excellently organized in each of the ten editions I took part in. Somehow this was simply not my year. My best game I played in Round 1.

Nils Grandelius
Nihal Sarin
Malmö 2021 (1)
Ruy Lopez, Smyslov Defence

The last time we played, Nihal Sarin went for the Sicilian, got out-prepared and lost, but after having been completely fine in-between. I expected something else this time. I just had no idea what.

1.e4 e5 2.♘f3 ♘c6 3.♗b5 g6

A first surprise, but at least I was expecting to be surprised! This is, I think, a somewhat dodgy opening, but it fits Nihal's style of avoiding main lines, and nowadays almost anything is playable if checked properly...

4.c3 a6 5.♗a4 ♗g7 6.d4 exd4 7.cxd4 b5 8.♗c2 d5

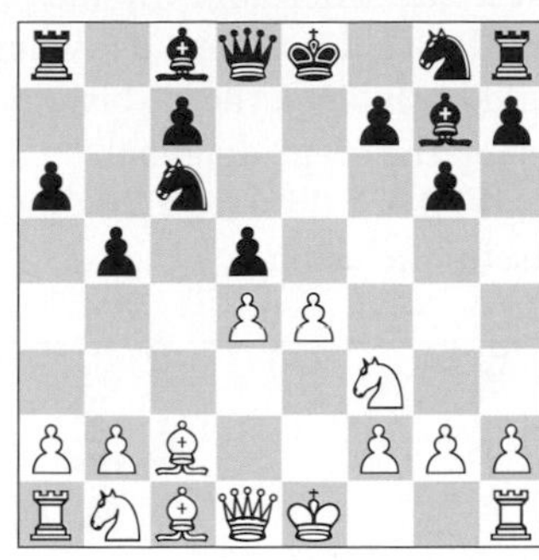

A topical move, introduced a few years ago. It looks risky to open the centre with the knight still on g8, but ...d5 in itself is also a logical reaction when White's bishop goes to c2 rather than b3 in the Ruy Lopez.

9.♗g5 A month before this game, I had published a course on Chessable, a repertoire for White in the Ruy Lopez. In that course I described the move 9.♗g5 as 'rare and interesting', so I was especially curious to see what Nihal had in mind against it. However, judging by his time management in the next couple of moves, it became clearer and clearer to me that he hadn't studied the course!

9...♘ge7 10.♘c3 h6

11.♗xe7 This is White's idea. By giving up the bishop pair, the centre is secured and the influence of the g7-bishop is reduced.

11...♘xe7 12.e5 0-0 13.0-0 ♗g4 Undoubtedly the strongest move, but at the same time a slightly sad one to make. By giving up the bishop pair, Black basically gives up all hope of taking the initiative later, but if he hadn't played it, the break with ...c5 would have been impossible to achieve, leaving White with a very pleasant space advantage.

14.h3 ♗xf3 15.♕xf3 c5!

This looks risky, but Black desperately needs to fight back in the centre.

16.dxc5 ♕c7 17.♖fe1

17.b4 looks more natural, but 17...♕xe5 creates unpleasant threats along the long diagonal.

17...♕xc5 17...♗xe5 18.b4 is now safe for White.

18.♗b3

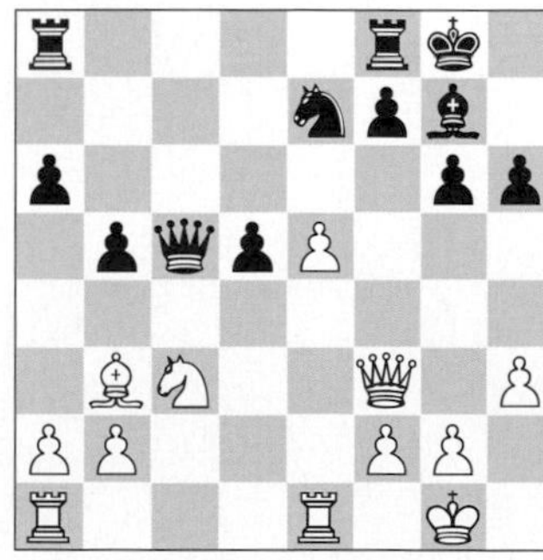

With opposite-coloured bishops, the main aim is usually to make one's

What struck me the most was the eagerness everyone exuded to be back at the board playing classical chess

own bishop strong and the opponent's bad. Therefore my idea is to lure Black's d-pawn to d4, where it would both block the g7-bishop and open up the b3-g8 diagonal.

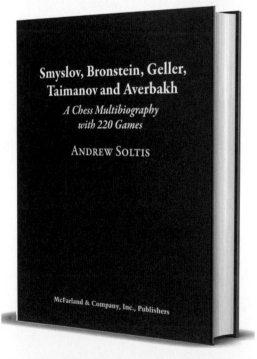

18...d4 19.♘d5 ♘xd5 20.♖ac1
A useful inclusion.

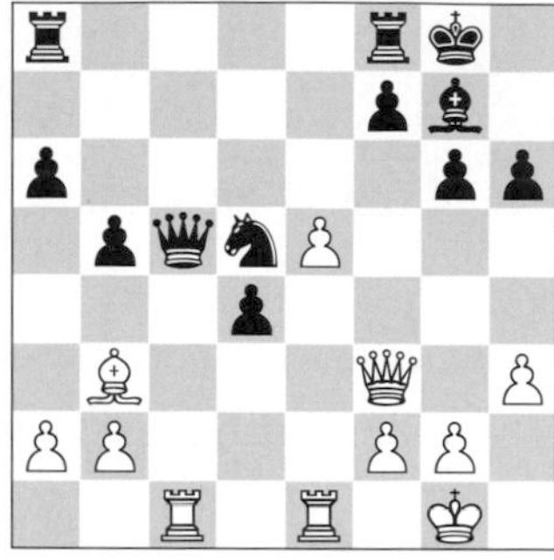

20...♕b4 A serious strategic error that allows me to realize my goals.
In my Chessable course I mention that 20...♘c3! is the only good move. The point is that after 21.bxc3 Black can play 21...♖ae8!, after which White can't hold onto the e5-pawn in the long run. This means that the g7-bishop will come alive. After something like 22.cxd4 ♕xd4 23.♖c6 White still keeps some initiative, as f7 is still a bit soft and g6 a tactical weakness, but compared to the game this is far, far better for Black.

21.♕xd5
Now the d-pawn will be safely blocked and the e5-pawn can always be supported by f2-f4. Long term, White's plan is to push his kingside pawns and launch an attack. Additionally, both the d-pawn and the c-file are annoying for Black to handle. As a final point, it should be mentioned that the pawn being on h6 rather than h7 is a serious concern for Black, since this weakens the whole kingside structure.

21...♔h8 22.♕e4!
A good, prophylactic move. I make sure that the d-pawn would never move. With such a long-term advantage there is no reason to rush things, as the lack of counterplay makes the position very difficult for Black in a practical game.

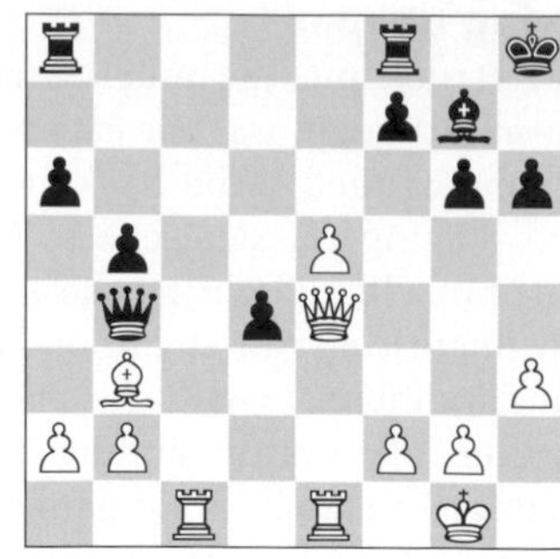

22...♖ae8 23.f4 ♖e7 24.♖ed1 ♖d8 25.♖d3 Not so much to attack the d-pawn, but to make even more sure that it will never advance. Again, the issue for Black is the lack of any meaningful counterplay.

25...♕a5

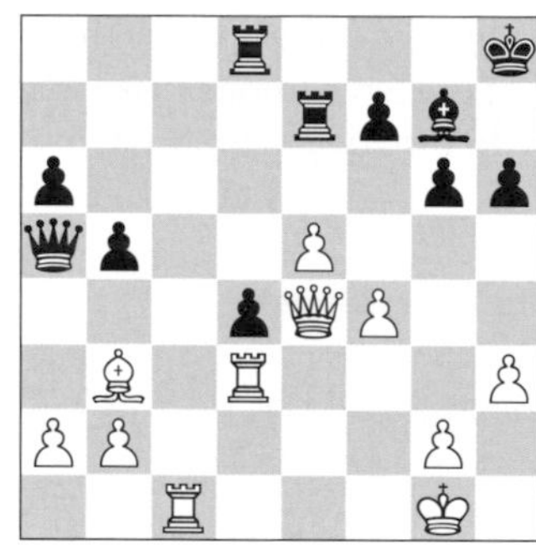

26.h4?! A good move in principle, since the plan of h4-h5 makes a lot of sense, but the timing wasn't the best. 26.♖c6 was natural and far stronger. I didn't want to trade rooks after 26...♖c7, but the simple 27.♔h2! would highlight just how hopeless Black's position is. Trading a set of rooks would leave f7 even weaker than before, and there is also the possibility of ♖d6 on the next move. Black is just collapsing.

26...♖c7 27.♖cd1 ♕b6 28.h5

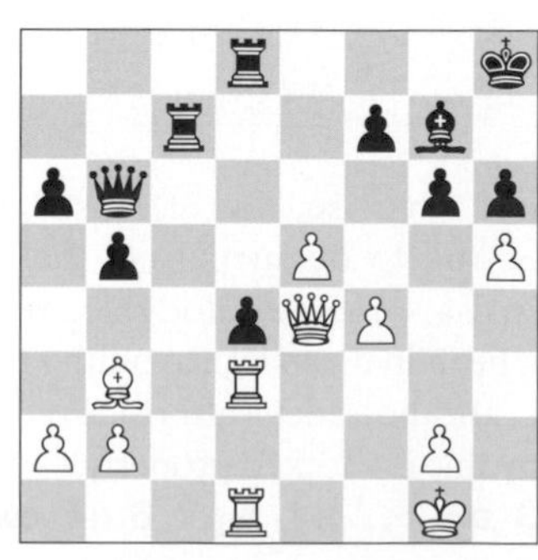

LARS HEDLUND

Nils Grandelius was not too happy about his play this time, but the Swede won an excellent game against Nihal Sarin in the first round.

Played without much thought, as I considered it the logical follow-up. Still, there is no rush and I should perhaps have considered a move like ♔h1 instead.

28...gxh5 28...g5 29.g3 would not change much. Sooner or later I will be able to put my bishop on the b1-h7 diagonal, with fatal consequences.

29.♔h1?
Played on general grounds. I didn't play 29.♔h2, because it's on the same colour square as Black's bishop, possibly allowing for tactical tricks, but if I had taken a more concrete look at the position, I would have seen that in the game continuation the king is simply much better placed on h2, because it's closer to the centre.

29...♕g6

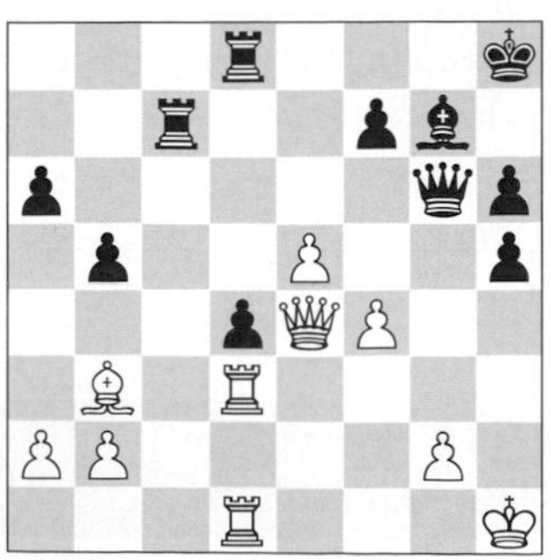

30.♕xg6! Very tempting was 30.f5, but 30...♕g4! 31.♕xg4 hxg4 actually gives Black some counterplay: 32.f6 ♗f8, and here it is clear that my king would have been much better on h2, because then the black idea of ...g3 and a back rank mate would not have existed!

30...fxg6 31.♖xd4 ♖xd4 32.♖xd4
With a protected passed pawn on e5, White is of course still much better. But the reduced material gives Black drawing chances.

32...♗f8 33.♖d8 ♔g7

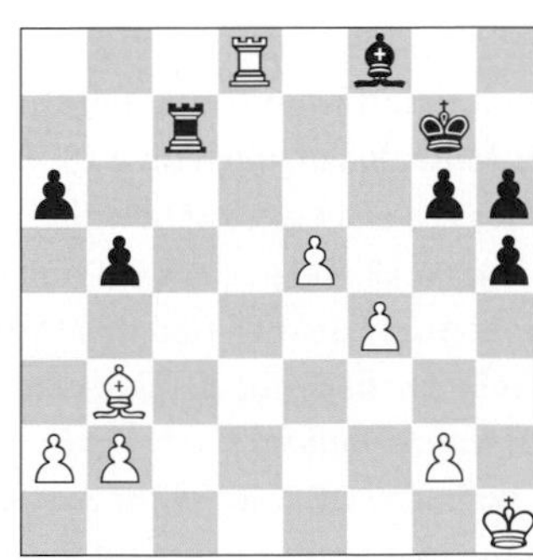

34.♖a8?
A greedy move, which could have cost me half a point. I had underestimated the potential for counterplay. 34.g3! was much better, simply bringing the king into the game and stopping all counterplay. It allows 34...a5, but that wouldn't help Black much. After 35.♔g2 a4 36.♗d5 Black still can't really get out, as abandoning the 7th rank with the rook would be too risky.

34...h4! Nihal immediately seizes the only counterplay available.

35.♔h2 ♗c5! 36.♔h3

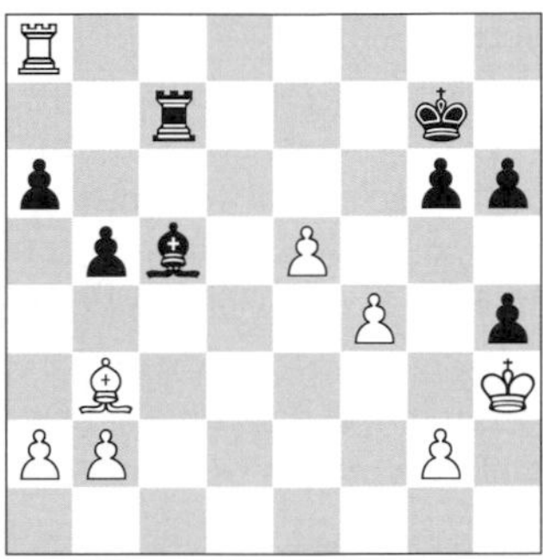

36...♗d4?
We both completely missed 36...♖d7!, even in the post-mortem. The rook lands on d3 with great effect: 37.♔xh4 ♖d3!, followed by ...♗f2+, with enough counterplay for a draw.

37.♖xa6 g5 Undermining the e5-pawn, but the white king's activity is much more important.

38.f5! ♗xe5 39.♖g6+ ♔h7 40.♔g4!

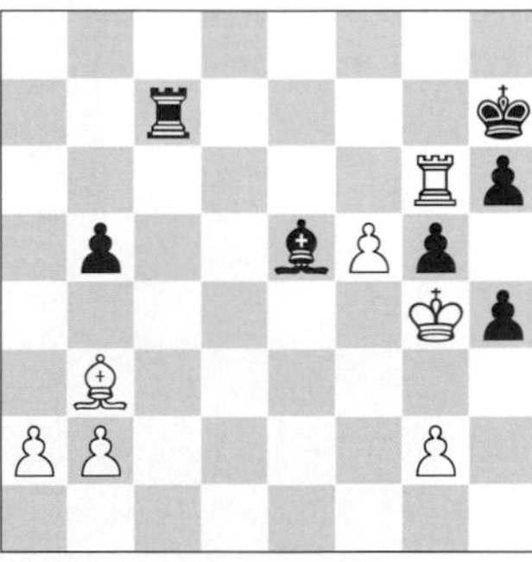

The key move. The king enters on h5, and in combination with the passed f-pawn and mating threats, White is again completely winning.

40...♗g7 41.♖a6
There is simply no defence against f6, followed by ♔h5, so the game is over.

41...h3 42.gxh3 ♖d7 43.f6 ♖d4+ 44.♔f5

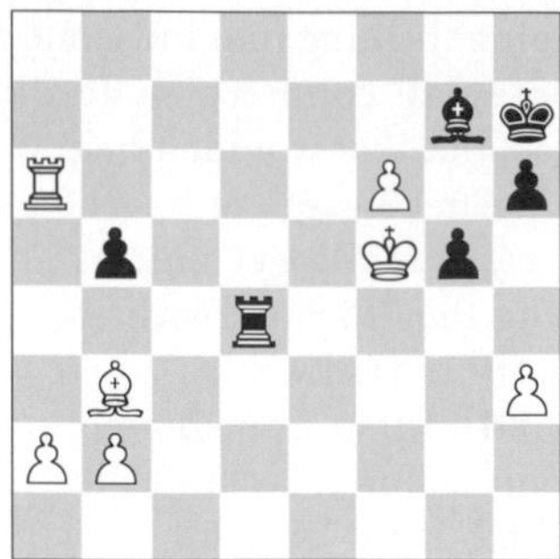

Black resigned.

Jorden van Foreest, who sensationally won this year's Tata Steel tournament in Wijk aan Zee, was also the winner in Malmö. He won very convincingly, showing good preparation, expert handling of the initiative, and excellent defensive skills when necessary. He annotated his best wins, that against the veteran in the field, Nigel Short (56), and that against the youngest participant, 17-year-old Jonas Bjerre from Denmark.

NOTES BY
Jorden van Foreest

Jorden van Foreest
Nigel Short
Malmö 2021 (3)
Scotch Opening, Mieses Variation

1.e4 e5 2.♘f3 ♘c6 3.d4 On the two previous occasions that I played against Nigel Short, I went for the Ruy Lopez. This time around, I wanted a sharp struggle in the Scotch Opening.
3...exd4 4.♘xd4 ♘f6

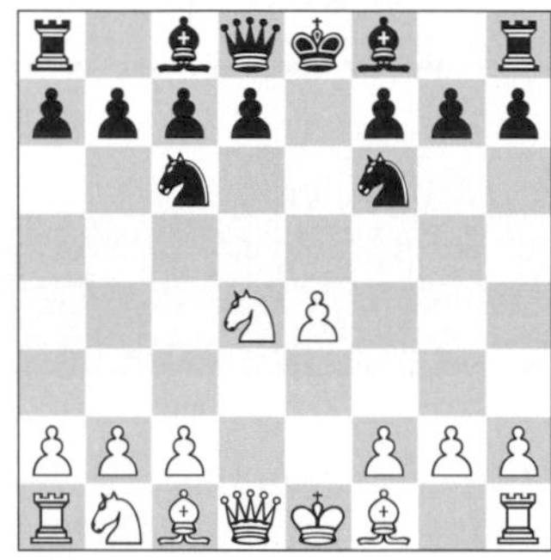

Throughout his long career, Short has tried virtually every move against the Scotch. With the text and over the next moves, he follows his most recent game with this opening: that against Deep Sengupta from 2017.
5.♘xc6 bxc6 6.e5 ♕e7 7.♕e2 ♘d5 8.c4 ♘b6 9.♘c3 a5
Still following the aforementioned game. Somewhat surprisingly, I had also found several half-forgotten games of my own in my preparation for this game.
10.f4

A small twist that seemed to throw Short off, as he sunk into deep thought.
The main move is 10.♕e4, although I have tried the subtle 10.♗d2 as well.
10...g6? I assume that this move was intended to take me out of my preparation. However, there is nothing against the natural and most popular 10...♗a6. The text weakens the dark squares around the black king, which will become a salient factor later in the game.
11.♗e3 ♗a6

12.♗xb6! A remarkable decision, giving up the strong bishop.
I did not want to play the natural 12.b3 in view of moves like 12...a4 and 12...♘d5. In return for the lost bishop, the white pieces get quick access to the d6 and f6-squares, while the bishop on a6 has lost its purpose.
12...cxb6 13.0-0-0

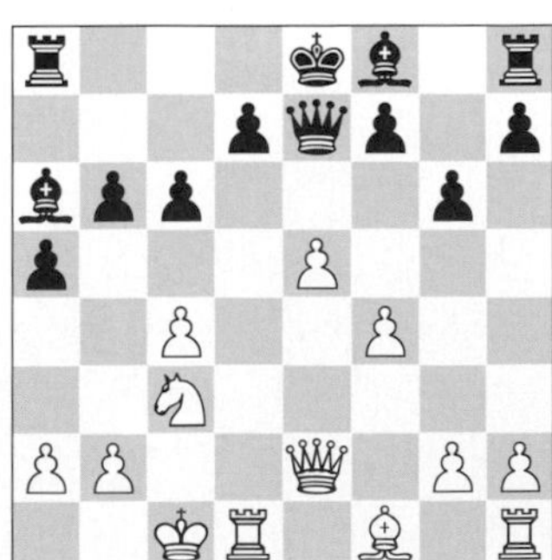

13...♗h6?! During the game, I thought this was a strong move to gain time to complete development. Interestingly enough, the contrary is the case, and Black should have played 13...♗g7, aiming for a quick central pawn break: 13...♗g7! 14.♘e4 0-0 15.♖d6. I assessed this position as overwhelming for White, but it turns out that things are not so simple after 15...♖ae8 16.♕d2 f6 17.♖xd7 ♕e6. This is a key variation, in which Black manages to free his position, obtaining decent counterplay at the cost of a pawn.
14.g3 0-0 15.h4 Such Dragonesque moves can be played without too much thought. The black king is a clear target. After 15.♘e4, 15...♕xe5! is the point behind 13...♗h6.

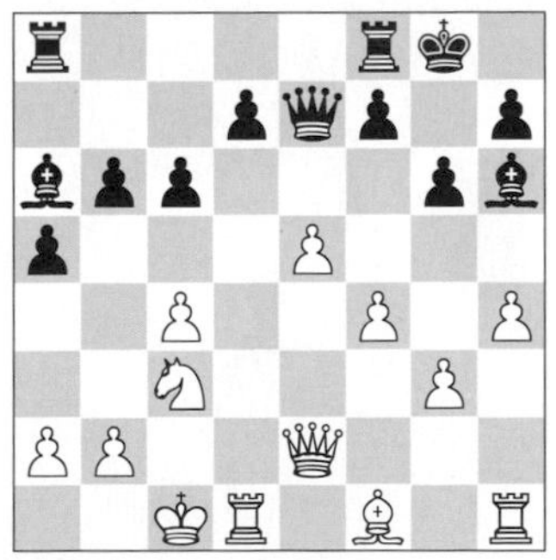

15...♖ae8 Preparing ...f6, and also threatening to capture e5.
16.♔b1?
Too slow. I should have continued with a somewhat brainless push of the h-pawn, as it fulfils the dual purpose of also preventing 16...♕xe5: 16.h5 ♕xe5? 17.♕xe5 ♖xe5 18.hxg6!, and Black loses material.

LARS HEDLUND

A subtle rook manoeuvre gave Jorden van Foreest a paralyzing grip on Nigel Short's position, leaving the Black player no chance to free himself.

16...f6 17.h5

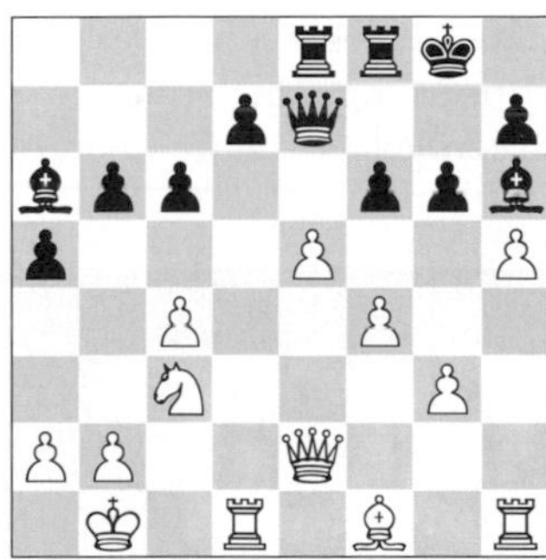

17...g5?
Missing his one chance to get back into the game. With the bishop on a6 already buried alive, it is necessary to have the other one play at maximum capacity: 17...fxe5 18.hxg6 ♗g7! 19.f5!? (19.gxh7+ ♔h8 is a typical theme, using the enemy pawn as a shield) 19...hxg6 20.fxg6 e4.

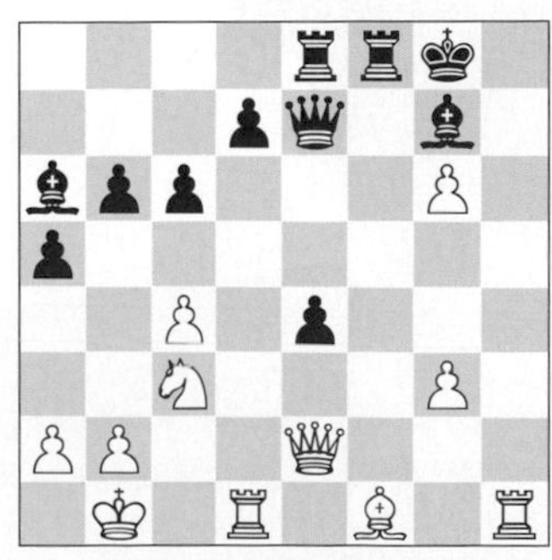

ANALYSIS DIAGRAM

It certainly looks scary for Black, but if there is no quick mate, the white king will soon start feeling the heat from the powerhouse of a bishop on g7 as well.

18.♘e4! The d6-square is starting to look highly enticing. There is not much Black can do about the white pieces invading.

18...fxe5 Perhaps Short was pinning his hopes on the advance 18...d5, intended to finally liberate his languishing a6-bishop. It's just too late, however, since 19.♘d6! comes with a multitude of threats. Not only is the rook hanging, ♘f5 is a cute move to watch out for as well.

19.fxg5 ♗xg5 20.♕g4 h6 21.♖d6!

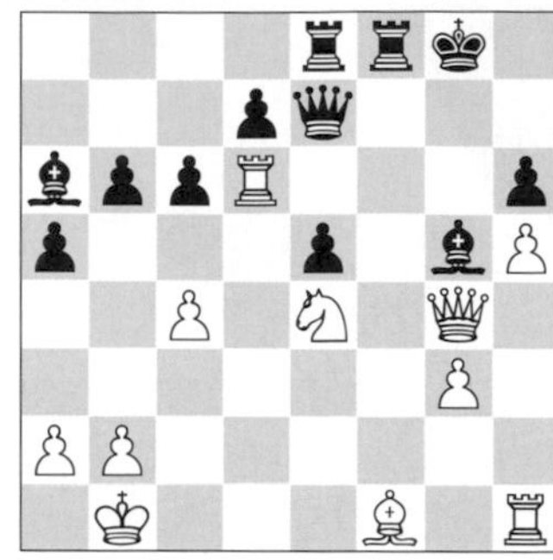

The key move! Cutting the board in half and stopping any pawn breaks Black might have been considering. In an online blitz game this could have been one of those accidental mouse slips that turn out to be good – since at first glance it seems far more logical to take: 21.♖xd7. However, this runs into the rejoinder 21...♗c8!. After the text Black's position is in a total state of paralysis, and there is surprisingly little he can even try.

21...♔h8 22.♗d3 ♗c8

A sad move to make, but at least here the bishop is fulfilling the function of defending d7.

23.♖d1 ♖g8

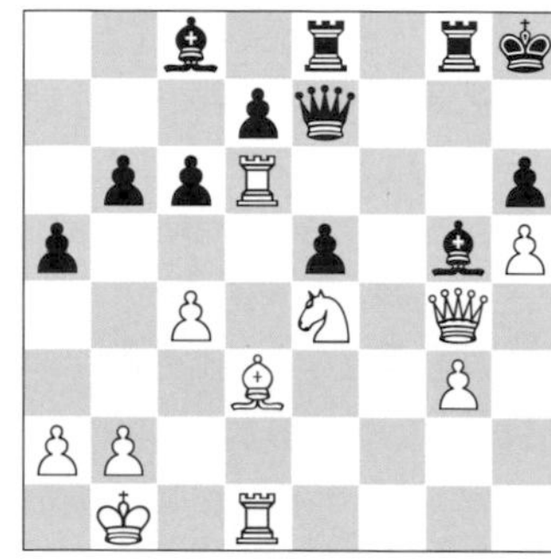

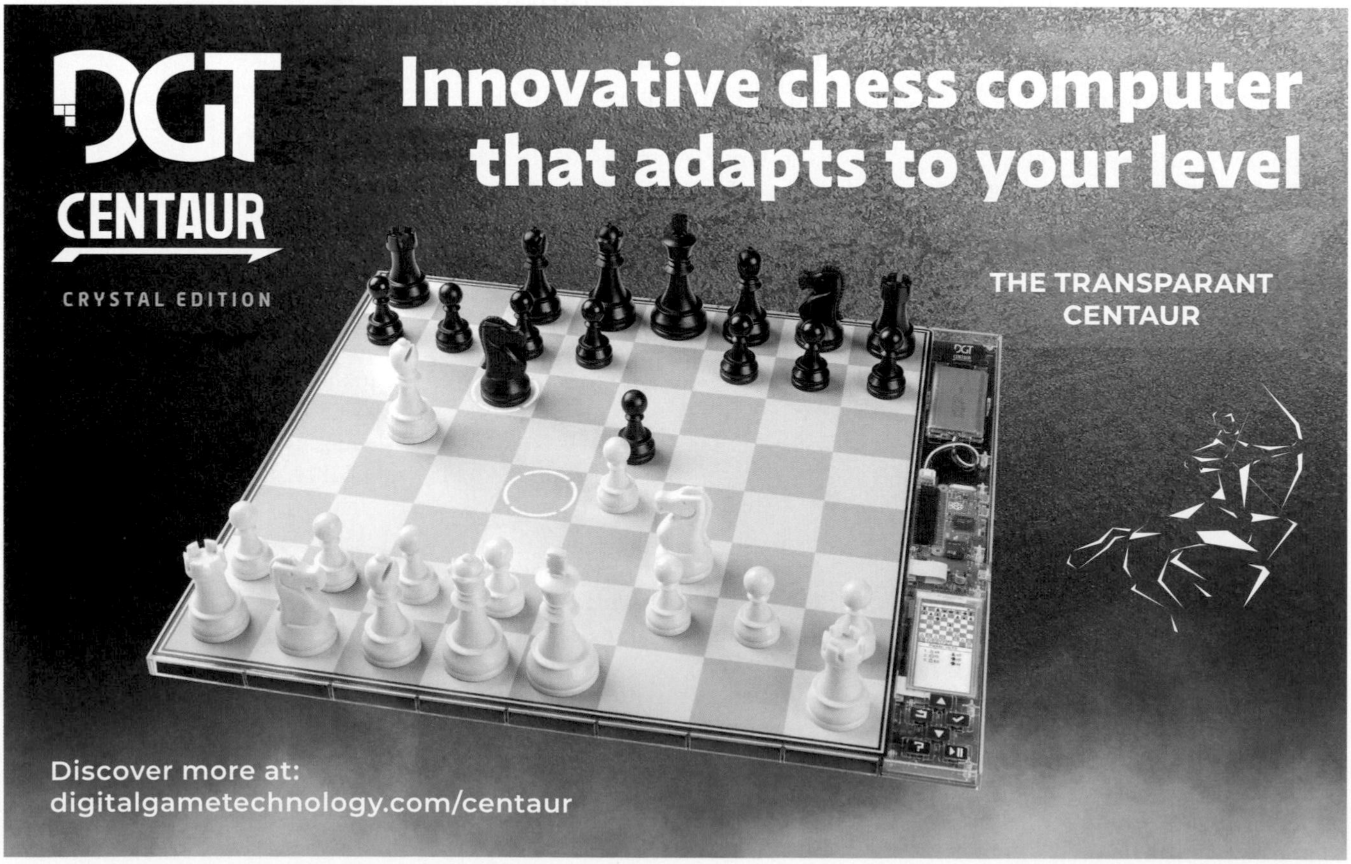

This allows a direct attack, but I can suggest little to improve Black's chances. White can even reinforce his position further with little moves like ♗c2 and a3.

24.♘xg5

A somewhat surprising trade, one might think. After calculating some variations, I noticed that in return for giving up the proud knight I get direct mating threats that are extremely difficult to deal with.

24...♕xg5 25.♕e4 The point of trading off the knight; the e4-square can now be accessed by the queen.

25...♖g7 26.♖f1!

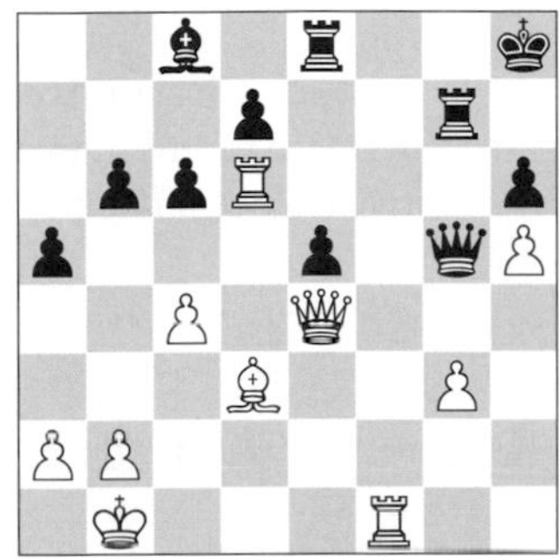

This is the position I envisioned when considering my 24th move. It is of crucial importance that I take direct control of the f-file.

26...♔g8

The best defence: prophylaxis against a potential ♖xh6+, since this will now no longer come with check.

27.c5 Attempting to access the a2-g8 diagonal with my bishop. Short, however, is not so obliging.

27...b5 28.a4

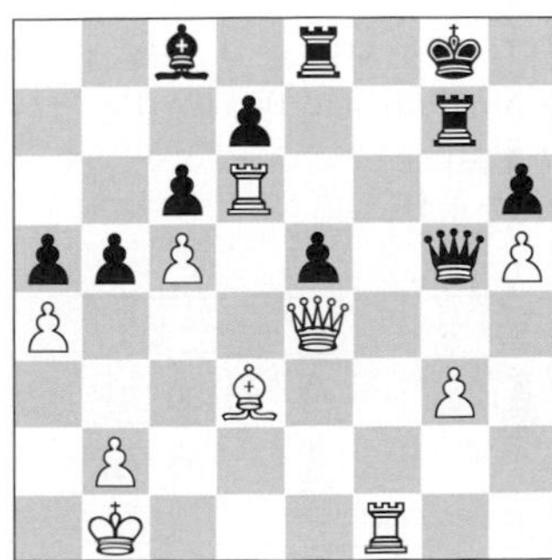

28...♗a6!

Tenacious defending by Short, who is keeping the position shut for the moment. Still, I felt the win should be only a few moves away. I sunk into thought, attempting to find the most direct one, but to my surprise I could not find anything. Black has just one idea in the position: to go ...♕g4.

One does not see an Alekhine's Gun along the sixth row every day

Even the endgames might be better for me, but Black is up a pawn, after all. After some twenty minutes of thinking, and becoming slightly flustered that I couldn't finish Black off at once, I finally thought I had hit on an accurate way.

The immediate 28...♕g4 was far more hopeless, allowing a trivially won endgame after 29.axb5 ♕xe4 30.♗xe4 cxb5 31.♖xh6 ♖xg3 32.♗d5+ ♔g7 33.♖b6, with h6 to follow.

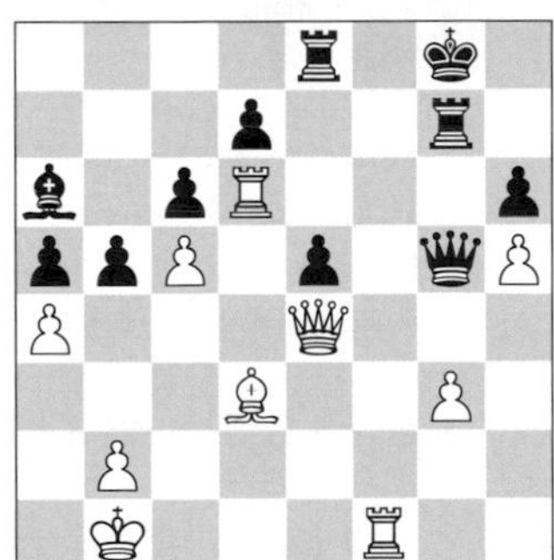

29.♖g6!? I was not sure about this move, as my rook stood so nicely on d6, but I finally decided I had calculated all the variations up to and including a win.

However, 29.axb5 might have been the simplest move. I considered it but did not want to allow Black the pleasure of exchanging his doomed bishop: 29...♗xb5 30.♗xb5 cxb5 31.c6!. This is the point:, the white queen finds a way into Black's position with decisive effect: 31...dxc6 32.♕xc6 ♖b8 33.♖ff6. One does not see an Alekhine's Gun along the sixth row every day. Black has nothing left but to throw in the towel, since his king is for the chopping block.

29...♖xg6 30.hxg6 The threat of ♕f3, followed by ♕f7, forces Black to retreat. **30...♕e7** So as to meet ♕f3 with ...♖f8. **31.♖f7**

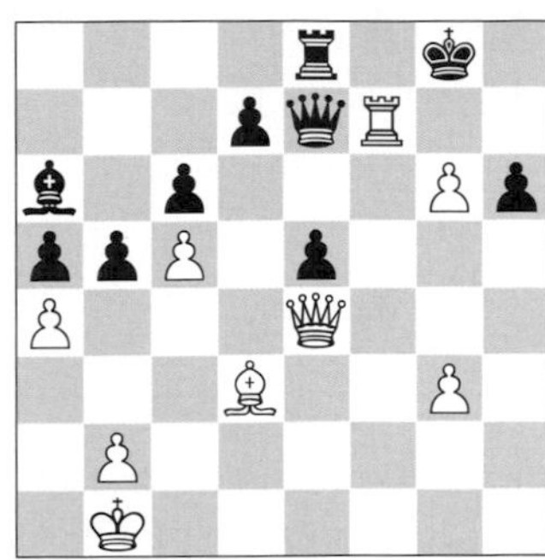

31...♕e6 There was no time for greedy pawn grabbing excursions. After 31...♕xc5 32.♕f5 the dual threat of ♖g7+ and g7 will be unstoppable: 32...♕d5 33.g7.

32.♕h4?! I had calculated this far and thought that it should really be game over now. Surely, ♕xh6 cannot be prevented and there is no way Black can give more than a couple of spite checks? The next move was an absolute shocker!

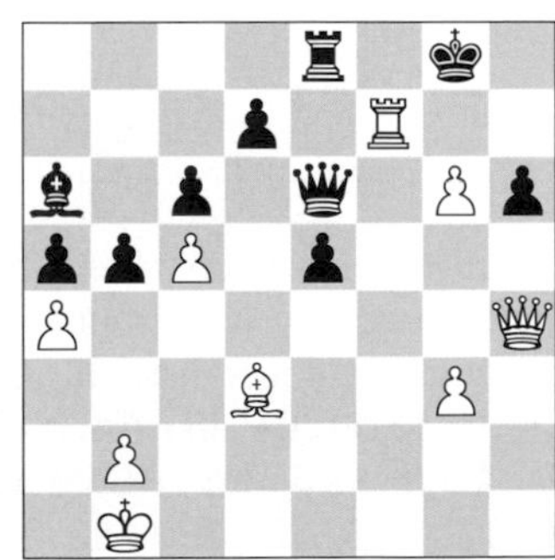

32...b4! I had completely overlooked this resource. My first thought was that I had bungled fatally. After a few moments of recollecting myself I noticed that I was fortunately still winning. Still, allowing such resources is not for the faint of heart, and the next time it might cost me dearly.

33.♗c2 Not, of course, 33.♗xa6 ♕xg6+, and the tables have turned!

33...b3

Black has no better, but now we transpose into an easily won endgame.

34.♕xh6 bxc2+ 35.♔c1 ♕xf7 36.gxf7+ ♔xf7

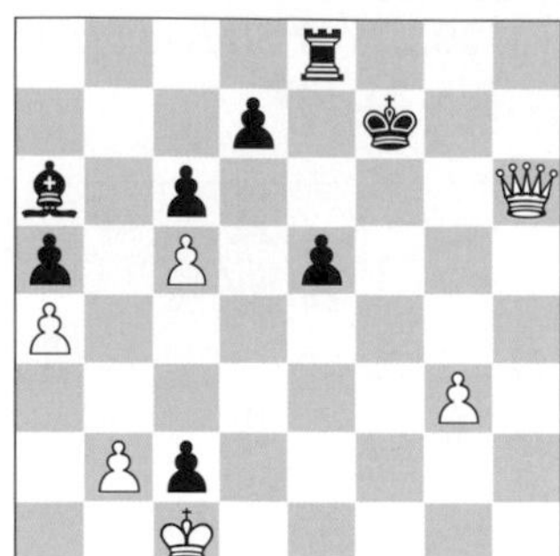

The material situation is, in fact, still balanced, but fortunately for me Black loses most of his remaining pawns.

37.♕h5+ ♔f8 38.♕f5+ ♔g7

38...♔e7 39.♕xe5+ ♔d8 40.♕c3 was hardly a better defence.

39.♕xd7+ ♔f8 40.♕xc6 ♗c8 41.♕e4 ♔g7 42.♔xc2

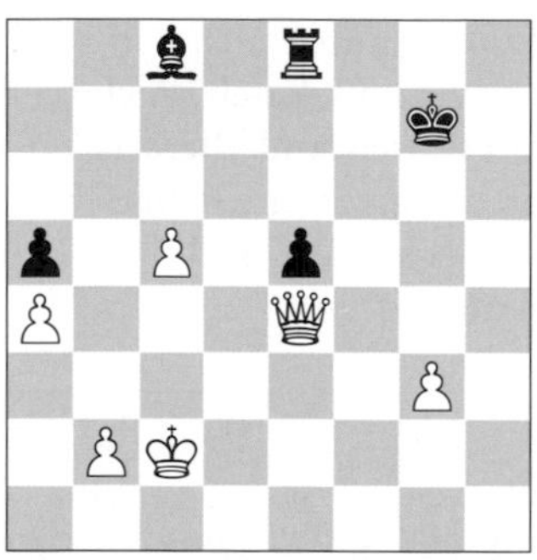

The game is effectively over. Short still tries to stir up some trouble, but even I could no longer mess this up.

42...♔f6 43.♕c6+ ♔f7 44.♕c7+ ♔f6 45.♕xa5 e4 46.♕c3+ ♔g6 47.♕e3 ♖f8 48.♔d2 ♗b7 49.♕d4 ♖f3 50.b4

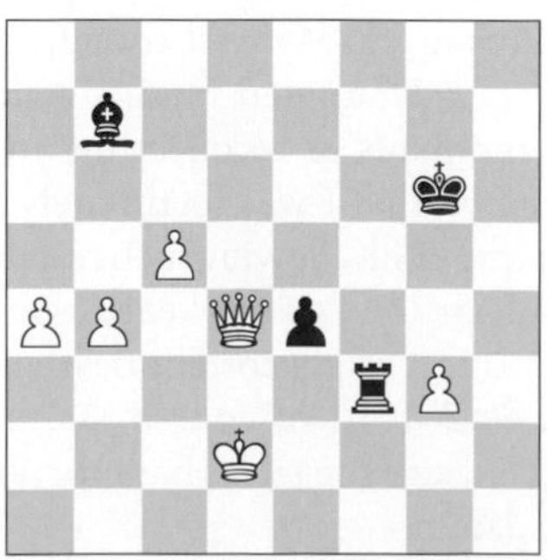

This was an easy calculation, since the three pawns are too much to deal with for the poor bishop.

50...♖d3+ 51.♕xd3 exd3 52.b5 ♗e4 53.c6 ♔f6 54.a5 ♔e7 55.a6 ♔d6 56.a7 ♗xc6 57.bxc6

Black resigned. A huge win over a legendary player, and one that I am very happy with.

NOTES BY
Jorden van Foreest

Jorden van Foreest
Jonas Buhl Bjerre
Malmö 2021 (6)
Sicilian Defence, Grand Prix Attack

1.e4 c5 2.♘c3 d6 3.f4

The Grand Prix Attack! One doesn't see this opening all too often at such high level these days, but I was inspired by Nigel Short's win against Jonas Bjerre in Round 4.

3...g6 4.♘f3 ♗g7 5.♗b5+ ♗d7

6.♗c4

The afore-mentioned game featured 6.a4. One might be puzzled by the bishop retreat, but as it turns out, the black light-squared bishop is worse placed on d7 than on c8 in several lines. For example, the d6-pawn will often be unprotected and become a target after an eventual ...e7-e6.

6...♘c6 7.d3 ♘a5

The most popular move in this position, but surprisingly it turns out to be an inaccuracy. I had seen the danger of the black position with my own eyes in the game Jobava-Giri, Batumi European Team Championship 2019, in which Giri survived by the skin of his teeth in this line.

The alternative is 7...e6 8.f5 gxf5.

8.♗d2

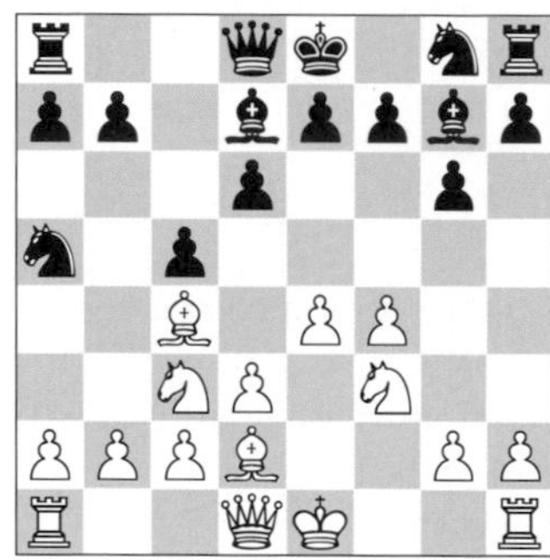

8...♘xc4?

Once again the most popular move, but in fact a serious mistake! This gives White much improved central control after the knight-for-bishop exchange. At the same time, Black struggles to develop his pieces.

Better was Giri's 8...e6, keeping options open and not giving White a clear plan.

9.dxc4 ♘f6

10.♕e2?

It is beyond me why I didn't push 10.e5 at once, forcing the knight to a highly awkward square. Somehow I'd forgotten that after Black castles, the knight has the e8-square at its disposal. 10.e5 ♘h5 11.♕e2 looks like a complete disaster for Black.

10...0-0 11.0-0-0 b5! My opponent correctly assessed that he had no time to waste and created counterplay.

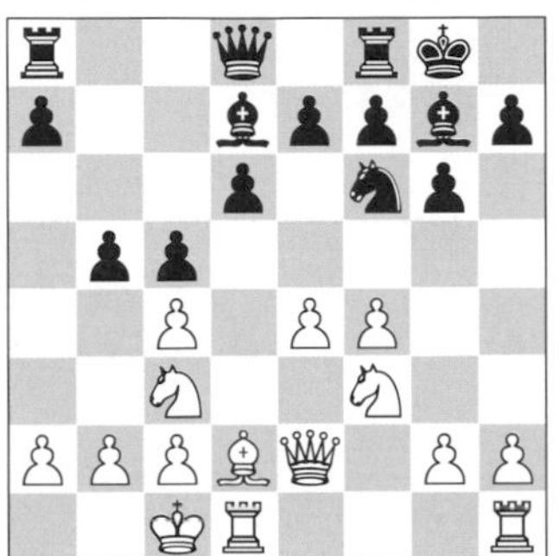

Jonas Buhl Bjerre is the youngest GM in Danish history. He earned the title two years ago, at the age of fifteen.

12.cxb5? A huge mistake, choosing the wrong move order. I should have started with 12.e5 for reasons that will become clear on the next move.

12...a6! Of course! Black is playing in the style of the Benko Gambit, with the added benefit of my king being on the wrong side of the board.

13.e5

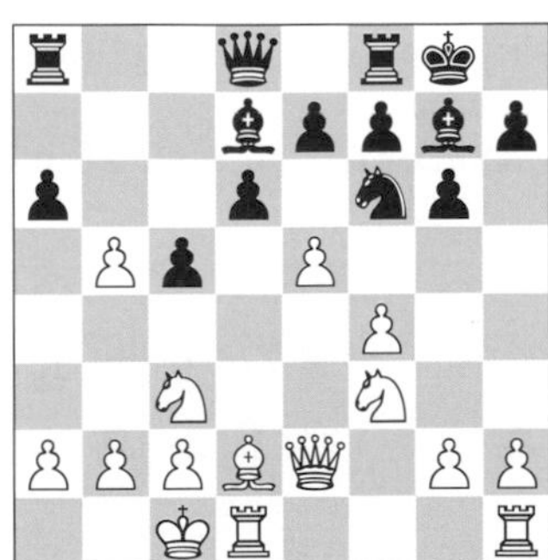

13...♘e8? Missing a golden opportunity for a stunning piece sacrifice! 12. e5 would not have allowed this and would still have given me a comfortable position.

True, 13...axb5, just leaving the knight to be captured like that, is not something one comes across every day. In fact, I had seen this possibility for my opponent but I could not believe it would actually yield him enough compensation: 14.exf6 exf6! (this is the most accurate follow-up, and one that I had missed, having only considered the more human 14...♗xf6. During the game I saw 15.♘d5 ♖xa2 16.♗c3, but this, too, is fine for Black).

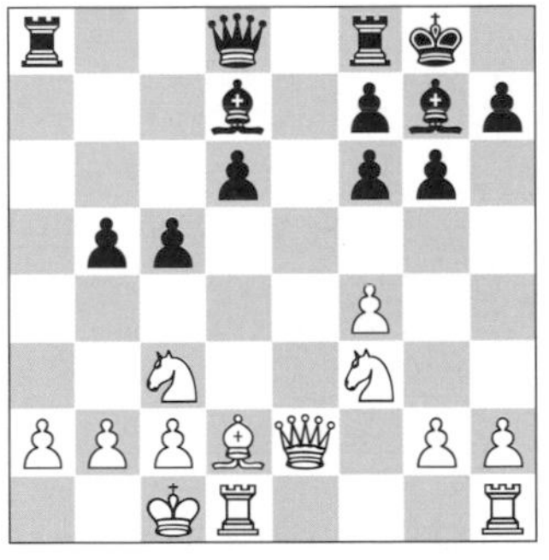
ANALYSIS DIAGRAM

As it turns out, opening the e-file and making sure the powerhouse of a bishop on g7 will not be exchanged is more important than keeping a healthy pawn structure. White has no adequate way to prevent ...b4, and should in fact be careful to maintain the balance, so as not to lose in short order: 15.♗e3 b4 16.♘b1 ♕e7, with tremendous compensation for the sacrificed piece. Although the silicon monster gives 0.00, I surely would not have enjoyed this position one bit.

14.b6!

I didn't think about this for long, as I was very happy to close the enemy files near my king.

14...♕xb6 15.♘d5 ♕b7!

Correctly giving up the e7-pawn with check! 15...♕d8 would have been far too passive in a position in which time and activity are of the essence.

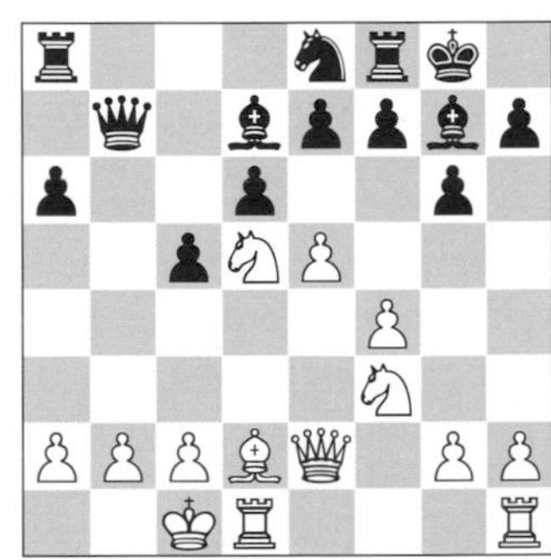

16.♗c3?!

I did consider the adventurous 16.♘xe7+, but I was quite worried my knight would not make it back alive. As it turns out, the variations do work out in White's favour: 16...♔h8, and now:

– 17.f5 (for some reason I thought ...♗b5 was a threat, so I barely considered this move) 17...♗b5 18.♕e1 ♕xe7 19.♗g5! ♕b7 20.f6, and White

wins back the piece while retaining a highly dangerous attack.
– I had only considered 17.♕e1, intending ♕h4. Fortunately, I did not opt for it, as I would have been completely busted after 17...♗g4 18.♕h4 ♗xf3 19.gxf3 ♖a7!.

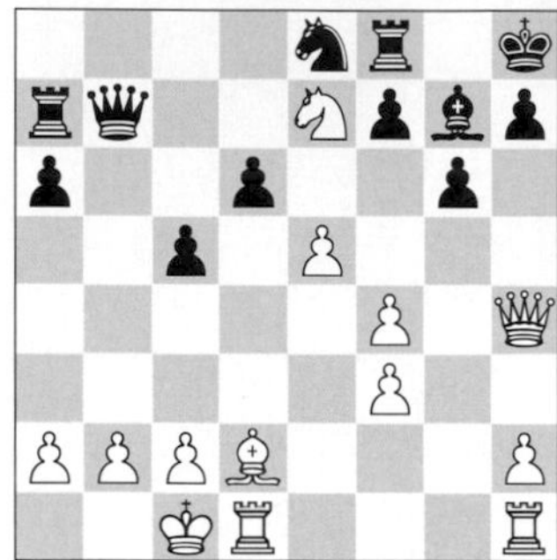

ANALYSIS DIAGRAM

The point – and the resource I had missed.

16...♗e6 17.exd6

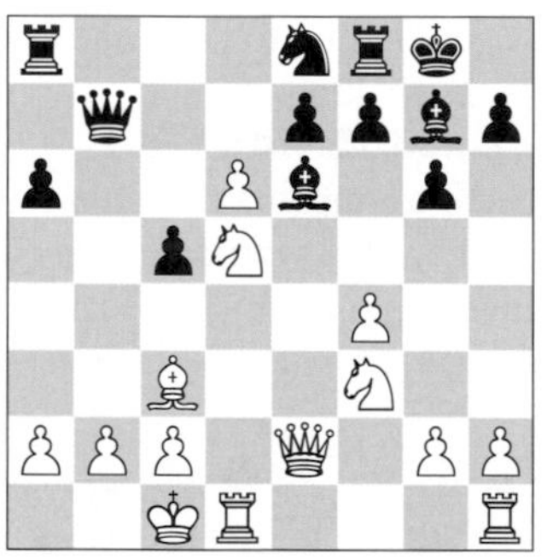

17...♗xc3?

This is simply too much. Instead, after 17...exd6 matters would have been far from simple. During the game I was sure I was much better after 18.♗xg7 ♔xg7 19.♕d3, due to my strong d5-knight and the backward pawn on d6. However, I had underestimated that Black had decent play of his own on the queenside after either 19...♖b8 or 19...a5. The game should be balanced.

18.♘xe7+ ♔h8?!

18...♔g7 would have been the better defence. The knight can possibly go to f6 later on, where it is far more active than on g7, as in the game. Still, the black situation is similar to the game: quite desperate.

19.bxc3 ♖b8

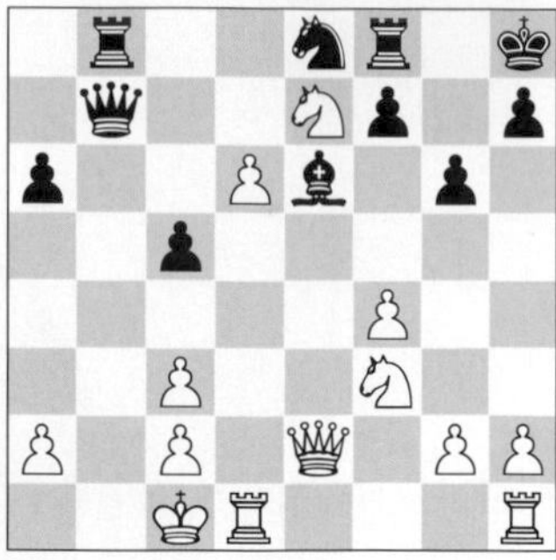

At the first glance, it may look as if dangerous threats are looming over the white king, but upon closer inspection it becomes clear that all Black has is just one check, and no way to follow it up. The white knight on e7, protected by the mighty d6-pawn, is a thorn in Black's side, leaving him with no real possibilities of generating counterplay.

20.♕e5+ ♘g7 21.♕xc5

There is no reason not to take this foot soldier. It also has the added benefit of vacating the d4-square for my knight.

21...♖fd8 22.♘d4 ♕xg2

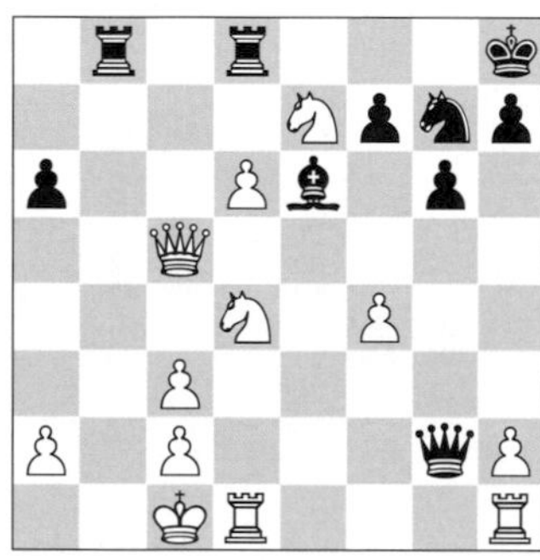

23.♖hg1 The most accurate reply, forcing the queen away before jumping in with the other knight.

Malmö TePe Sigeman 2021					
					TPR
1	Jorden van Foreest	NED	2691	5	2792
2	Gawain Jones	ENG	2684	4	2685
3	Vincent Keymer	GER	2607	4	2696
4	Nigel Short	ENG	2626	4	2694
5	Nils Grandelius	SWE	2666	3½	2638
6	Nihal Sarin	IND	2652	3	2590
7	Etienne Bacrot	FRA	2658	3	2589
8	Jonas Buhl Bjerre	DEN	2550	1½	2424

In chess there is always a way to butcher a winning position. After 23.♘xe6, the following line is a prime example: 23...♘xe6 24.♕e5+ ♘g7 25.♘f5 with the idea of 25...gxf5 26.♖hg1, and wins. After 25...f6 26.♕xf6 gxf5 White would be in for a cold shower, however, as 27.♖hg1 is met by 27...♕b7!.
23.♘dc6 ♗xa2 24.♘b4 should have won as well, but why let Black enjoy the prospect of a mate-in-one threat at all?

23...♕h3 24.♘dc6

24...♖b5 Keeping the rooks, but not holding the position.
24...♗xa2 won't save Black either: 25.♘xd8 ♖b1+ 26.♔d2 ♕xh2+ 27.♔d3, and the checks run out.

25.♕d4 ♖d7 26.♖g5

I was quite happy with this move, exchanging Black's last remaining active piece.

26...♖xg5 27.fxg5 ♕g2 28.h4

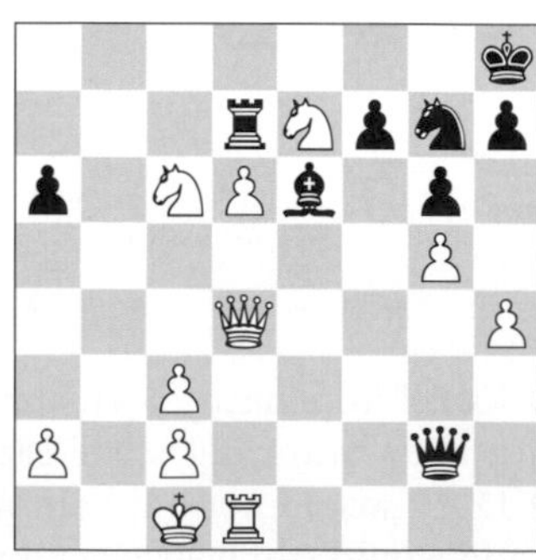

White has all the time in the world to protect the pawn, since his pieces completely dominate the board.

28...♖b7 29.♘d8

Black resigned. ■

Fair & Square

Sir Tom Stoppard: 'If I retire, I'll retire into chess.' *(The acclaimed playwright speaking in the new BBC documentary on his life and career, Imagine... Tom Stoppard: A Charmed Life)*

Dr Phil: 'When you look that 90 percent of the people that are dying are not vaccinated, do the math, this isn't hard. This is not chess, it's checkers. This is easy to figure out.' *(The American daytime talk show and TV series psychologist, in a recent show, on the perils of not being vaccinated)*

Nigel Short: 'Magnus Carlsen is stylistically universal. He can play all formats. Perhaps you can compare him to Brian Lara, who could play just about any shot.' *(In the September cricketer.com website, for their regular guest feature, 'Why I love cricket')*

Rachel Reeves: 'Chess is the perfect preparation for going into politics.' *(The Labour MP and Shadow Chancellor, who was once the British U14 girls champion, interviewed on BBC Radio 4's Political Thinking with Nick Robinson)*

William Horberg: 'What can I say? You brought the sexy back to chess, and you inspired a whole generation of girls and young women to realise that patriarchy has no defence against our queens.' *(The executive producer of The Queen's Gambit, gesturing to star Anya Taylor-Joy, as he accepted the award for Outstanding Drama series at the Primetime Emmys)*

Simon Kuper: 'Playing top-class football is something like playing chess with your feet at the speed of Formula One.' *(The British author in his latest book Barça, The Inside Story of the World's Greatest Football Club)*

Maggie Haberman: 'Sounds like four-dimensional chess to me.' *(The CNN political analyst weighs in on former President Donald Trump's latest attempt to overturn the 2020 US Election, by officially asking the Secretary of State for Georgia to decertify his state's election result)*

Rustam Kasimdzhanov: 'It's like a divorce. When you work together intensively for six years, a special personal relationship develops. You can't say the collaboration is purely business. We were together too often and too long for that. And there are still a number of unresolved issues, just like a divorce.' *(The long-time coach of Fabiano Caruana, speaking on the recent ending of his collaboration with the world No 2)*

Louis Persinger: 'I do believe that musicians have had a very special hypnotic fascination for the 32 little figures and have always been very willing slaves to those little characters' inexhaustible intrigues and pranks.' *(The renowned American violinist and chess fan in the July 1961 Chess Life)*

Anatoly Karpov: 'I didn't picture myself as even a grandmaster, to say nothing of aspiring to the chess crown. This was not because I was timid – I wasn't – but because I simply lived in one world, and the grandmasters existed in a completely different one. People like that were not really even people, but like gods or mythical heroes.'

Matt Selman: 'Chess isn't a game of speed, it is a game of speech through actions.' *(The six-time Primetime Emmy-winning writer and producer of The Simpsons)*

Bent Larsen: 'Nimzowitsch became then for me more or less the author of the only book which could help me get away from these Euwe books, which, I admit, are very good for the ordinary club player. But once you've reached a certain strength you get the impression that everything that Euwe writes is a lie.'

Henry Atkins: 'Music seems to me one of the few things (like chess) which really last through life, and gives one almost as much pleasure towards the end as in the early days.' *(The early 20th century schoolmaster and nine-time British champion)*

Vishy Anand: 'In chess, knowledge is a very transient thing. It changes so fast that even a single mouse-slip sometimes changes the evaluation.'

James Altucher has written 25 books. About 21 of them are bad but one or two are OK. He has started several companies and has a popular podcast called 'The James Altucher Show'. Among others, Garry Kasparov and Judit Polgar have been guests on his podcast, as well as Kareem Abdul-Jabbar, Richard Branson and 963 others. He has played chess since he was 16 but stopped when he hit 2204 USCF in 1997, and is now starting to play again.

Is it crazy to think adults can improve at chess?

Can you still get better at chess once you've reached 'a certain age'? It's easy to become discouraged, but **JAMES ALTUCHER** tells you that you can. And tells you how to do it.

Chess can sometimes be depressing. Everyone telling you, 'You can't do this – you're too old to get better.' Or, 'Your memory is worse now.' Or, 'You can't calculate like these kids.'

The kids! The kids! God save us from those kids!

I last studied chess in 1997. 24 years ago. GM John Fedorowicz was my coach. I would make a move and his face would scrunch up and he'd say, hmm, that doesn't feel right. And five moves later I'd be lost. I went from 2048 USCF to over 2200+ in a six-month period in 1997 with Fedorowicz. But that was then.

Did I have a chance now? I didn't know. Covid was the storm that left me stranded again on Chess Island. For the first time in 24 years I decided to take it seriously. I was a bit depressed perhaps, so I returned to my first love, left at the altar so many years ago. I was disappointed that I was weaker than I had been in 1997. The world had grown up and I stayed behind.

One of the only non-online games I had played in the past few years was when I did a podcast with a talented young chessplayer named Garry Kasparov. He, of course, crushed me. You can find that game on YouTube.

Six months ago I was rated 1899 in rapid chess on Lichess. I am now 2402. I haven't washed my keyboard since I made it over 2400 (my name on Lichess is 'FleetWalker'). Some days it's exhilarating ('I'm better!') and some days I'm the biggest loser. So disappointed. 'I can't believe I missed that!' Or this! Or those! When will I get better? The beauty of these past months is seeing an entirely new game. With older eyes.

I can't memorize openings anymore. Or calculate as deep. So I had to actually 'learn' chess for the first time. What a beautiful game it is. I wish I had learned it earlier.

If you like the below suggestions for adult improvement, let me know, and I'll write more of what I am doing as an 'adult improver'. My goal: infinite.

Plus, minus, equal

Frank Shamrock told me about his favourite learning technique. He was Mixed Martial Arts world champion for about ten years in a row. He constantly had to learn new martial arts quickly. He told me: 'Find a PLUS, someone to coach you and give you feedback.'

I had to actually 'learn' chess for the first time. What a beautiful game it is. I wish I had learned it earlier

When I was 19, in 1987, I played in the US Junior Open and I remembered a game against a 15-year-old master named Jesse Kraai. Now he's a grandmaster and I'm the same as I was then. I can remember a game from 1987 but I can't remember if I ate breakfast this morning. He agreed to give me lessons. In the first lesson he looked at my opening and said, 'This is awful! You're a madman!' He still thinks I'm insane. But he convinced me not to play 1...h6 anymore.

Frank Shamrock also told me, 'EQUALS are the people who you are competing with. Who are trying to improve just like you.' 70,000,000 people are members of Chess.com. Plenty of equals to choose from.

'Most important is the MINUS. Someone you can teach. If you can't explain something simply then you don't truly understand.' I called Merrick Furst. He was the professor in graduate school who had to officially throw me out when I failed every class several semesters in a row. A few years after that he saw me in a restaurant and asked if I could give him chess lessons. We became best friends for the next 30 years. And now I give him lessons again. Our main focus: avoiding blunders.

Microskills

For many years I was an entrepreneur and started several businesses. At first nothing would go right. Clients would fire my company in the middle of a project. We'd miss deadlines. I'd negotiate poorly but thought I was doing great! I realized there is no such skill as 'Entrepreneurship'. It's really a basket of mutually exclusive microskills. And each one I had to learn: Ideas, Execution, Management, Motivation, Sales, Marketing, Negotiation, etc. Everything that is difficult requires breaking it down into microskills and start training in each microskill. Chess also is a basket of microskills. Chess has openings, endgames, middlegames, attacking, tactics, strategic play, prophylactics, time management, space advantages, time advantage, etc.

I put together a training regimen for each microskill. Ulf Andersson games for the endgame. Tal for attacking. 'Mate in Two' puzzles from Laszlo Polgar's book. Jesse shows me ideas from the openings he suggested I play. The key is to learn just ONE thing from every game I study. From every lesson I have. From every puzzle I attempt. It adds up. A friend told me that it doesn't add up unless you actually 'add it up'. So I keep a diary of what I learn each day and review it often.

The key is to learn just ONE thing from every game I study

I'm nervous now because in a few weeks it will be my first over the board tournament in over two decades. Jesse tells me it doesn't matter if I do good or bad. That I have to think 'in the long run' studying tournament games is the best way to get better.

When someone says, 'You can't do X', it means they can't do it

For the six years before Covid I performed standup comedy all over the world. Everyone told me I couldn't start standup at the age of 47. Or I couldn't be an investor. Or an entrepreneur. And now, at the age of 53, an improving chessplayer.

They are wrong. When someone says, 'You can't do X', it means they can't do it. At least, when I log in at three in the morning for 'just one game', this is the story I tell myself.

Every game I study I try to learn one thing. Here's the game:

Kasparov-Shirov
Horgen 1994

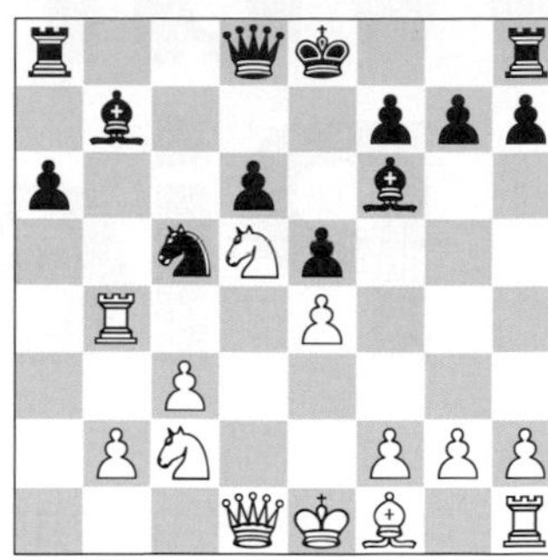

position after 16...♘c5

White to move and... not quite win. Not even to have a massive advantage. White to move and create a position where his ideas are easier to come up with than Black's.

17.♖xb7! ♘xb7 18.b4!

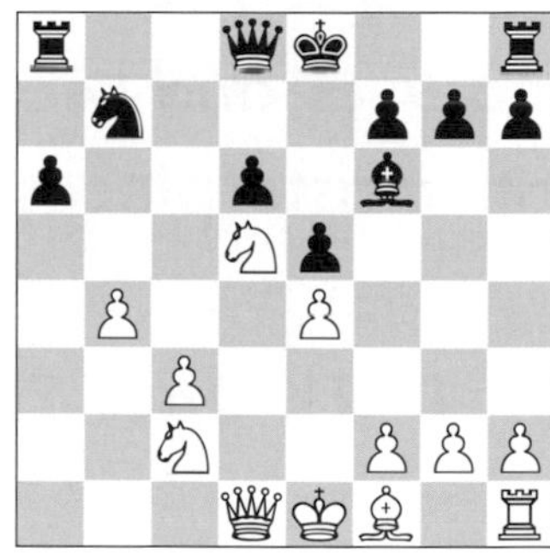

What just happened? White gave up his rook for Black's good bishop. But that's not enough for compensation. What made it worth it was b4! Guess how many squares the knight can now move to? Zero! He gave up a rook to DOMINATE every piece on the board. 'Domination' was a chess skill I never even heard of before. A rook for a good bishop and total domination.

What does the computer say? Equal!

But Garry knew this was a position he would like playing, and Shirov wouldn't. He won on move 38.

Someone once asked me if I was good at chess. Well, I said, I know the rules. I know how to move the pieces. But I don't really know where to move the pieces to. I know how to play b2-b4. But maybe one day I will know how to play b2-b4!? ■

War with Pieces

In another memorable episode of the 'Chess in the Museums' exhibitions staged by the Russian Chess Federation, ten GMs convened for a rapid tournament at Yasnaya Polyana, the legendary estate where Leo Tolstoy wrote *Anna Karenina* and *War and Peace*. Anish Giri had read both masterpieces and was truly inspired.

DIRK JAN TEN GEUZENDAM

On October 28, 1864, Leo Tolstoy, who was 36 years old at the time, wrote in a letter: 'I cannot imagine this life without chess, books and hunting.' The great Russian writer was passionate about chess and played the game throughout his life. Dmitry Oleynikov, the director of the Chess Museum in Moscow, told us: 'In his youth, Tolstoy considered chess an important tool for self-development. In maturity, he saw in the game a fascinating and effective way of resting from writing work. In old age, he considered meeting at the board an excellent way of communication. At Yasnaya Polyana, chess games became one of the evening rituals of the writer's daily life.'

However, Tolstoy was a complex personality who always questioned everything, and there was a period in which he entertained serious doubts about chess. As Oleynikov added: 'At one time, Tolstoy wanted to abandon the game of chess, because it contradicted his theory of "non-resistance to evil". He worried that the game resembled boxing and that, just like "boxing with fists", it inflicted "pain on one's neighbour" and caused "bad feelings" towards one's opponent. However, the writer soon found an excuse for his hobby: the essence of the game for

ETERI KUBLASHVILI

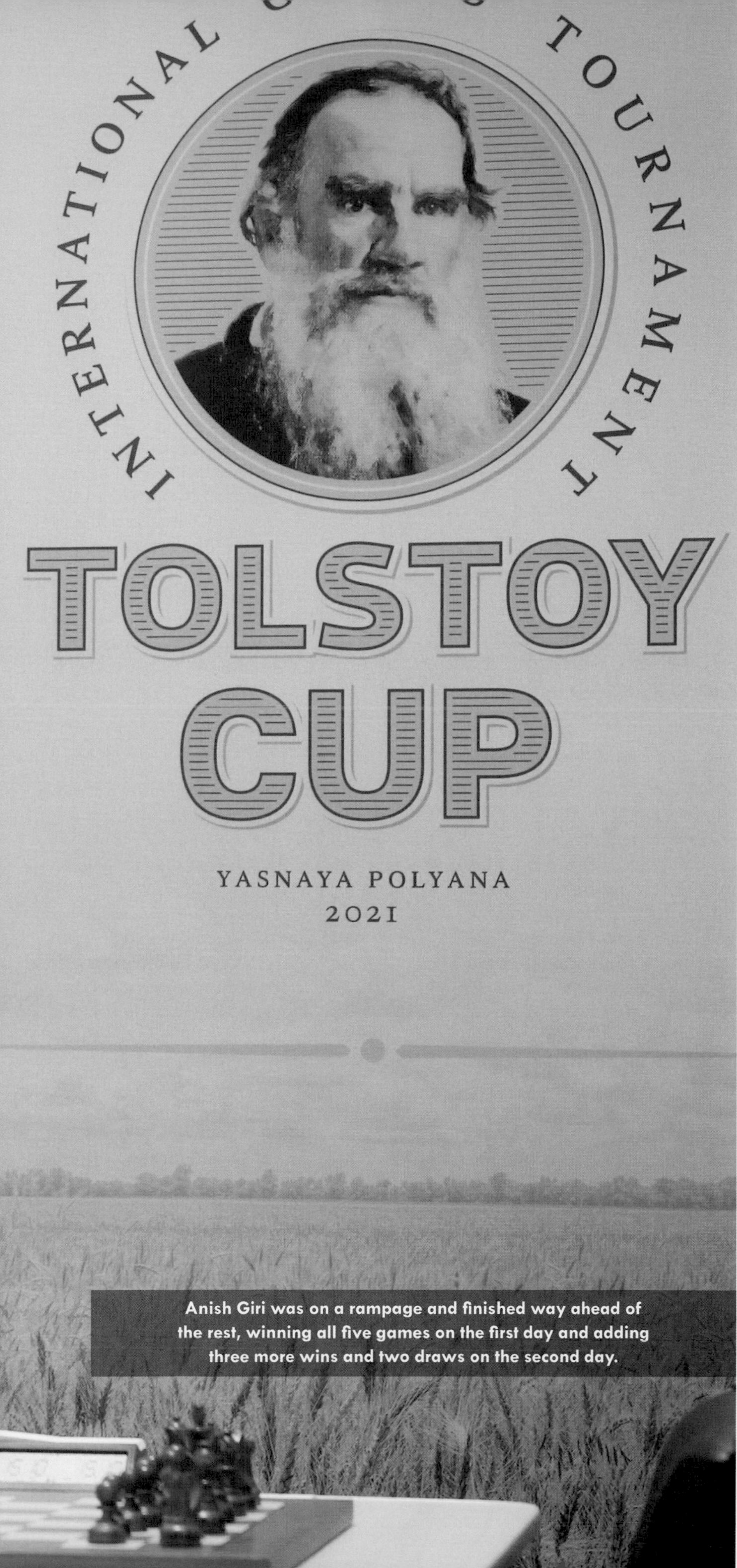

Anish Giri was on a rampage and finished way ahead of the rest, winning all five games on the first day and adding three more wins and two draws on the second day.

him was not defeating an opponent, but searching, in co-operation with an opponent, for the best, most beautiful continuation.'

Napoleon

Inevitably, chess often appeared in his books as well. Napoleon's Russian campaign, which ended in the emperor's failed attempt to conquer Moscow, gets the following comment in *War and Peace*: 'A good chess player having lost a game is sincerely convinced that his loss resulted from a mistake he made and looks for that mistake in the opening, but forgets that at each stage of the game there were similar mistakes, and that none of his moves were perfect. He only notices the mistake to which he pays attention, because his opponent took advantage of it. How much more complex than this is the game of war, which occurs under certain limits of time, and where it is not one will that manipulates lifeless objects, but everything results from innumerable conflicts of various wills!'

In the year of the centenary of the Leo Tolstoy museum-estate Yasnaya Polyana, the Russian Chess Federation, together with the Elena and Gennady Timchenko Foundation,

Leo Tolstoy: 'I cannot imagine this life without chess, books and hunting'

organized another of their 'Chess in Museums' tournaments. Ten grandmasters from Russia, Uzbekistan, Ukraine, Israel and the Netherlands – all of them able to read Tolstoy's books in Russian – were invited for a two-day rapid event. The winner's trophy was an ornamental

Leo Tolstoy playing chess with his son-in-law Mikhail Sukhotin at Yasnaya Polyana in 1908. On the board is a position from the Kieseritzky Gambit, which was popular at that time and was recommended by Ian Nepomniachtchi in his recent Chessable course 'Long live the King's Gambit'!

vase especially made at the Imperial Porcelain Factory.

During their stay, the players got a guided tour of the estate and could see with their own eyes that Tolstoy had two beautiful Staunton chess sets in his home, as well as two travel sets. (They also saw dumbbells that Tolstoy still trained with when he was 80 years old.)

A passionate chess player

The tournament was a sweeping performance by Anish Giri, who scored a massive 8 out of 9 and finished 2½ points ahead of runner-up Nodirbek Abdusattorov from Uzbekistan. On the first day, Giri won all five games, on the second day he won another three and made two draws. Looking back he said, 'It was a combination of things, as always. I was very fortunate with how the cards played out, how the openings worked out and the order of the pairings. And sometimes my opponents made mistakes at critical junctures, and I picked the right move, sometimes on purpose and sometimes by accident. But I also played quite well by my own standards. For a score of 8 out of 9, clearly a lot of things have to go well.'

Giri had read Tolstoy's two most famous novels and found it fascinating to visit the writer's home. 'That he was a passionate chess player was new to me. In his main room, there was a chess set that apparently he used all the time. Because he was concerned about so many real-life matters it was interesting to see what his own life looked like. It was a place with a lot of quiet and a lot of nature. I had assumed it would be a bit more isolated, but in the village there was more than only his estate. On the other hand, the estate was really big; much bigger than I had expected.'

Giri read *Anna Karenina* when he was 16 or 17 years old, at an age when the bigger social questions that Tolstoy wrote about – What is the right approach to the serfs working for you? How do you make sure their lives are not miserable? – were not the first thing on his mind.

Light and humorous

It was years later that he considered reading *War and Peace*. 'Of course we had *War and Peace* at our place in Russia [where he lived till he was 14, before the family moved to the Netherlands – ed.], but these volumes were so high on the bookshelf and they looked so imposing and old... Somehow they looked like books that you would never actually read, that you're not supposed to read (laughs). So I never dared to touch them. It didn't feel that they were meant for me.'

This changed when he spent several weeks in Tbilisi for the 2017 World Cup and walked into a Russian bookshop, where he saw a one-volume copy of *War and Peace*. 'I just opened the book on the first page to see what it's like, and I was extremely surprised to find how accessible it was. I had assumed it would be some completely indigestible philosophical work of art, but it was very accessible, light and humorous, and I finished it very quickly. I found it a very entertaining read, apart from the deeper philosophical points that are there throughout the book.'

Thinking about this experience. he almost inadvertently draws a parallel with chess. 'But surely you have to read such works more than once, because they are multi-layered

Anish Giri: 'I had assumed *War and Peace* would be some completely indigestible philosophical work of art, but it was very accessible, light and humorous'

and offer different things, depending on how and when you read them. I noticed the same with chess. There is this thing, when you analyse an opening position, and then you come back to this position a year later, and you analyse it again. And even if you have the same engine, and even if you see the same position and see the same computer assessments, you perceive them differently. Because in that year you encountered things that changed your understanding, your outlook on chess, a little bit. That's why I return to the same variations over and over again, because every time I look at them, I see them a little bit differently.

'And I would guess that this applies even more to a book like *War and Peace*. You read the same book, the same text, but now that you've encountered certain things yourself, you suddenly are more perceptive to aspects that had seemed less important before. Even now that I have been at Yasnaya Polyana, my interest has been reignited. I didn't read *War and Peace* that long ago, but reading it again would give me more insight. You now know that some characters were based on people in his life and you now know more about its background, so now it's even more interesting to read it again. That's certainly inspiring.'

Anish Giri annotated the two games that he liked best. 'I was under the impression that I had played many "coherent" games, but once you look at them with an engine, you see that most of them are not as coherent as you wanted them to be. These two were the cleanest, the most straightforward. The game against Boris Gelfand was played in the first round. I didn't make many mistakes, but he made one big one. Not a bad game on my part. The game against Nodirbek Abdusattorov was the final game of the first day. He didn't play the opening well, but I converted it very well.'

NOTES BY
Anish Giri

Anish Giri
Boris Gelfand
Yasnaya Polyana 2021 (1)
Slav Defence, Semi-Slav

1.d4 ♘f6 2.c4 e6 3.♘f3 d5 4.♘c3 c6
One can never be sure these days, as most players have quite a broad opening repertoire, but the Semi-Slav is one of Boris Gelfand's favourites.
5.♕d3

Developing the queen this early doesn't seem very healthy, but I had noticed a pretty idea down the main line and wanted to try it for this game.
5...dxc4 6.♕xc4 b5 7.♕d3 a6
This is the main line nowadays. Back in the day, the theory went on with 8.e4 c5, but recently the move 8.g4!? popped up at some point.
8.g4!?

This was first played by Berkes in 2017, but it really took off once Matlakov played it in 2019. The idea is not new and exists in the Anti-Meran, but in this particular version I felt it had still gone somewhat unnoticed.
8...c5
So far nobody has dared to grab the pawn, and most players have gone for this counter-push.
9.g5
Here Black has three choices: 9...c4, 9...cxd4 and the game-move, which may be the most natural one.
9...♘d5
The engine is slightly less enthused about this move compared to 9...c4, but it is more human to keep the tension in the centre. Also, while the engine is slightly concerned about the upcoming endgame, a human player often doesn't mind trading queens in the face of a dangerous g-pawn march.
10.dxc5 ♗b7

11.♘xd5
The engines claim that going for an endgame is the only way to fight for an advantage, and so I obeyed.
11...♕xd5 12.♕xd5 ♗xd5 13.♗e3
White gets to keep the pawn for now. I hadn't gone all too deeply into this endgame, since it is just one of the scenarios, but I was still quite familiar with it. I thought it was quite hard for Black to understand what is going on and how reliable it is to play for long-term compensation with 13...♘c6.
13...♘c6
The only way. Black cannot regain the c5-pawn quickly. Instead, he should focus on quick development and aim for counterplay down the road.
14.♗g2

14...h6!

While preparing, I saw that this is one of the engine's top choices and also that the line goes 15.g6! ♗e7!. I found this all too unhuman and unlikely. To my surprise, this was exactly what happened. Possibly, Boris was aware of this position, or perhaps he just has a very good feel for dynamics.

The point of the move 14...h6 is that Black is trying to activate his f8-bishop and h8-rook as quickly as possible. If Black goes for the ...♗e7/...0-0 plan, which I found far more natural, his counterplay will be far slower, since the dark-squared bishop will have trouble getting to the long diagonal, hitting the b2-pawn.

14...g6, aiming for ...♗g7, was also natural, but compared to ...h6 gxh6 gxh6, Black doesn't have any open file for his rook on h8: 15.h4 (hinting at a potential h5) 15...♗g7 16.0-0-0.

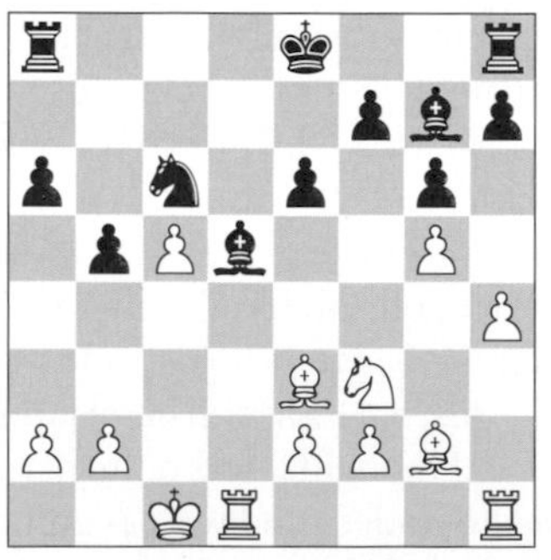

ANALYSIS DIAGRAM

This is a nice idea – White protects b2, but also develops his rook to d1, hinting at the ♖xd5 sacrifice. Castling is a wonderful invention. 16...h5 17.♖xd5 exd5 18.♖d1 is a beautiful sample line – White has superb compensation for the exchange, as the d5-pawn will probably fall as well and my c5-pawn will only get stronger.

15.g6!

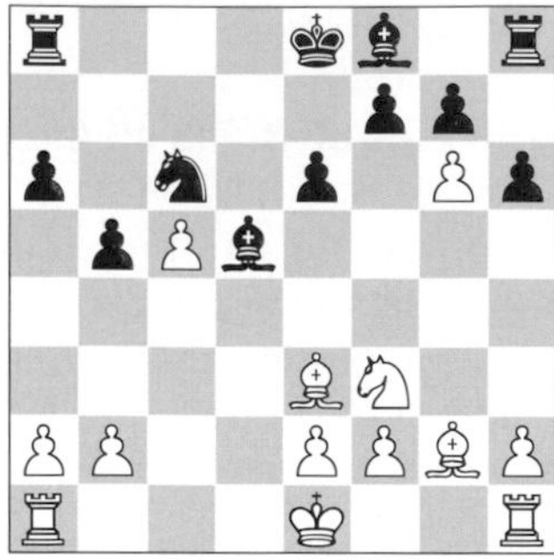

I spent some time here, even though I was pretty sure that this was where the engine suggested this move. Frankly, I didn't go too far in this direction, once again because Black has at least five other ways that are equally good and no less challenging. I tried to understand what the engine's point was, and why we give up a pawn just like that, but essentially I realized that the computer probably found it worth a pawn to slow down Black's activation of the f8-bishop and h8-rook. Allowing ...hxg5 would give the black h8-rook too much scope, while 15.gxh6 gxh6 gives Black the opportunity to get in both ...♖g8 and ...♗g7, quickly mobilizing his kingside forces.

15...♗e7!

I was extremely surprised that once again, after some thought, Boris picked the engine's first choice.

Yasnaya Polyana, Tolstoy Cup 2021					
					TPR
1	Anish Giri	NED	2777	8	3051
2	Nodirbek Abdusattorov	UZB	2648	5½	2783
3	Boris Gelfand	ISR	2680	5	2739
4	Dmitry Andreikin	RUS	2728	4½	2696
5	David Paravyan	RUS	2660	4½	2703
6	Anton Korobov	UKR	2685	4	2662
7	Evgeny Tomashevsky	RUS	2708	4	2660
8	Maxim Matlakov	RUS	2683	4	2662
9	Kirill Alekseenko	RUS	2693	3½	2622
10	Nikita Vitiugov	RUS	2727	2	2479

Of course, if you understand the position very deeply, it becomes clear that ...♗f6 is important and that gxf7+ ♔xf7 is not a big issue.

I figured that after 15...fxg6 the point was to just castle and then trade with ♘d4, trying to unblock my c5-pawn, though frankly I can't say this looked crushing: 16.0-0 ♗e7 17.♘d4 and, as we trade away the d5-bishop and the c6-knight, it gets harder for Black to deal with the c5-pawn: 17...♔d7 18.a4 b4 19.♖fd1.

16.a4

I thought it was good to clarify the situation on the queenside before deciding whether to castle short or keep the option of castling long.

16...bxa4?!

This is logical if Black tries to simplify the game and get more trades in, but it clarified my task a lot and made my opening advantage more understandable.

I was far less sure of what's going on after the more ambitious and murkier 16...b4!. Now 17.♖g1! is probably the best move, keeping the option of castling queenside in order to protect the b2-pawn: 17...♗f6 (alternatively, 17...fxg6 can be met by 18.♘d4, with a small plus after all the trades, thanks to the better pawn structure) 18.0-0-0 fxg6 19.♘d2, and it is likely that if we trade the light-squared bishops and enter on the d6-square at some point, the c5-pawn is more of a strength than a weakness. But these last three moves had to be found, and I am not sure they were very obvious.

17.♖xa4 fxg6 18.0-0

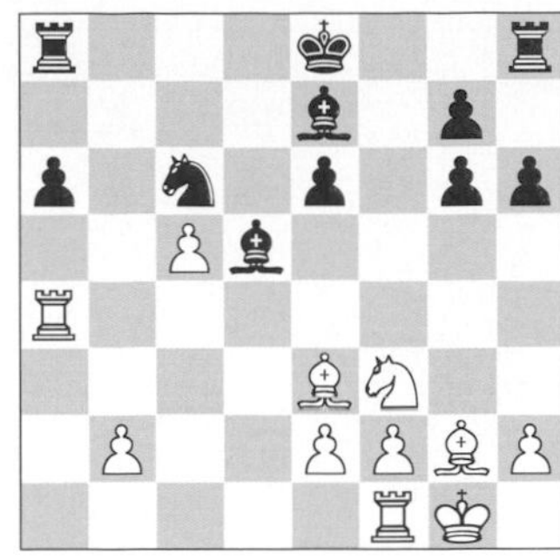

Here I was pretty happy with my position, although I did realize there are quite some drawish tendencies. It is quite clear that White can put pressure on the a-pawn and Black has to try to target my b-pawn. Many trades are likely to happen, as well as a better endgame, possibly a rook ending in which White will have a better pawn structure, but which may be defensible.

18...♗f6?! A very natural mistake and one that went unpunished. The engine starts with 18...a5!. Besides transposing to the game with 19.♖fa1 ♗f6, White also has the option of going 19.♘d4 (19.♖fa1 ♗f6) 19...♔d7, and as expected, we are likely to land in a drawish position with decent chances for White to cause serious practical problems thanks to a better pawn structure.

19.♖fa1?! My idea was to double on the a-file and then trade everything with ♘d4 (or ♗d4) and get a good rook ending. There was the very strong 19.♗f4!, aiming for the d6-square and stopping a potential ...♖b8. For me, this was too deep for a rapid game. White apparently has a massive advantage.

19...a5

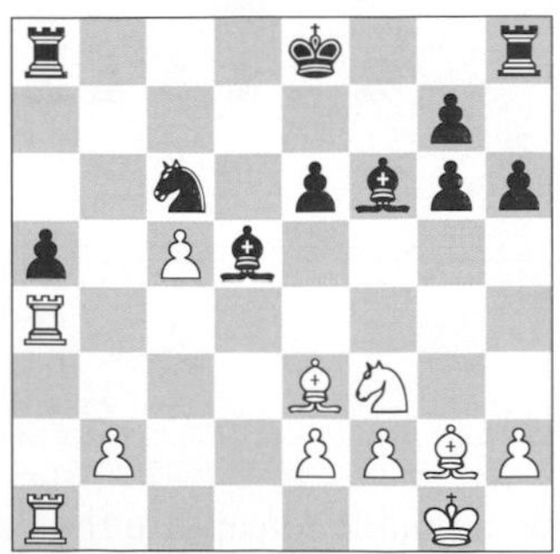

ETERI KUBLASHVILI

Protected from head to toe, Maxim Matlakov and Nikita Vitiugov pay tribute to Leo Tolstoy as they play a King's Gambit in the great writer's museum.

20.♗d4

This was bad judgement, but it did win me the game, as Boris fell for the trap I didn't even know I had set.

The natural 20.♘d4 was stronger. After 20...♗xg2 21.♔xg2 ♗xd4 22.♗xd4 I obviously disliked that Black doesn't have to take on d4 (otherwise I would have gone 20.♘d4).

Still, 22...♘xd4 is probably best anyway: 23.♖xd4 ♔e7. This endgame is obviously unpleasant for Black, as his extra pawn on the kingside is badly doubled, while White has a passer on the queenside. Still, it seems that with accurate defending,

This was bad judgement, but it did win me the game, as Boris fell for the trap I didn't even know I had set

Black should be able to hold: 24.c6 ♖hd8 (accurate) 25.♖c4 ♖dc8, and the computer doesn't show a win or anything big.

In case of 22...0-0 23.♗c3 ♖f5 (I also wasn't sure if I'd have something after 23...♖b8, but I believe I may have missed 24.♖d1 ♖f5?, and now 25.♖d7! e5 26.♖d6)

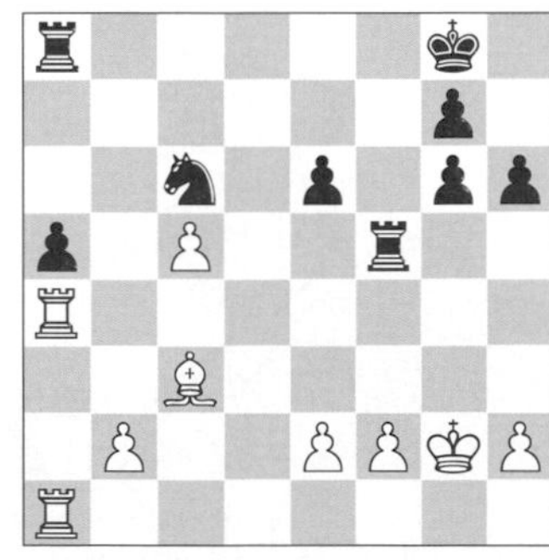

ANALYSIS DIAGRAM

there is 24.♗xa5 – I don't know why, but somehow I dismissed this natural and strong move as yielding too little, because it is unlikely that I didn't realize that the a5-pawn is hanging.

I could not make 24.b4 ♖af8! work, and I dismissed the immediate

24.♖c4 in view of 24...♖ab8 25.♖d1 ♖d5.
All correct, but why not the simple 24.♗xa5 ? I do not know. 24...♖xc5 25.♗c3 – of course Black has drawing chances here, but it is definitely more promising than what I went for.

20...♔e7?
A very unfortunate move that loses on the spot. Boris wanted to get the best version of the ♗xf6 exf6 ♘d4 position, which would lead to a rook ending, but missed a much more relevant detail. Instead, the following two moves lead to a very drawish endgame.

20...♔f7 21.♗xf6 gxf6 22.♘d4 ♗xg2 23.♔xg2 ♘xd4 24.♖xd4. In fact, I was feeling optimistic here, but it seems that with some minimal accuracy Black should be able to hold. The easiest is probably 20...0-0 21.♗xf6 gxf6 22.♘d4 ♗xg2 23.♔xg2 ♘xd4 24.♖xd4 ♖fc8. Black should definitely hold this one.

21.e4!
Suddenly this cheapo works, as the f6-bishop lacks squares.
21...♗b3 22.e5!
The bishop on f6 is kind of trapped, and Black suddenly loses by force in all variations.

YOU NEVER KNEW FOR SURE IF TOLSTOY
HAD MADE A MOVE
VONK
BEREND VONK

22...♗xa4 I didn't finish calculating the endgame arising after 22...♗g5, when Boris decided to go for the rook vs two pieces position, but that endgame is also lost: 23.♘xg5 ♗xa4 24.♖xa4 ♘xd4 25.♖xd4 hxg5 26.♗xa8 ♖xa8 27.c6. All forced. Here I noticed 27...♖d8, but before I could calculate the pawn ending, Boris moved. After 27...♖d8 White wins as follows: 28.♖xd8 ♔xd8

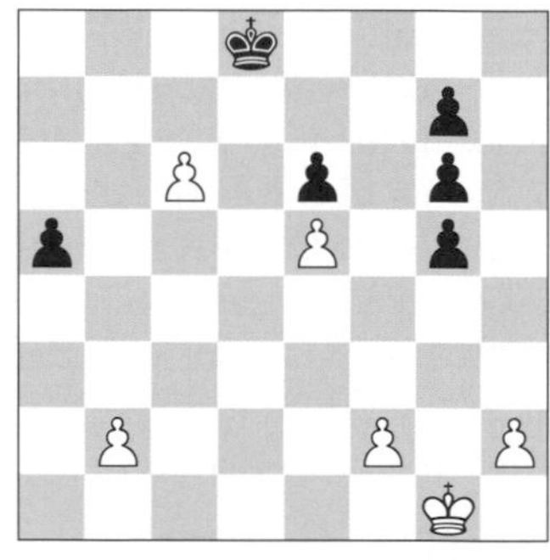
ANALYSIS DIAGRAM

and the following line is as straight as an arrow: 29.♔g2 ♔c7 30.♔g3 ♔xc6 31.♔g4 ♔d5 32.♔xg5 ♔xe5 33.♔xg6 ♔f4 34.♔xg7 e5 35.h4. Boris may have seen it, since it's all completely forced.
23.exf6+ gxf6 24.♖xa4

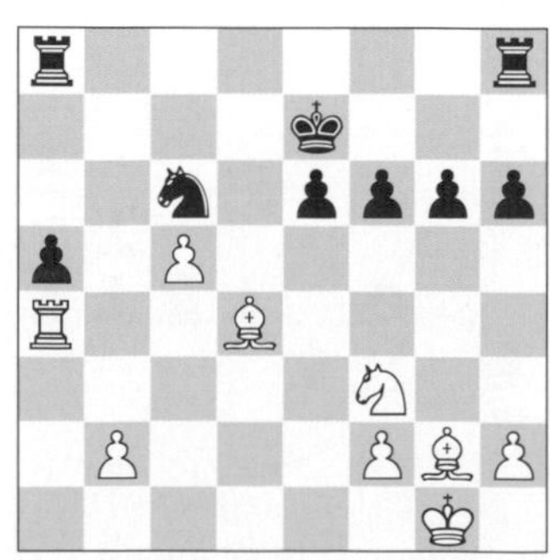

Black is unable to capture the dark-squared bishop because of the concrete issues that would follow. As I get to keep the bishop pair and the dangerous c-pawn, Black is completely lost.

24...♖ab8 25.♗c3 ♖hc8 26.♘d2
With the knight rerouting, Black's position collapses like a house of cards. **26...♖b5 27.♘e4**

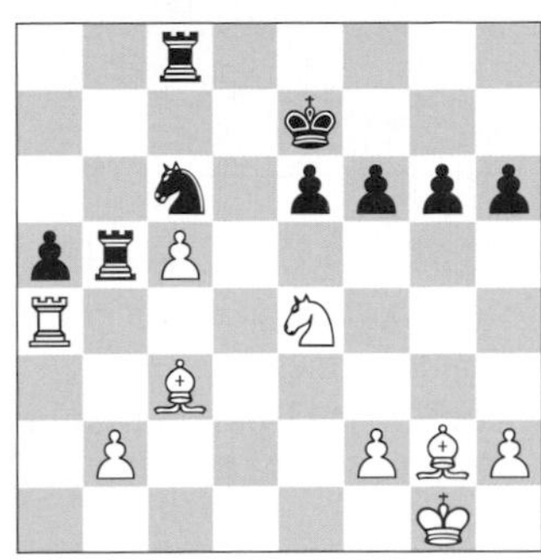

Too many threats, with ♗xf6 and ♘d6 coming.

27...♖cb8 28.♗xf6+ ♔f8 29.♗c3 ♖d8 30.♗f3 c5 31.♘d6

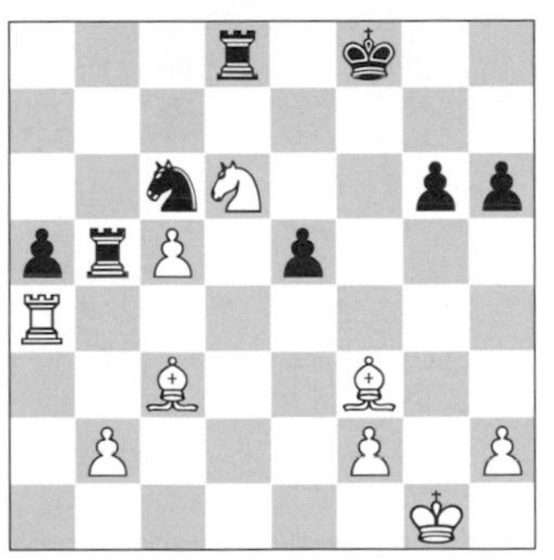

And as 31...♖xc5 will be met by 32.♘b7!, Black resigned.

NOTES BY
Anish Giri

Nodirbek Abdusattorov
Anish Giri
Yasnaya Polyana 2021 (5)
Grünfeld Indian Defence, Exchange Variation

1.d4 ♘f6 2.c4 g6 3.♘c3 d5
Sometimes I play the Grünfeld, sometimes I don't.
4.cxd5 ♘xd5 5.♗d2
A solid system, which I have also played with the white pieces. White wants to recapture on c3 with the bishop to effectively neutralize the pressure of Black's dark-squared bishop along the long diagonal.

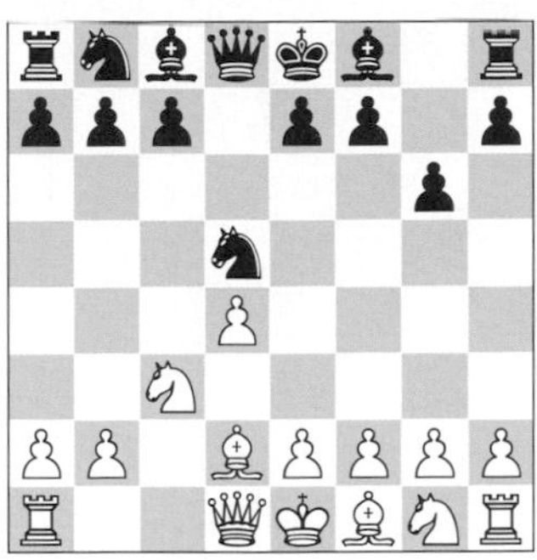

5...c5!? I noticed this rare move a while back. Black is trying to confuse White with the move order. I had already played it against Gukesh in the Champions Tour online, and later Carlsen also used it to win a good game in the first round of the World Cup against Martinovic.

6.dxc5
Gukesh went 6.e4, while Martinovic chose 6.♖c1, both of which are critical as well. Nodirbek Abdusattorov, however, grabs the pawn.

6...♗g7 7.♖c1 0-0 In the Grünfeld it is not unusual to sacrifice a pawn and not rush to regain it.

8.♘f3 ♘c6!? It was also possible to try and target the c5-pawn, with a set-up like 8...♗e6, and later ...♘d7, but just developing the knight is interesting as well.

9.e3?
This natural move is inaccurate. White weakens the d3-square and my knight is heading straight for it.

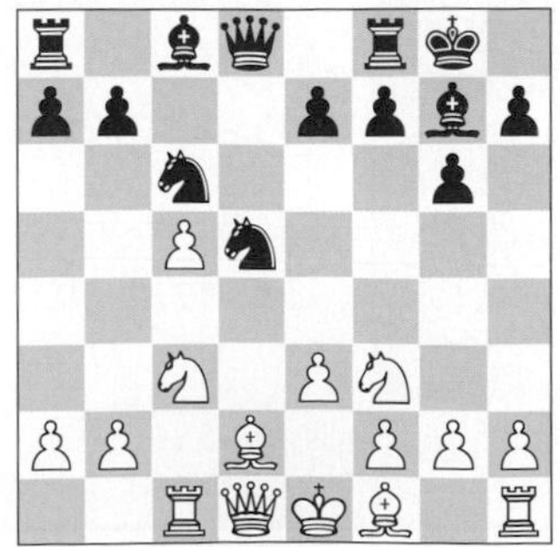

9...♘db4!
Not a difficult move, especially since I had seen this idea in the game Martinovic-Carlsen (after 6.♖c1 ♘c6 7.dxc5 ♗g7 8.e4 ♘db4). Curiously enough, my game almost fully transposed to their game later on.

10.a3 ♘d3+ 11.♗xd3 ♕xd3 12.♕e2

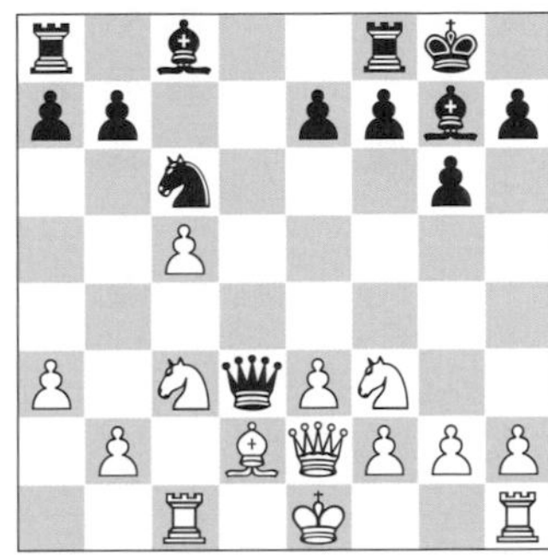

12...♗f5
A decent idea. The alternative was also very good.
I thought 12...♕xe2+ was a little less precise, but I had underestimated 13.♔xe2 ♖d8!. I didn't realize that White will be too late to regroup here, since after 14.♖hd1 ♗e6 he is still unable to play 15.♗e1 due to 15...♗c4+, so the d1-rook will be sent packing with ...♗b3. I only thought about 13...♗e6, but that would allow 14.♘d1 followed by 15.♗c3, neutralizing some of the pressure.

13.e4? This is a mistake. White could still hold things together with accurate play:
13.♕xd3 ♗xd3 14.♘a4 (intending ♗c3, trying to neutralize the powerful g7-bishop) 14...♖fd8 15.♗c3 e5. This was my intention, but now

White has a strong response: 16.b3, intending ♘b2, getting the knight back into the game. White's position is far from dashing, but he should still be able to hold the balance.

13...♕xe2+

Forced.

14.♔xe2 ♗g4!

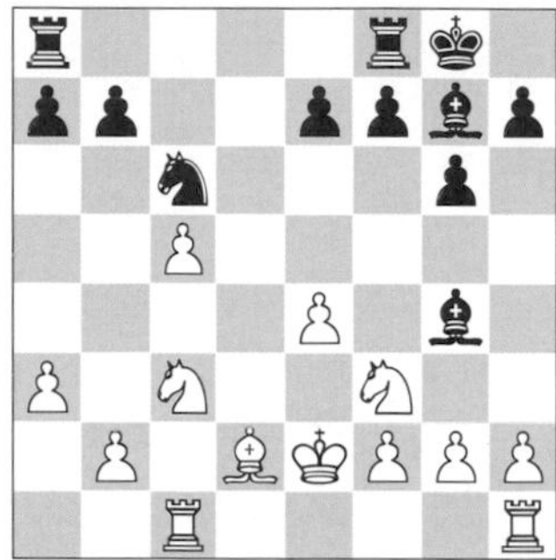

Actually improving on Carlsen's game. Magnus had the bishop on c8 and developed it to e6 instead. The text-move is more forcing.

15.♗e3? This is right up my street. 15.h3 was the lesser evil: 15...♘d4+ 16.♔e3 ♗xf3 17.gxf3 f5 18.f4 (White manages to keep things together and avoids immediate disaster) 18...♘b3 19.♖cd1 fxe4 20.♘xe4 ♗xb2, and Black has the better pawn structure, but White can still hope for a successful defence with relatively limited material and a reasonably safe king.

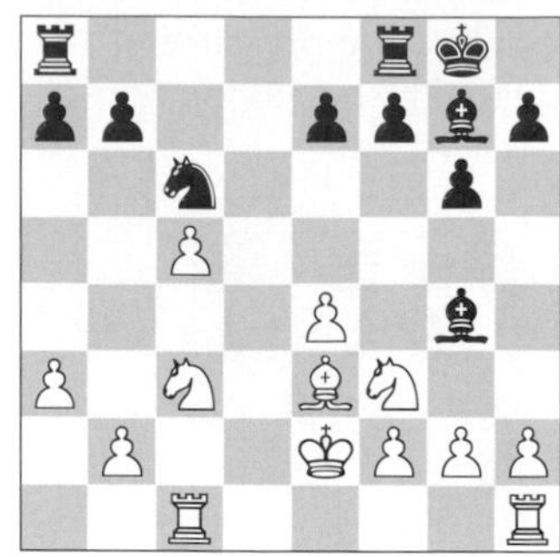

15...f5!

Now White is in a great deal of trouble. The key is that after 16.exf5 gxf5 17.h3 Black gets to keep the pin with 17...♗h5!. Threats are aplenty (...f4 and ...♘d4), and White will not be in time to get the h1-rook into the game and his king to safety at the same time. Basically, it all comes down to White needing a ♖hd1/♔f1 regrouping and not having time to achieve it. The immediate ♔f1 is not a solution, with the h1-rook locked up.

16.h3

This gives Black a pleasant choice. 16...♗h5 is good here, but the direct option is winning by force.

16...♗xf3+!

The forced line allows Black to first regain the sacrificed pawn and then to also gobble up another one.

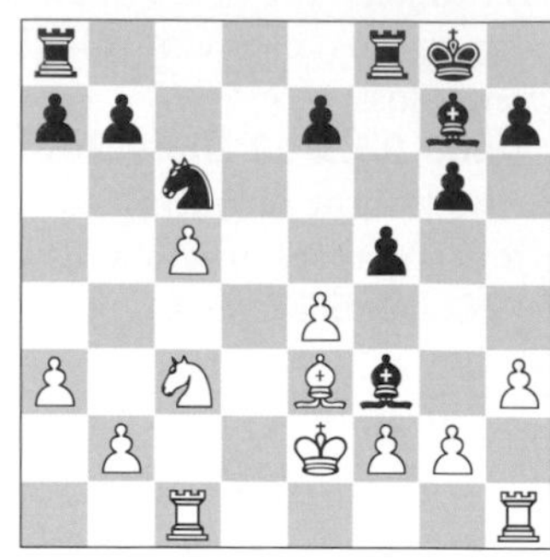

17.gxf3 f4! 18.♗d2 ♘d4+ 19.♔d3

There is no good square for the king, including this one.

19...♖ad8 The f3-pawn will not run away. **20.♖cd1 ♘xf3+** Picking up the first pawn.

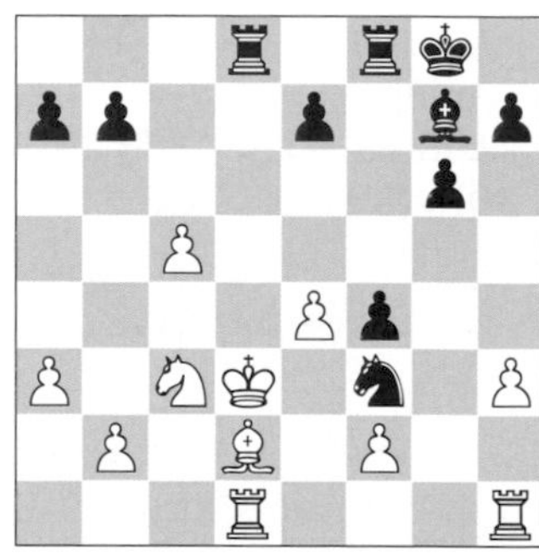

21.♔c2 ♘d4+ The knight is now doing another round.

Leo Tolstoy looks on in approval as Anish Giri receives the winner's cup, an ornamental vase especially made at the Imperial Porcelain Factory.

22.♔b1 ♘b3
Picking up the second pawn.
23.♗c1 ♘xc5
Black ends up being a pawn up and, as they say in such cases, is having the compensation, too.
24.♖xd8 ♖xd8 25.♗xf4

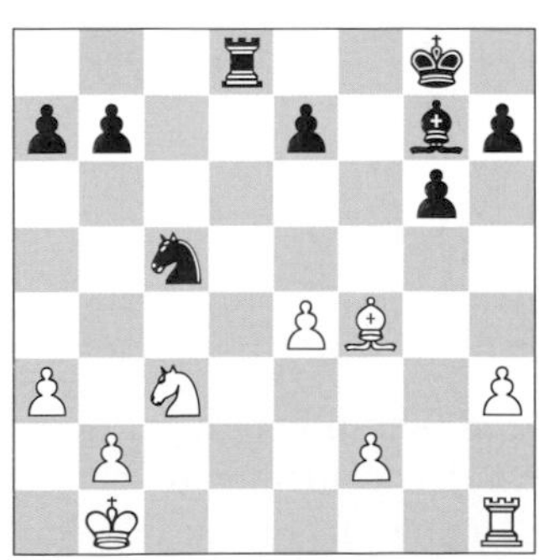

This loses another pawn, but Nodirbek is trying to set up a desperate defence at the cost of a bunch of pawns. Not a bad attempt, given how dire the situation is at this point.
25...♗xc3 26.bxc3 ♘xe4
Black is one up already and one more is falling.
27.♔c2 ♘xf2

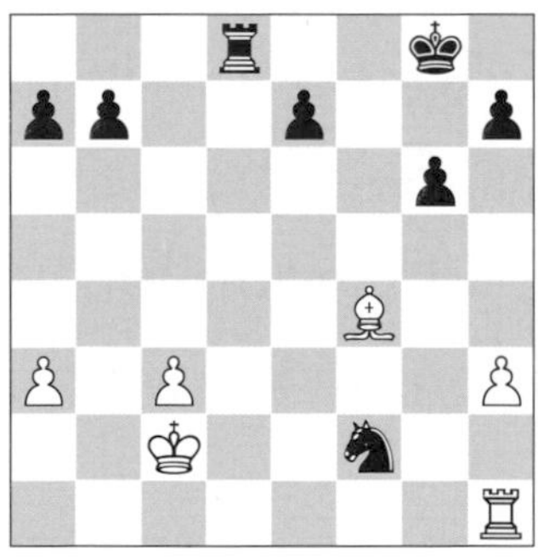

28.♖e1
A clever attempt, but it doesn't work. 28.♖h2 ♘d3 is what I had expected, when Black is just two pawns up and should be able to convert without much trouble, as after 29.♖d2 there is 29...♘e1+!.
28...♘xh3 29.♗h6
I was a bit puzzled, because somehow it was hard to make a pretty move here. After a while I realized I should make an ugly one. Three pawns is a lot; there is no need for pretty moves at this point.

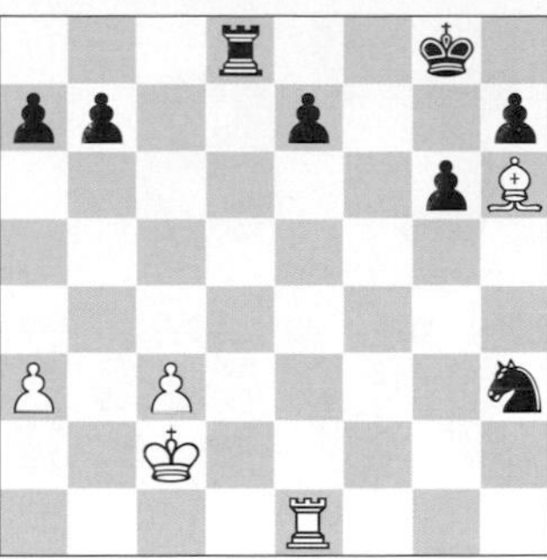

29...♖e8! The knight can't be trapped. Black is happy to return one pawn to eventually bring back the knight, as two pawns is enough to guarantee an easy conversion.
30.♖d1 g5

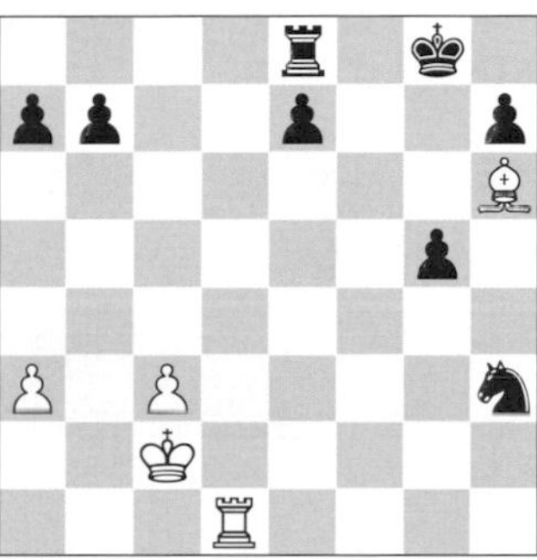

This pawn will eventually be lost, but for a good cause.
31.♖d3 ♘f4 32.♖e3 ♔f7 33.♗xg5 e5 Black has given up one of the three pawns, but now the knight is back and piece coordination has been restored.
34.c4 h5 35.♔d2 b6 36.♖e1 ♖e6 37.♖f1 ♖d6+ 38.♔e3 ♖d3+ 39.♔e4 ♔e6

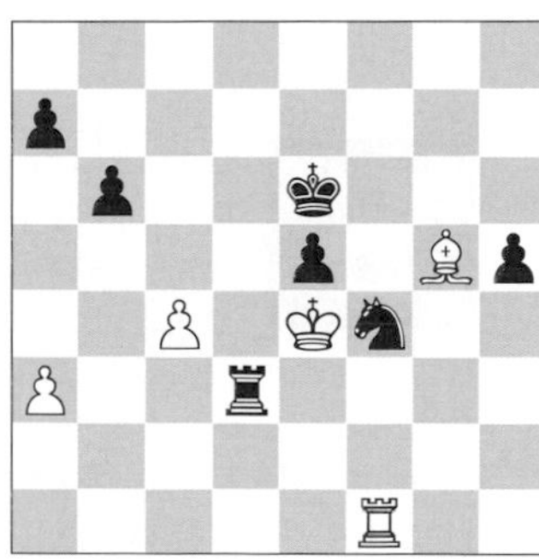

A nice final trick. 40.♗xf4 ♖d4+! wraps things up.
White resigned. ■

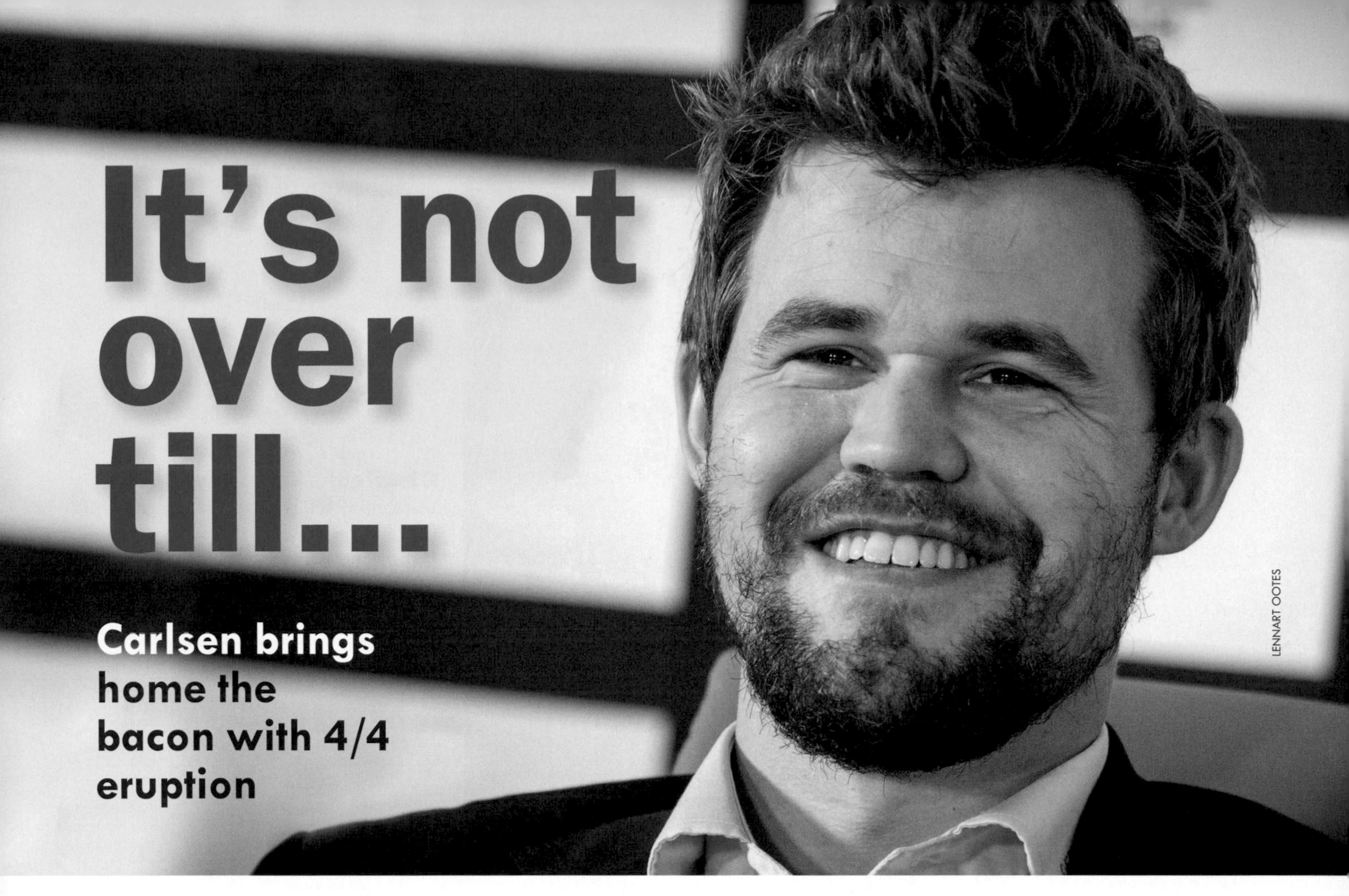

It's not over till...

Carlsen brings home the bacon with 4/4 eruption

Even though he can be a notorious slow starter, his fans may have been worrying when Magnus Carlsen failed to win a single classical game in the first half of Norway Chess. Such trepidation was unwarranted. With four straight wins, the World Champion secured first place in Stavanger, ahead of the sensations in his wake, Alireza Firouzja and Richard Rapport.

DIRK JAN TEN GEUZENDAM

Stories repeat themselves, even if they have long lost their veracity. When the first Norway Chess tournament, riding on the waves of Magnus Carlsen's fame, was held in 2013, many Norwegians were flat-out perplexed that their hero didn't win it. And they were still puzzled when it was only in the fourth edition that he finally took first prize. What was it that kept him from showing his best in his own country?

It's a question that continues to be asked, even though it has lost most of its relevance after Carlsen's further wins in 2019 and 2020. Now that he had won his fourth title – the third in a row – he could barely hide his annoyance when he smugly tweeted: 'Maybe next year the Norwegian media can do a different build-up than: Magnus usually struggles at Norway Chess'.

Indeed, shouldn't they know by now that the format of classical games, followed – in case of a draw – by a tie-breaking Armageddon game, suits him very well? They should. When Norway Chess introduced the format in 2019, it was even criticized for favouring Carlsen too much. A win in the regular, classical game was worth two points, but a win in the Armageddon game (after a draw) only half a point less. It turned out to be a poor incentive to fight in the classical games. In these classical games, Carlsen made the same score as Ding Liren that year, but whereas the Norwegian won six Armageddon deciders (finishing way ahead of the rest), the Chinese player *lost* six.

Last year, the scoring system was refined, with three points for a classical win and only one-and-a-half for a win in the Armageddon. In 2020, however, Carlsen, although collecting the same classical score as Alireza Firouzja, again took first prize thanks to his better results in the Armageddons.

This year, the format seemed to approach the desired balance. While there was nothing wrong with the fighting spirit in the classical games, in which over half saw a winner (quite shockingly, this was less than 25 percent in 2019), the Armageddon games added further excitement without being disruptive. In fact, the final standings would have been the same if only the classical games had been counted.

Magnus Carlsen, happy and relieved about his fourth overall win in the Norway Chess tournament in Stavanger: 'I worked really, really hard at the board.'

Visa issues

The main story of this 9th edition was the final clash between Carlsen and Nepomniachtchi before their world title match. Of course, the importance of such games should be taken with a grain of salt. After all, you may wonder what they will really reveal. It didn't help either that Nepomniachtchi arrived late due to visa issues and had to play his postponed first-round game against Karjakin on the only free day, leaving him with an unpleasant schedule.

Their two classical games ended in draws, and Carlsen won both Armageddons. Understandably, Nepomniachtchi qualified his result in Stavanger as 'totally disgusting, considering all the chances I spoiled', and shrugged off the following loss in the first Armageddon game as 'just a blitz game'. On the other hand, Magnus Carlsen did little to hide his contentment when he talked about the game in the studio and flashed a broad grin when he spoke about the torture he had managed to subject his opponent to.

NOTES BY
Jonathan Speelman

Magnus Carlsen
Ian Nepomniachtchi
Stavanger 2021 (4, Armageddon)
King's Indian Attack

1.♘f3 ♘f6 2.g3 d5 3.♗g2 g6 4.0-0 ♗g7 5.c4 c6 6.b3

The most important thing for White in an Armageddon game is to keep it going. If you can get something from the opening then great. But a slow burning game is much better than one that flares briefly but then subsides into equality. In totally different circumstances, this was the approach that Garry Kasparov took in a must-win situation in the famous last game of the 1987 World Championship match against Anatoly Karpov in Seville – a slow opening and plenty of long-term tension rather than too much too soon.

6...♘e4 7.d4 0-0 8.♗b2 a5

Gaining some space on the queenside. For the moment it's more or less equal, but of course either player could aspire to the advantage.

My engine, Houdini, also likes 8...♘d7 and 8...♗f5, for some reason very slightly favouring them. But at this stage that's unimportant. Black should play what he wants.

9.♘c3 ♗f5 10.e3

10...♘xc3 Carlsen said that 10...♘d7 is slightly inaccurate because White can later exchange on d5 and play ♕b5: 11.♕e2 ♘xc3 12.♗xc3 ♗e4 13.cxd5 cxd5 14.♕b5 ♕c7 15.♖fc1 ♕c6 16.♕xc6 bxc6 17.♘e1.

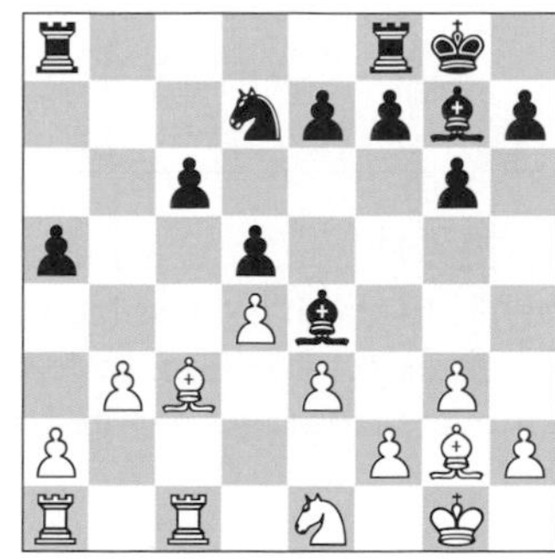

ANALYSIS DIAGRAM

White is a tad better here, but presumably with best defence it shouldn't amount to much. Not that that bothered Magnus who won nicely

Magnus Carlsen flashed a broad grin when he spoke about the torture he had managed to subject his opponent to

after 17...g5 18.♗xe4 dxe4 19.♖c2 ♖fb8 20.♖ac1 a4 21.b4 a3 22.♗d2 e6 23.♖xc6 ♗f8 24.♘c2 ♘f6 25.♖b1 ♘d5 26.♖b3 g4 27.b5 ♖b7 28.♗c1 ♖ba7 29.♖c5 ♖a4 30.♗xa3 ♗xc5 31.dxc5 e5 32.♘b4 ♘xb4 33.♗xb4 ♖xa2 34.b6 ♖c2 35.♗c3 f6 36.b7 1-0, Carlsen-Duda, Aimchess Rapid, 2021.

11.♗xc3 ♗e4

12.♕e2

12.♗h3 was a more direct way to move the knight and maybe embarrass the black bishop. Speaking to Judit Polgar after the game, Carlsen said that he hadn't thought about it but might have played it if he had.

12...a4 13.♖fc1 axb3 14.axb3 ♖xa1 15.♖xa1

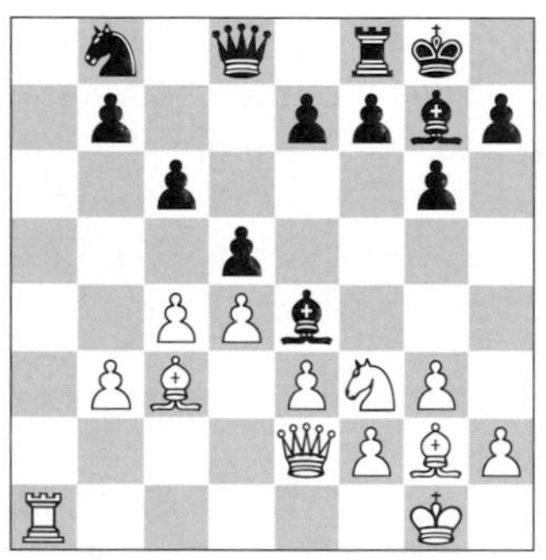

15...♕b6?! 15...c5 is a move that you'd like to play if it's possible and the engine finds no objection. Instead, the text-move encourages White to play for c5.

16.b4 Starting to gain space. The position is allegedly still equal, but Carlsen now has a plan. He will try to get in c5 followed by b5. If Black takes this pawn, then both the d5- and b7-pawns will be weak. Otherwise White can possibly attack c6, but more likely perhaps press on with b6, establishing a huge bind on the queenside. The b7-pawn will then be a very juicy target and if White can arrange a sacrifice to free his b-pawn – ♗a6 is the obvious one – then it will be very close to touchdown. There's a famous Capablanca game against Treybal from Carlsbad 1929 in which he got space both on the queenside and the kingside, which you may look at for comparison:

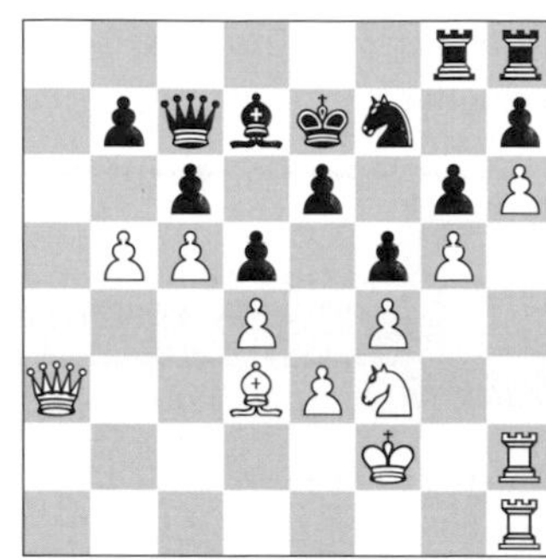

(Capablanca-Treybal, Carlsbad 1929, position after 38...♔e7)

However, this is far more extreme than anything that a world-class player today would ever succumb to (White continued 39.b6 ♕b8 40.♖a1 – 1-0, 58).

16...♘d7 17.c5 ♕c7

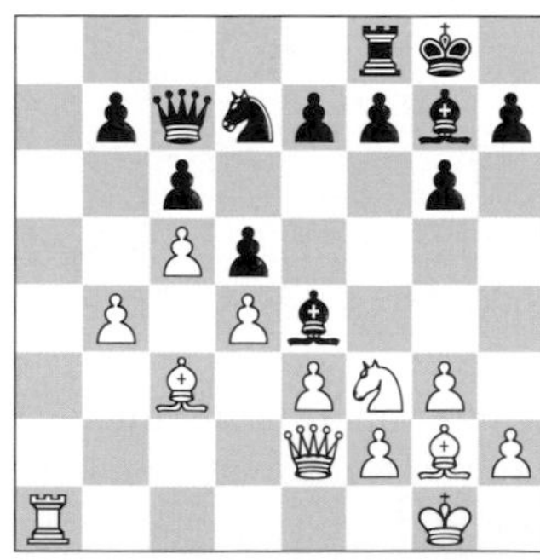

18.♖a7 For the moment, White can't get in 18.b5? because of 18...♘xc5, but he has the a-file and a real plan to achieve b5, after which, if ...cxb5 ♕xb5, the b7-pawn will hopefully be weak, or if he gets in b6 too, then that's a lot of space and in endings Black will have to watch out for ♗a6 to free the b-pawn.

18...♕b8 19.♕a2

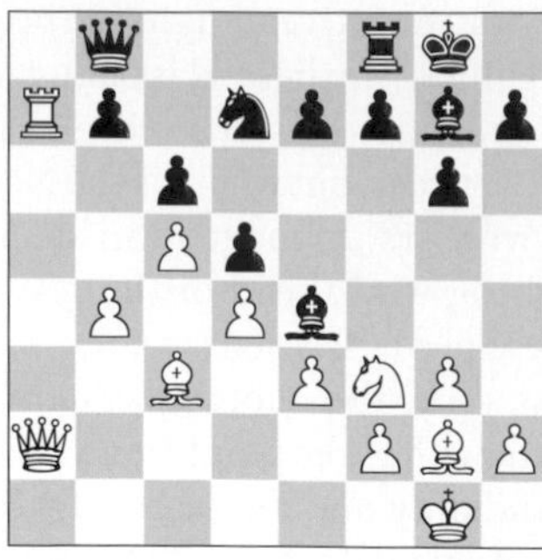

19...♗xf3?! Trying to equalize at once, but he had presumably missed that Carlsen can play 21.b5 in a moment. Here 19...e5 20.♘xe5 ♘xe5 21.♗xe4 dxe4 22.dxe5 is clearly better for White, but 19...♗d3 looks pretty okay.

20.♗xf3 e5 Counterattacking against d4, but allowing Carlsen to play the very move he wants to, as explained in the note to 16.b4.

21.b5!

21...e4 21...exd4 22.♗xd4 ♗xd4 23.exd4 ♕c8 is clearly better for White. Instead, Nepo tries to fight fire with fire, but Carlsen has seen more.

22.♗e2 ♘xc5 Of course this was the idea. **23.♗b4 ♘a6 24.♗xf8 ♗xf8**

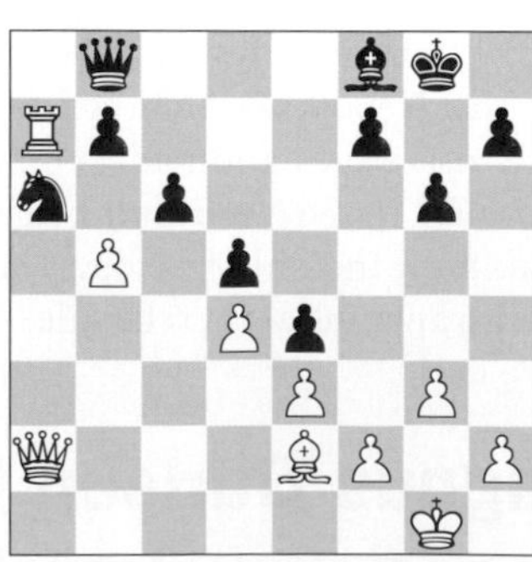

25.♖xb7! Much the cleanest win, and simpler than 25.b6 which of course

LENNART OOTES

When in Norway... Supermodels Ian Nepomniachtchi and Magnus Carlsen show the new Norway Chess sweater collection.

should also have been more than enough. After the game Carlsen said – with a smile: 'I wanted to be 100% sure... and also to torture him (before the World Championship match – J.S). I realized before playing into it, that I had h4 and g4 to break his structure.'

25...♕xb7 26.♕xa6! ♕b8 Of course if 26...♕xa6 then 27.bxa6 and the pawn queens.

27.♕xc6 ♕d6

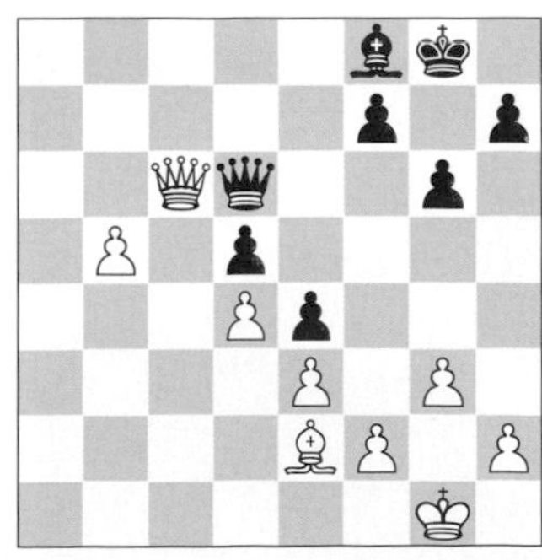

28.♕xd6 A very confident decision. The d5-pawn now drops off too and Carlsen was convinced that this would be enough.

28...♗xd6 29.♗d1 ♗c7

I wondered whether Black could preempt g4 by playing ...h5 and ...f5 and allowing b7, but then the g6-pawn is too weak: 29...h5 30.♗b3 f5 31.♗xd5+ ♔g7 32.b6 ♗e7 33.♔f1 ♗d8 34.b7 ♗c7 35.♔e2 ♔f6 36.♔d2 ♔e7 37.♔c3 ♗b8 38.♔c4

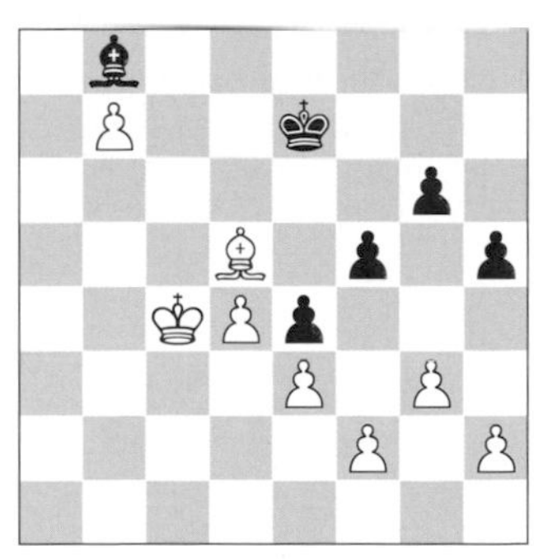

ANALYSIS DIAGRAM

and now White can play his king up to c6 and then ♗g8-h7 if he likes.

30.♗b3 ♔g7 31.♗xd5 f5 32.g4! ♔f6 33.h4

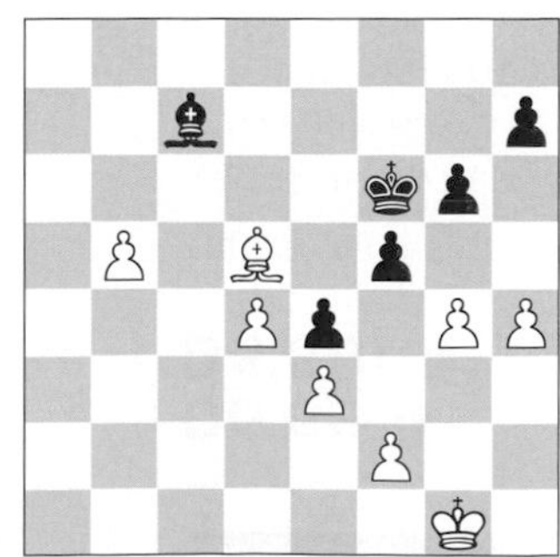

33...h6

Creating a further light-square weakness, after which it looks pretty easy, but if he waits then Carlsen should be able to play g5, to fix a kingside weakness and then break it to get his king to the queenside while Nepo's is tied to the kingside.

I could imagine something going wrong in the middle of this White plan but as long as he's careful it should win, for instance: 33...♗b6 34.♔g2 ♗c7 35.g5+ ♔g7 36.f3 exf3+ 37.♔xf3 ♗b6 38.♗c4 h6 39.e4! hxg5 40.hxg5 f4 41.♔xf4 ♗xd4 42.e5 ♗b6 43.e6 ♔f8 44.♗d3 ♗c7+ 45.♔g4 ♔e7 46.♗xg6 ♔xe6 and with the pawns so far apart it's a pretty easy win.

34.♔g2 ♗d8 35.h5!

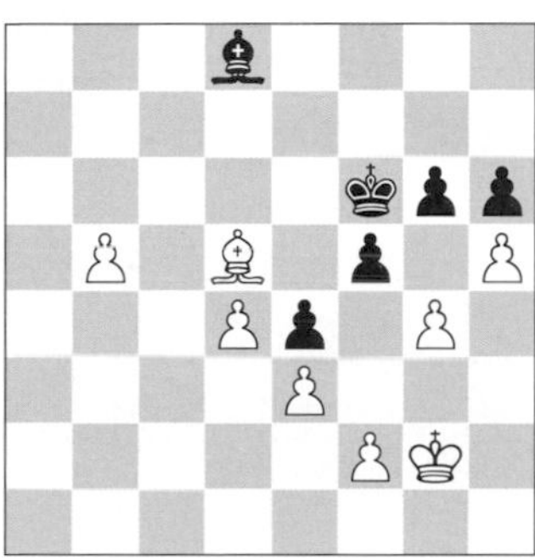

35...fxg4 36.hxg6 ♔xg6 37.♗xe4+ ♔g5 38.f4+ ♔f6

After 38...gxf3+ 39.♔xf3 the white bishop will stop the h-pawn and the king and centre pawns gently advance.

39.♔g3 h5 40.♔h4 ♗a5

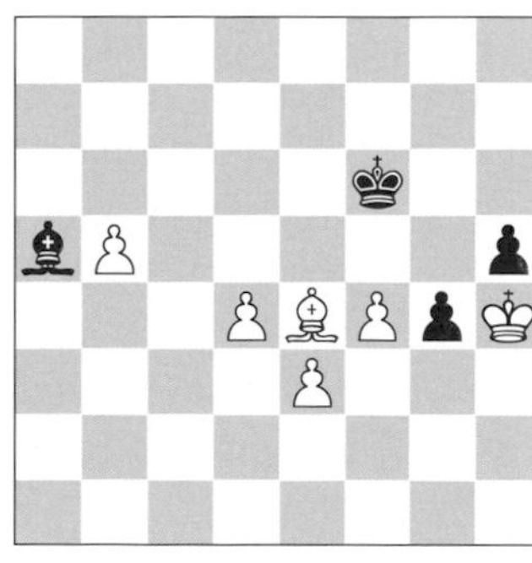

41.b6!

Deflecting the bishop so that he has time to take on h5 and get back to defend e3, removing the g-pawn on the way. Therefore Nepo resigned.

Modest and unassuming

Looking at the final standings after 10 rounds, it is hard to imagine that after seven rounds the supreme leader was Richard Rapport. The Hungarian was 3½ points ahead of Magnus Carlsen, and could even afford to lose to the World Champion in the next round (which he duly did) without losing the lead (for one more round; and then the story got sad). Rapport was playing wonderful chess and conquering the hearts of many, not only with his play, but also with his modest and unassuming manner. Typically, one of his comments after the last round was: 'Finally it's over – this is always my favourite part of every chess tournament, when the misery ends!'

It was painful to hear these words from a player who had been so impressive in the early rounds, in which he won four classical games. In Round 4, he won this fine game.

NOTES BY
Jan Timman

Richard Rapport
Alireza Firouzja
Stavanger 2021 (4)
Grünfeld Defence, Three Knights Variation

1.d4 ♘f6 2.c4 g6 3.♘c3 d5 4.♘f3 ♗g7 5.cxd5 ♘xd5 6.♗d2 0-0 7.♖c1 The ancient Smyslov System.
7...♘xc3 8.♗xc3

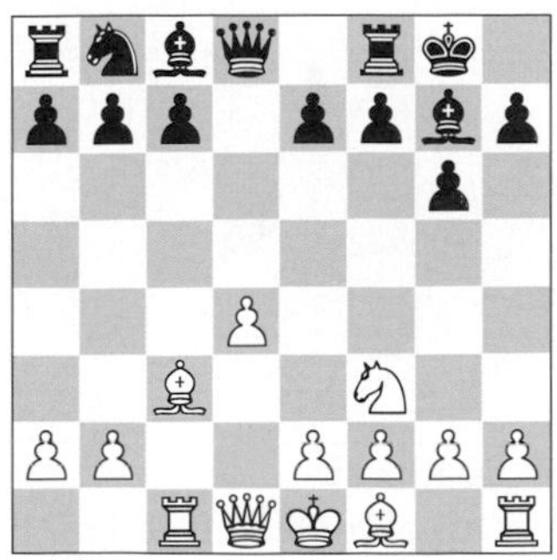

8...♘d7 Rarely played and new at top level. In Smyslov-Hort, Monte Carlo 1969, there followed 8...♕d5 9.b3 ♗g4, and now White should have continued with 10.e3 (instead of Smyslov's 10.♘e5).
9.e3 b6 10.♗e2 ♗b7 11.b4!
Thematic. White prevents the advance of the c-pawn.

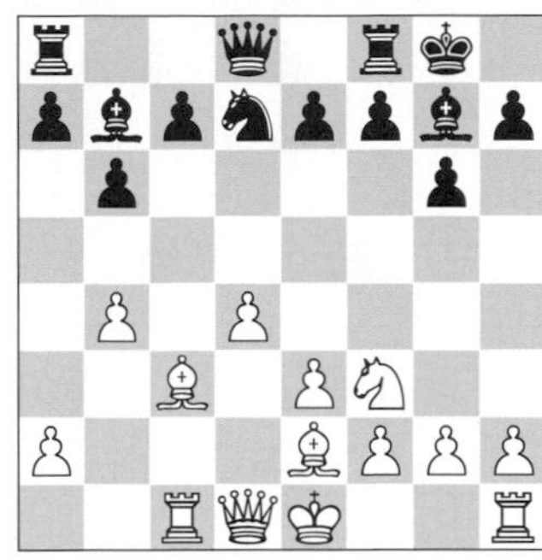

11...♘f6 Sharp and playable was 11...a5, to meet 12.bxa5 with 12...c5!. After 13.0-0 cxd4 14.♘xd4 bxa5 15.♗a1 or 15.♗f3 White is slightly better.
12.0-0 ♘e4 13.♗a1 ♕d6 14.♘e5!
Strong play. White doesn't have to cover his b-pawn.
14...♖fc8 Black covers the c-pawn. The alternative 14...♕xb4 was unattractive. After 15.♖xc7 ♗d5 16.f3 ♘g5 17.♘c6 White has a clear positional advantage.
15.♕a4 Stronger was 15.f3 ♘f6 16.♘c4!, after which 16...♕xb4 will fail to 17.♖b1. This means that Black has to withdraw his queen, after which White builds up a very strong centre with 18.e4.
The text is also strong in practical terms, since it was hard to foresee that Black would be able to make a successful bid to free himself.

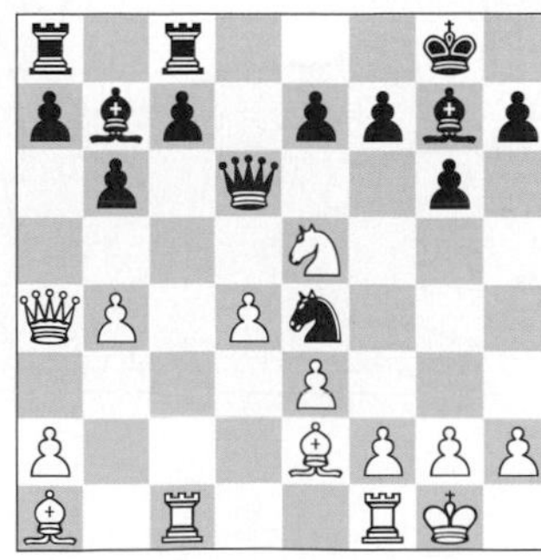

15...a6
Black could have freed himself with 15...c5, but it was very hard to see if this was justified tactically. The main line continues as follows: 16.♗c4 e6 17.dxc5 bxc5 18.♖fd1, and now Black has the surprising 18...♘d2!. Black escapes by the skin of his teeth, as witness: 19.♘xf7 ♔xf7 20.bxc5 ♖xc5 21.♗xe6+ ♔xe6 22.♖xc5 ♕xc5 23.♖xd2 ♗c6! 24.♕g4+ ♔f7 25.♖d7+ ♗xd7 26.♕xd7+ ♕e7 27.♕d5+ ♕e6 28.♕xa8 ♗xa1 29.♕xa7+, and the endgame is equal. A long and fascinating variation that is almost entirely forced.
16.♘c6 Consistent; but 16.♖fd1, preventing Black from freeing himself, would have been stronger.

16...b5
Firouzja accepts a weakening of his queenside to be able to effect a queen swap, but it will not be enough to solve all his positional problems.
The subtle 16...e6 would have been far more suitable, the point being that Black can meet 17.♖fd1 with the finesse 17...♘c5!. This line shows that the knight sortie to c6 had not been perfectly timed.
17.♕c2 ♗xc6 18.♕xc6 ♕xc6 19.♖xc6 a5

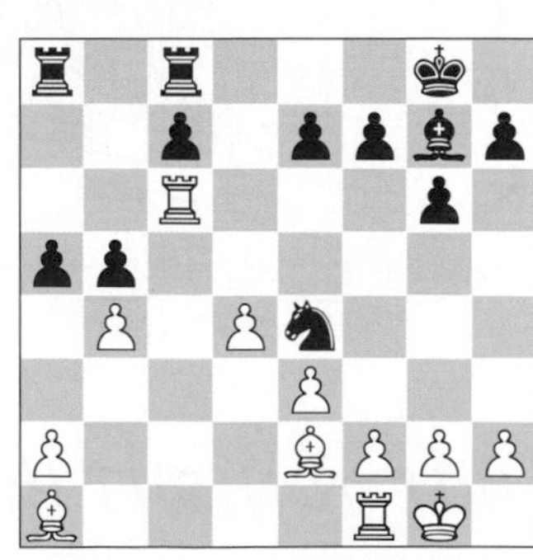

Alireza Firouzja was perhaps the most unpredictable player in the field

20.♗d3!
A strong move. Before taking on b5, White forces the knight back.
20...♘f6 21.♗xb5 axb4

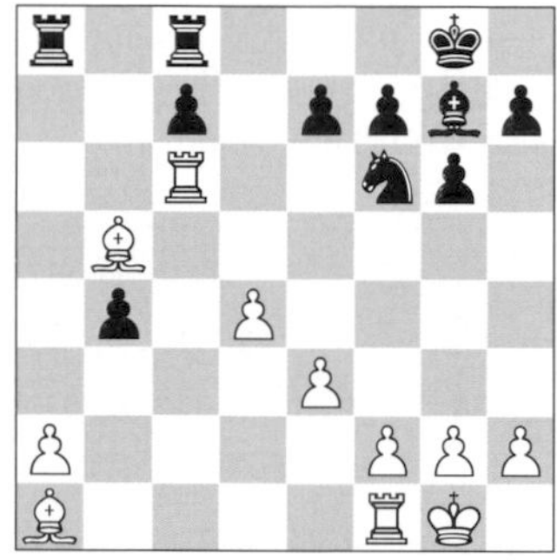

22.♗c4
The computer has a slight preference for 22.♗a6, only suggesting 23.♗c4 after 22...♖d8. After 23...♘d5 24.♗b3 e6 25.♖fc1 White has a clear positional advantage.
After the text Black has a knight manoeuvre to relieve the stress on his position considerably.
22...♘e4 23.♖c1

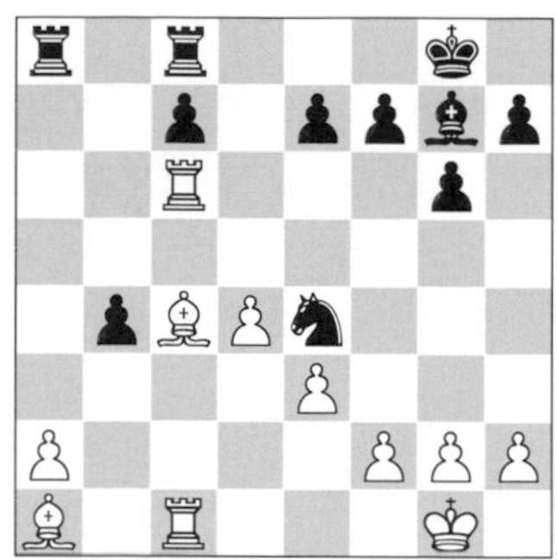

23...♘d2!
The point of the previous move. White will find it hard to maintain his bishop on the a2-g8 diagonal.
24.♗a6 ♖cb8 25.♖1c2 ♖b6
Black is aiming for simplification again. A better defence was 25...♘e4, seeing that 26.♗b2 ♘c3 27.♗c4 ♘xa2 28.♖xc7 e6 would offer him excellent drawing chances.
26.♖xb6 cxb6 27.♗b7 ♖a7 28.♗c6 ♘b1 29.♗d5!

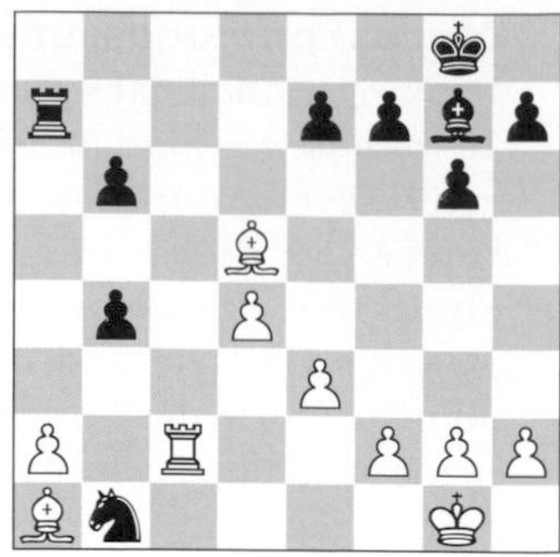

The bishop is back on the a2-g8 diagonal. White is in firm control.
29...♘c3 30.♗b3 ♖c7 31.f4 e6 32.g4 White increases his kingside territory unhindered.
32...♗f6 33.g5 ♗e7 34.♔g2 ♔g7 35.♔f3 h6 36.h4 ♖c8 37.♗b2 b5 38.♖c1 ♗d8 39.a3

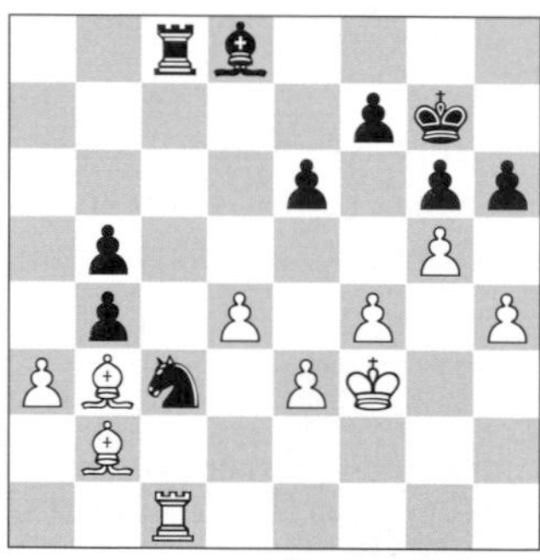

To make further progress, White will have to create space on the queenside.
39...♗a5 40.axb4 ♗xb4 41.e4 ♗a5 42.d5 exd5 43.exd5 hxg5
A tactical error. Black should have played 43...b4 at once.

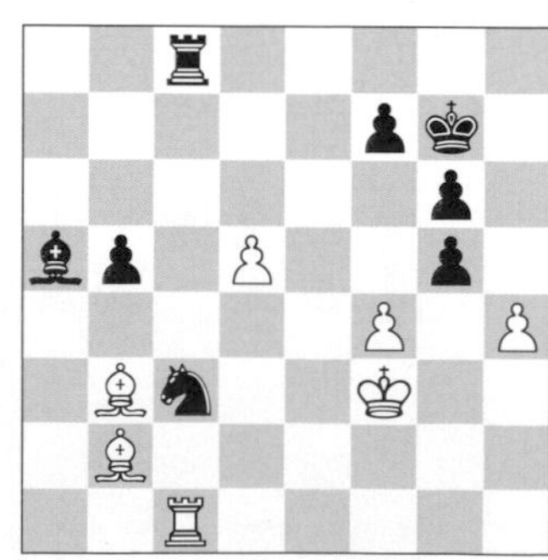

44.hxg5
An automatic reaction. But 44.♖a1! would have yielded White an immediate and winning advantage, because Black will be unable to prevent the

„NOT TONIGHT HONEY, I HAVE A HEADACHE"

white rook from crashing into a7 with force. A possible continuation is: 44...g4+ 45.♔xg4 ♗d8 46.♖a7 ♗f6 47.d6 ♖f8 48.♗a3, and Black will be unable to defend adequately.

44...b4

The immediate danger has been averted, but now White's passed pawn starts moving forward.

45.d6 ♖d8 46.♖d1 ♗b6 47.d7 ♔f8 48.♖d6 ♗a7 49.♗c4 ♗c5 50.♖c6 ♗d4 51.♖c8

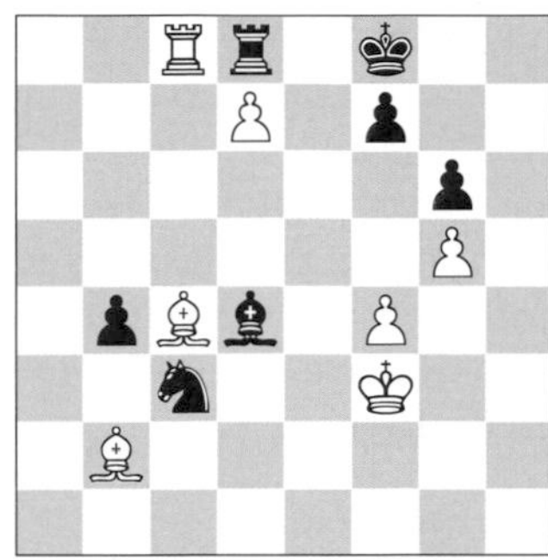

51...♔e7? Firouzja collapses under the pressure. After 51...♗b6 the issue remains open, although Black is still facing an arduous defence.

52.♗xf7 ♔xd7 53.♖c4 ♔e7 54.♗xg6 ♖d6 55.♖xb4

Black resigned.

Boundless energy and creativity

Alireza Firouzja was perhaps the most unpredictable player in the field, as can be seen from some simple statistics. The Frenchman started with three draws, followed by three Armageddons that yielded him nothing. Then he had seven decisive games, two losses and five wins, the highest number of all (and four of them in the final four rounds). One of his losses was another painful endgame experience against Magnus Carlsen, when just like last year Firouzja allowed himself to be tricked in a drawn endgame. But apparently nothing could break his spirit, and with boundless energy and creativity he kept fighting till the end.

In the final round he produced a brilliant attacking game that yielded him second place.

NOTES BY
Jorden van Foreest

Alireza Firouzja
Richard Rapport
Stavanger 2021 (10)
Sicilian Defence, Rossolimo Attack

1.e4 c5 2.♘f3 ♘c6

It is almost impossible to guess the openings of the creative Hungarian. This game is no exception, as it was the first time he played this variation of the Sicilian in the tournament.

3.♗b5

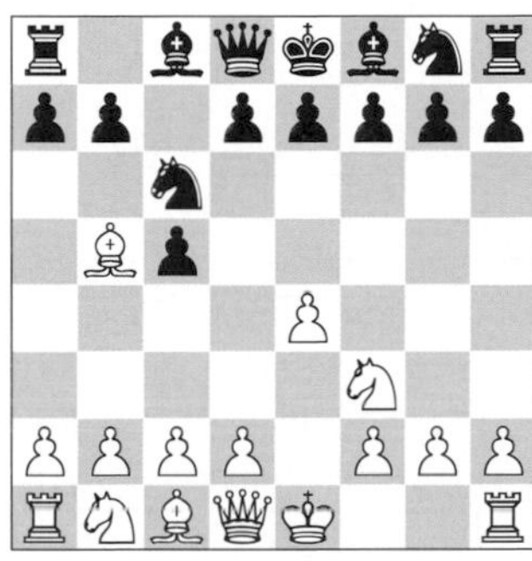

This was to be expected, as Alireza Firouzja had played the Rossolimo in Round 1 against Magnus Carlsen.

3...♘f6

This move is currently somewhat out of fashion. Most people seem to opt for 3...g6 or 3...e6. As usual, Rapport probably wants to take his opponent onto unfamiliar territory.

4.♘c3 ♘d4

The next couple of moves are almost universally played in this line.

5.e5 ♘xb5 6.♘xb5 ♘d5

White is at a crossroads here.

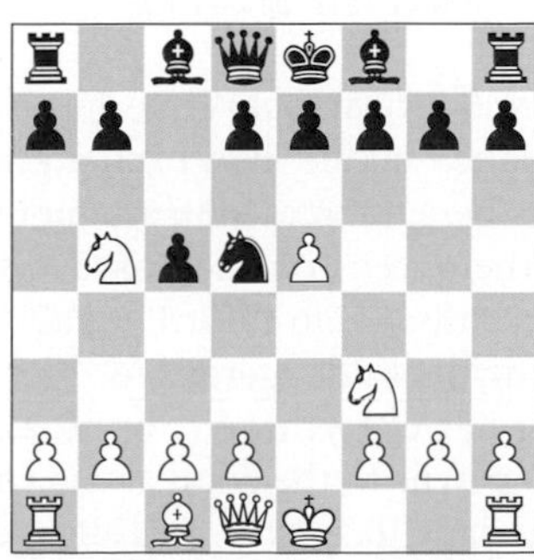

7.0-0

The main move is 7.♘g5 which, with the three knights on the fifth rank, looks pretty funny. It was seen on the highest level in a blitz game between Wesley So and Carlsen recently.

7...a6 8.c4

A useful move to include, forcing the black knight to an awkward square.

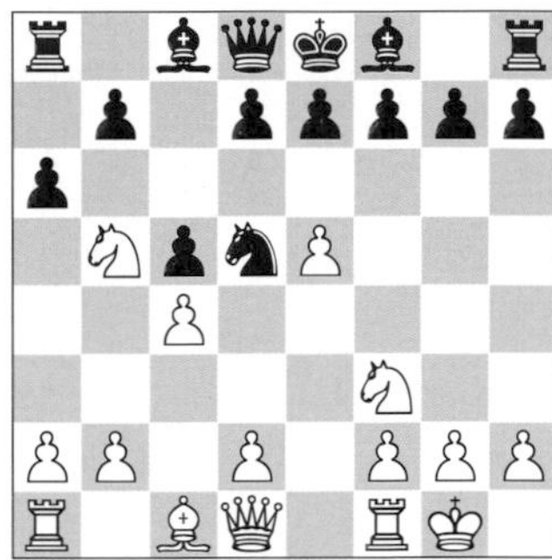

8...♘b4!

Black should not be going after the c4-pawn: 8...♘b6 9.♘c3 ♘xc4 10.d4, and Black has good chances of getting steamrolled.

9.♘c3 d6

So far, we are still following several games, among them one between Tukmakov and Sveshnikov dating back to 1978. However, I doubt the following move was something Rapport had expected in his preparation.

10.d4!

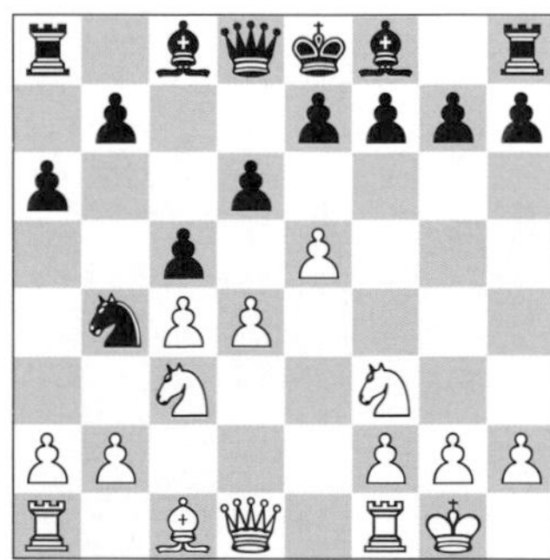

Firouzja must have planned the rook sacrifice that comes after this. A highly daring and creative decision by the French 18-year-old, which is further testament to his fearless playing style.

10...cxd4 11.♕xd4

Perhaps Rapport was already ambitious, rejecting the possibility to move the game toward a more risk-free position

There is no way back!

11...♘c2 12.♕e4 ♘xa1 13.♗f4

Firouzja spent a whopping 37 minutes on this move, which in fact turns out to be the best. The knight on a1 will be picked up on the next move, decreasing the material deficit to just an exchange. White's advantage in development yields him sufficient compensation, but no more.

13...♗e6 Rapport quickly tries to catch up on development. His real problem, though, is getting his king to safety, as developing the kingside will take a long time.

14.♖xa1 ♖c8 15.♘d5

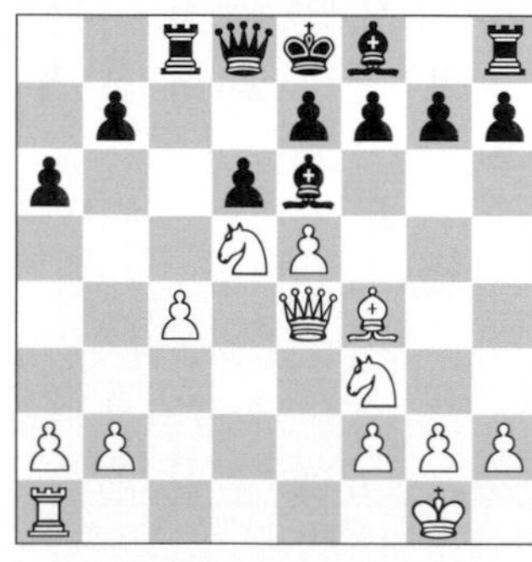

Definitely the most aggressive move, and the prospects for the black position certainly look daunting. Yet it might have been better to keep the tension with 15.b3 instead, not giving Black the chance to simplify as in the game.

15...dxe5 16.♘xe5

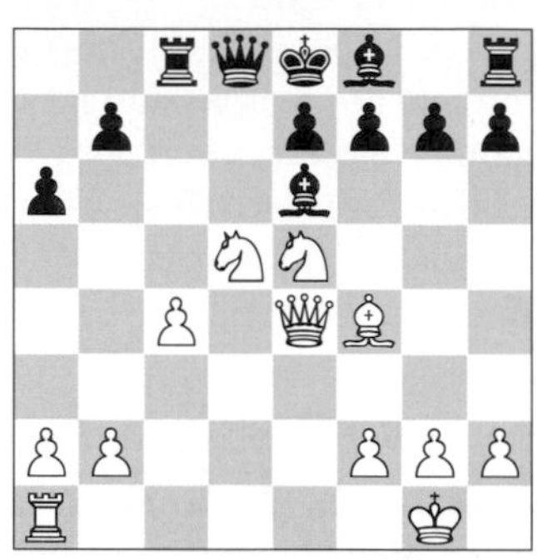

16...f6

Not a bad move, but quite a risky decision practically speaking. Perhaps Rapport was already ambitious, rejecting the possibility to move the game toward a more drawish and risk-free position.

Here, 16...♖xc4! was not a hard tactic, and Rapport must have considered it: 17.♕xc4

ANALYSIS DIAGRAM

17...♕xd5. It turns out White does not have much better than exchanging queens here: 18.♕xd5 (an attempt to keep the queens on the board with 18.♕c2 fails: 18...f6 19.♖d1 ♕xa2!. It certainly looks dangerous for Black, but he has everything covered and is two pawns to the good at the end of the day) 18...♗xd5 19.♖c1 ♗e6 20.♖c7, and White's activity should ensure a draw.

17.♘f3

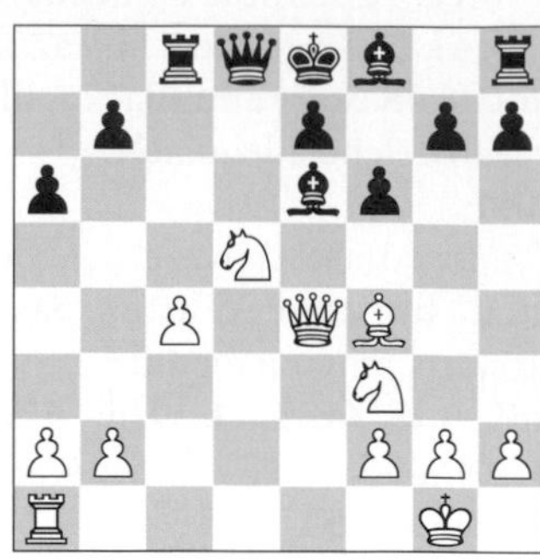

17...♗xd5?!

It looks as if Rapport is starting to lose the thread here. There was no reason to exchange the bishop just yet. Instead, getting the king out of the dangerous e-file now that he still can, would have saved him lots of headaches later on.

So, 17...♔f7 18.♖e1 ♗xd5 (only now!) 19.cxd5 ♕d7, stopping ♕e6+, and intending to slowly but surely develop his remaining pieces by means of ...g6 and ...♗g7. White's compensation is questionable at best.

18.cxd5

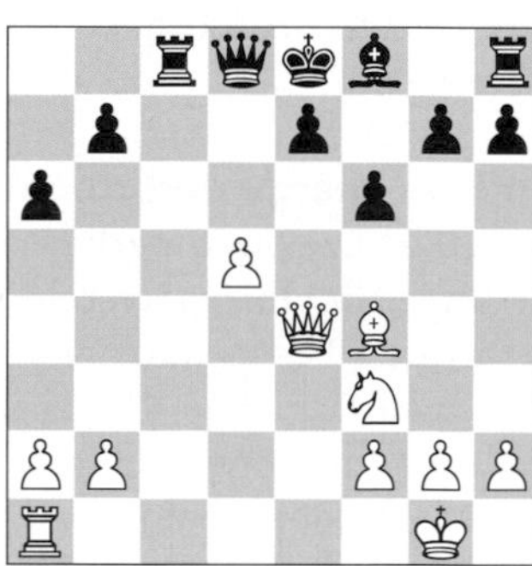

Compared to the position after 17...♔f7, Black is not quite in time to organize his forces here.

18...♖c5

Rapport is defending well for now. Note that 18...♔f7 now would be impossible due to 19.♕e6+.

18...e5!? would have been another interesting possibility. At the cost of giving White an extremely strong passed pawn, Black manages to get his kingside developed: 19.dxe6 ♗c5 20.♘h4

LENNART OOTES

With a brilliant last-round win, Alireza Firouzja claimed second place. In spite of this damper, Richard Rapport joined his opponent to break into the world's top 10.

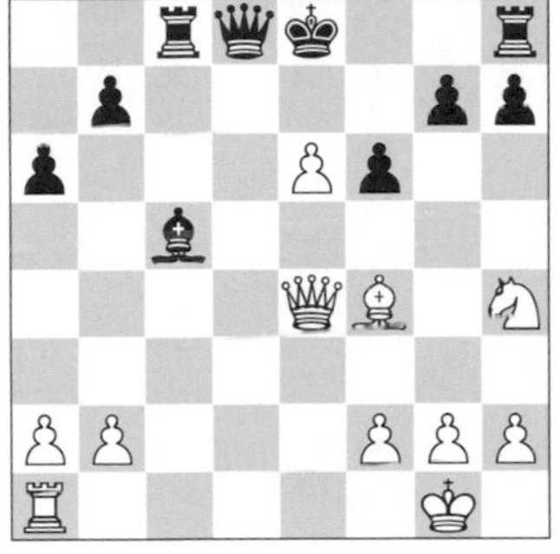

ANALYSIS DIAGRAM

Rapport may have been worried about this, since it looks highly dangerous with ♘f5 next. However, Black is just in time to create threats of his own: 20...♕b6!, attacking b2 and f2, gives Black enough counterplay.

19.d6! ♕d7 20.b4

Forcing the rook to an awkward square.

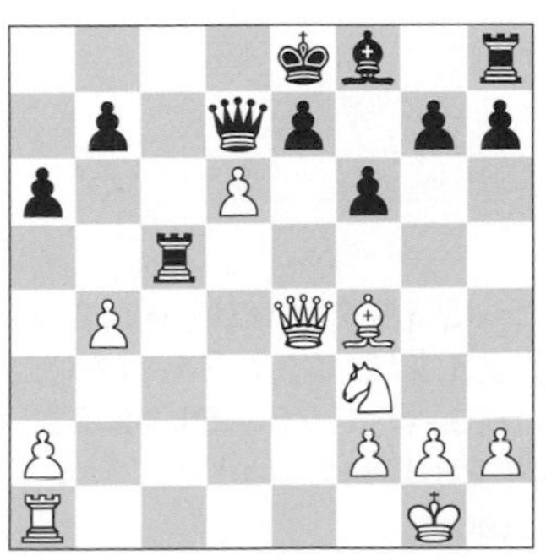

20...♖c6?!

Another inaccuracy, making Black's defensive task increasingly difficult. 20...♖c8! would have been better, an important difference compared to the game is shown in the following line: 21.♘d4 ♔f7 22.♖e1 ♖e8!, and the rook comes just in time to defend the e7-pawn a fourth time.

21.♖e1!

Firouzja is playing extremely well, and now deploys his final piece. The material deficit is not felt at all, since half the black army is still not participating in the game.

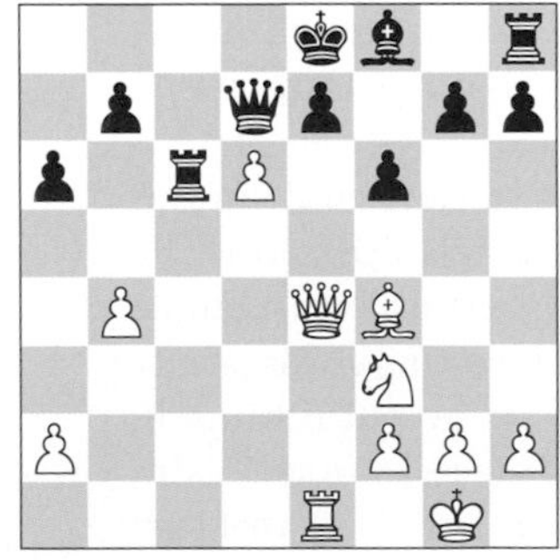

21...♔f7?

Beset by huge pressure, Rapport goes wrong.

There was just one way to keep the game alive, which was not at all trivial to find: 21...e5! 22.♗xe5 (22.♘xe5 fxe5 23.♕xe5+ ♔d8, and there is no mate) 22...♔d8!. Quite surprisingly, the black king finds a kind of safe haven on the queenside, and White has no good way to break through.

22.♘d4!

Now the white knight joins the attack, with crushing effect.

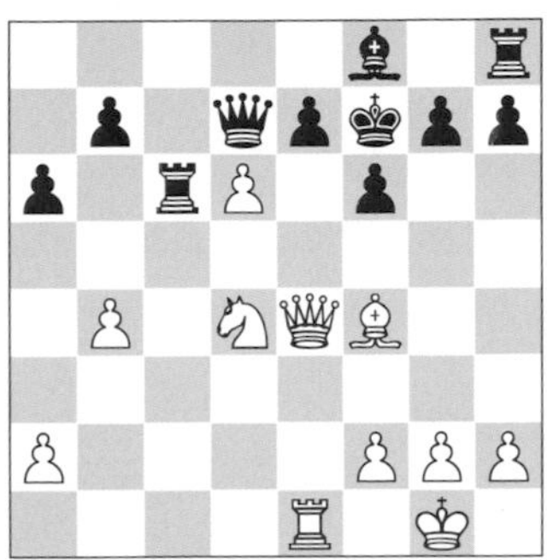

22...e5

The most human choice, desperately trying to keep the position closed, unfortunately to no avail. The computer points out an extraordinary line, in case Rapport had gone for 22...exd6 instead: 23.♕d5+ ♔g6 24.♗h6!!

ANALYSIS DIAGRAM

This has to be one of the most stunning moves I have seen! It prevents Black from playing ...h6 and ...♔h7 in the most violent way. The computer tells us Black is losing in every line. I will just give the prettiest variation here; the rest you can analyse and enjoy for yourself ☺: 24...gxh6 (24...♔xh6 25.h4!) 25.h4 (25.♖e3) 25...h5 26.♖e3 h6 27.♖g3+ ♔h7 28.♘e6 ♖g8 29.♘c5!! and White wins.

23.♕d5+
The white attack is crashing through, wherever the black king will flee. 24.♗xe5 will tear the position apart.

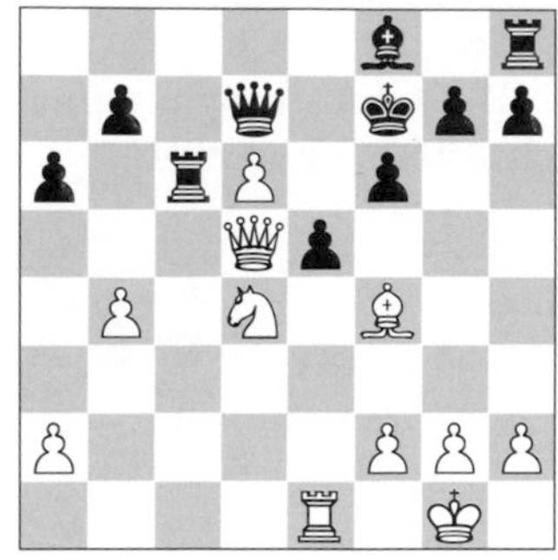

23...♔g6
After 23...♔e8 24.♗xe5 fxe5 25.♕xe5+ ♔d8 26.♘xc6+ ♕xc6 27.a4!

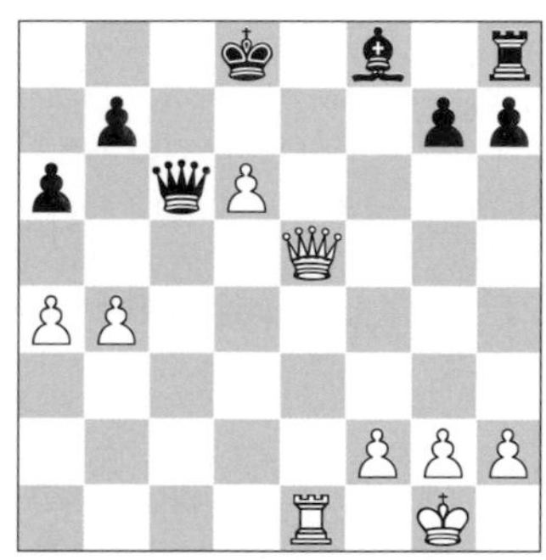

ANALYSIS DIAGRAM

there is, surprisingly, no direct mate, but Black cannot improve his position either. His position is bound to collapse sooner rather than later: 27...♗xd6 28.♕g5+ is an important point. Wherever the black king goes, Black will lose material: 28...♔c8 29.♖c1! or 28...♔d7 29.♕xg7+.

24.♗xe5!

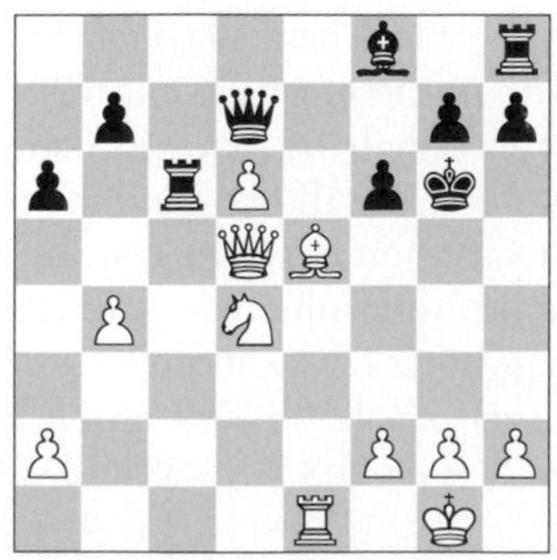

24...♖xd6
Capitulation, but there was nothing else. Now White restores the material balance, while continuing his attack. After 24...fxe5 Rapport had probably missed the devastating knight retreat 25.♘f3!. The fork on e5 will be decisive.

25.♗xd6 ♗xd6 26.♕e4+ ♔f7 27.♕d5+ ♔g6

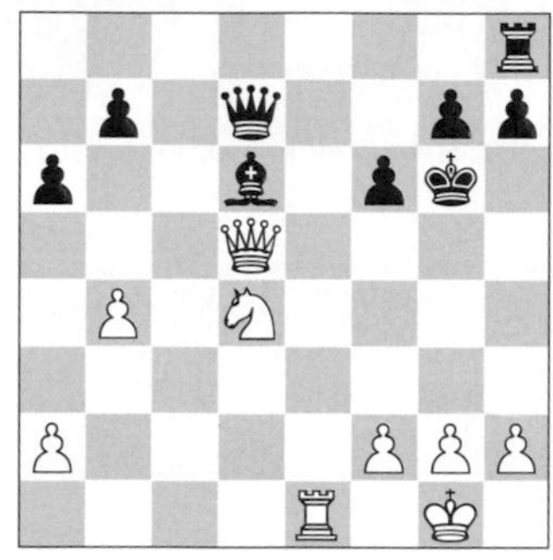

28.g3
It is important not to blunder (...♗xh2+ ☺).

28...h6 29.♖d1 ♖e8 30.♘f3 ♖e6 31.♘h4+ ♔h7 32.♕d3+
Black resigned, since ♘f5 next will win the piece.

Incredible work ethic

Just like Firouzja, Magnus Carlsen scored 6½ from 10 in the classical games (when a tiebreak would have favoured the Norwegian, thanks to a win in their second encounter), but the World Champion made the difference in the Armageddon games. Remarkably, Firouzja lost all Armageddon games (3), while Carlsen won them all (5).

A good part of Carlsen's win was due to his incredible work ethic. He was not in the best of forms, but he never stopped investing all his energy in his games. As he put it himself: 'What I would say is: I worked really, really hard at the board (...); that part I'm very happy with. Everything else, you know, there are a lot of things to improve, it wasn't sparkling at all, but I think under the circumstances I came away with absolutely everything I could have hoped for.'

Having lost against Sergey Karjakin in Round 5, Carlsen again got into trouble in Round 9. But he kept looking for his chances, and as they say, it's not over till...

NOTES BY
Peter Heine Nielsen

Magnus Carlsen
Sergey Karjakin
Stavanger 2021 (9)
Ruy Lopez, Berlin Defence

1.e4 e5 2.♘f3 ♘c6 3.♗b5 ♘f6 4.d3 ♗c5 5.♗xc6 dxc6 6.0-0 ♘d7 7.c3 h6 8.♘bd2 0-0 9.♘c4 ♖e8

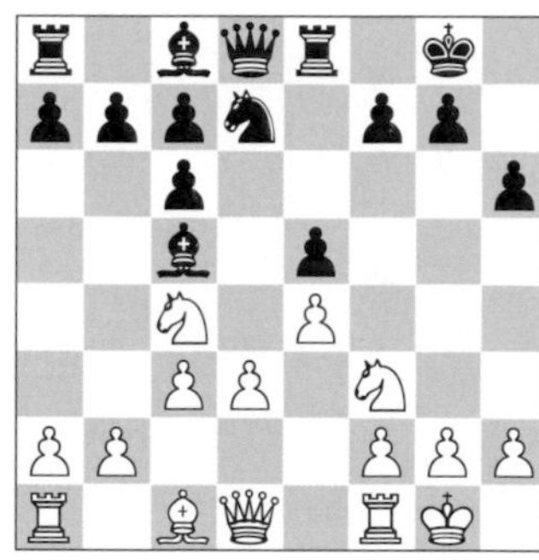

10.b4 ♗d6 11.♗e3 ♘f8 12.♘fd2 ♘g6 13.♘xd6 cxd6 14.a4 d5 15.♘b3 b6 16.a5 ♖b8 17.♕c2 ♗e6 18.♖fb1 ♖e7 19.c4 d4

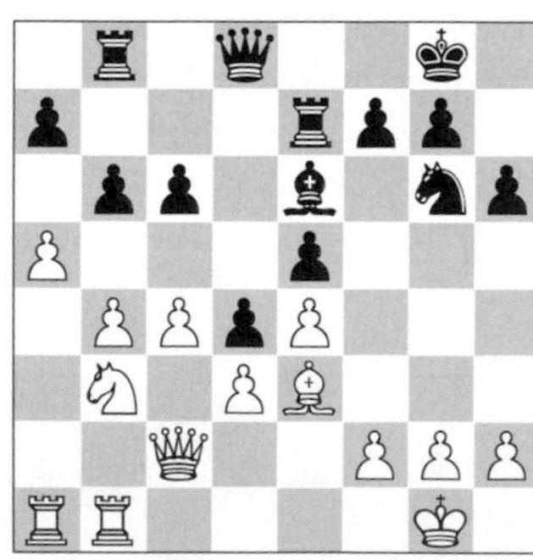

20.♗d2 f5 21.axb6 axb6 22.f3 ♖f7 23.♖f1 ♔h7 24.exf5 ♗xf5 25.♗e1 ♕g5 26.♖d1 h5 27.♗d2 ♕h4 28.♖de1 ♖a8 29.♖a1 ♖af8 30.♖a6

LENNART OOTES

Having defeated his old rival in their first game, Sergey Karjakin came close to beating Magnus Carlsen a second time. But it isn't over till...

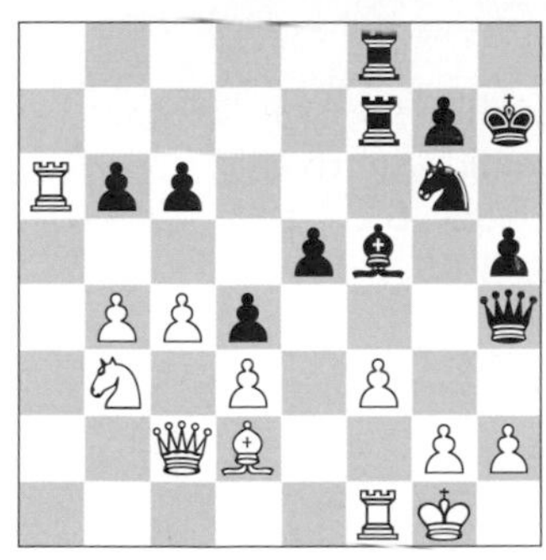

It is a commonly used trick by seconds for upcoming World Championship matches to refuse to say anything about the opening moves, claiming the need for secrecy and not revealing any secrets. Using that privilege to skip the first 30 moves is taking this too far [and the diagrams don't reveal anything either, since they were not suggested by the commentator – ed.], but the only thing to report up to now is that Karjakin has a strategically winning position and that after, for example, the retreat 30...♕d8!? the Norwegian computer Sesse, which is always following Magnus's games, gave as much as +3(!) for Black. But simply 30...h3 would undermine White's defences and win trivially. But having already beaten Magnus once during this event, Karjakin may have thought: why not make it 2-0 and in style?

30...e4?!

Magnus won four games in a row in Stavanger, and while in other sports or even in the earlier stages of chess history that would not be seen as something special, in modern top-level tournaments it certainly is. Streaks require a mixture of luck and skill, and, as Bent Larsen once pointed out, it is easier to win a bad position than a completely equal one.

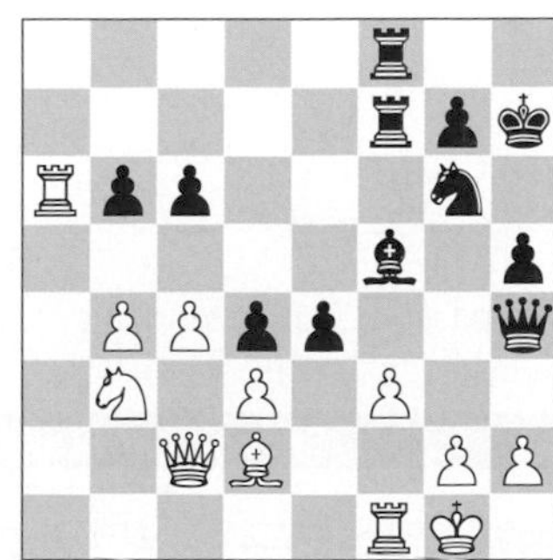

31.♘xd4!

Taking his chance (and a pawn!) immediately, but Karjakin was obviously expecting this and has a cunning plan up his sleeve:

31...exf3 32.♘xf3 ♗h3!?

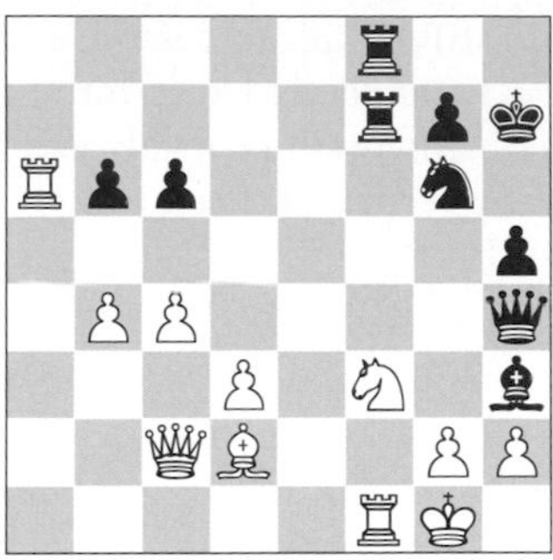

One can understand Karjakin's attraction to this move. Not only is it beautiful, but it's also logical. White has a stranded rook on the queenside, while all Black's pieces join the attack on the white king. It would not be unreasonable it Black was just winning, but Magnus has a resource:

33.♖f2!

Absolutely necessary and modest-looking, but exactly enough to fend off the black attack! Now 33...♗xg2 was perhaps what Karjakin had intended, hoping for 34.♘xh4 ♖xf2, but 34.♘g5+! turns the tables, as in this version of Black sacrificing his queen, after 34...♕xg5 35.♗xg5 ♖xf2 suddenly 36.♕xf2 has become available.

The computer suggests the calm 33...♔g8!?, with an ultimately balanced position, but Karjakin's move is not bad either:

33...♖xf3 34.gxf3

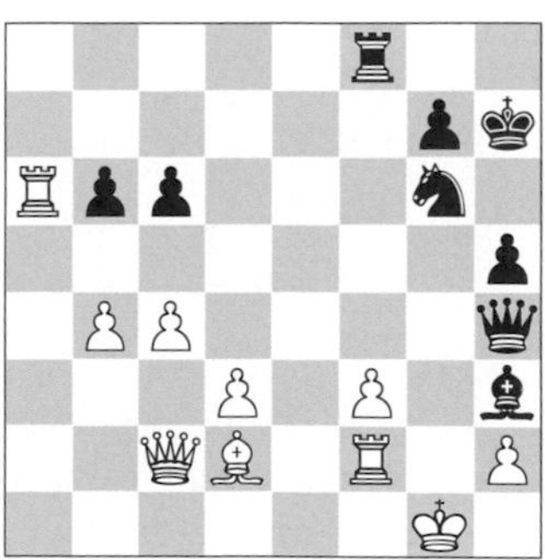

34...♖f5?

But here he falters. 34...♗g4! was the logical way to continue the attack with maximum energy, when after 35.f4 ♘e5! Black once again exploits the fact that White cannot take the offered piece. Surprisingly, White would still be able to defend, as both 36.♗c3 and 36.♗e3 keep him in the game, which will probably end in a draw by perpetual check.

35.d4!

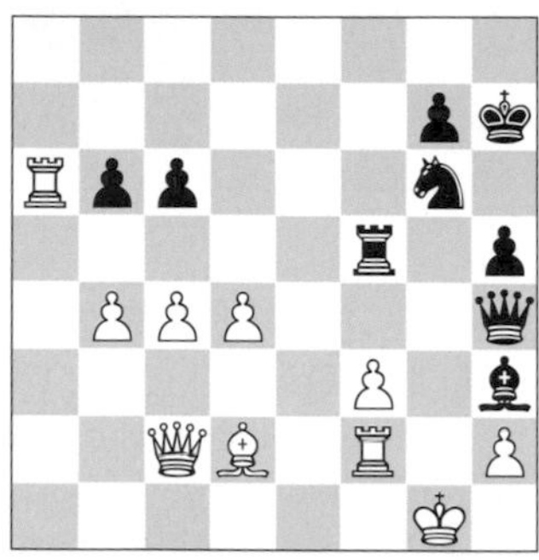

Materially, White is well ahead, but more importantly, this opens the diagonal of the white queen towards the king on h7, as well as the third rank, where the rook can join the defence via a3.

35...♕xd4 36.♖a3

36.f4! would have been more precise, as now 36...♖e5!? becomes an extra option.

36...♖f7 37.♖e3 ♗f5 38.♕c3 ♕d8

39.♖e1?!

Sesse gave 39.f4! as the winning move, but from a human perspective one can understand the logic behind leaving the pawn on f3 and giving the king somewhat more protection, as well as preparing the following manoeuvre. And, while tactically flawed, it does win the game!

39...♖d7 40.♕e3

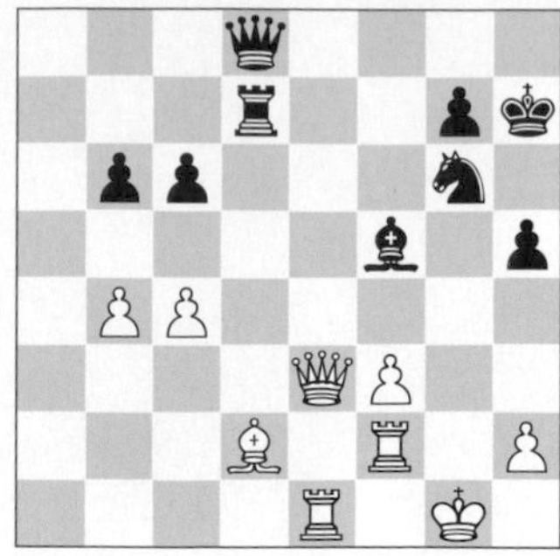

40...♖d4? When Karjakin played his 30th move, he had considerably more time left on his clock than Magnus, but in the ensuing complications he caught up and, being short on time, now blunders the game with his last move before the time-control.

40...♖e7! was possible, since 41.♕g5?? then loses to 41...♖xe1+, as 42.♗xe1 leaves the queen unprotected on g5. Thus 41.♕c3 would be necessary, but after 41...♖d7, according to the computers, White would not have better than a repetition draw after 42.♕e3.

41.♕g5

Now, however, White just wins trivially. The threat of exchanging queens as well as h5 and f5 hanging, is more than the black position can handle.

41...♕xg5+ 42.♗xg5 ♖xc4 43.♖b2!

Perhaps looking passive, but defending the b-pawn was necessary. And as Larsen said: while opposite-coloured bishop endings are often drawn, when they are winning, they often win easily! And this is the case here: White will rearrange to attack g7, and with Black's bishop having the opposite colour, there is no way to defend.

43...b5 44.♔f2 c5 45.bxc5 ♖xc5 46.♖c1 ♖d5 47.♖d2 ♖xd2+ 48.♗xd2 ♘e5 49.♖c7 b4!?

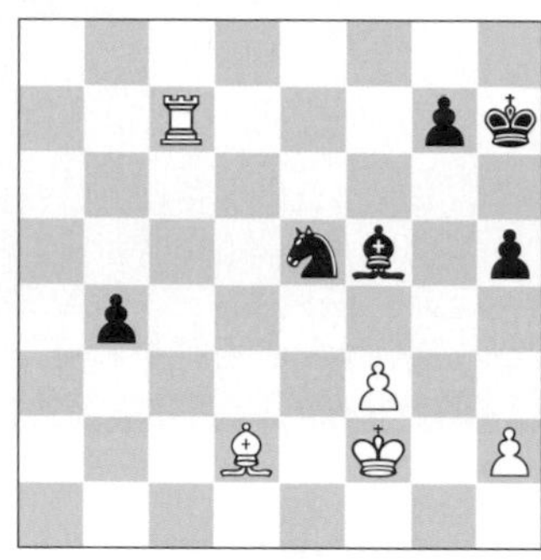

Trying to confuse the issue, as otherwise ♗c3 would win trivially.

50.♖b7 ♗e6 51.♖e7! ♘d3+ 52.♔e3 ♗c4 53.♔d4

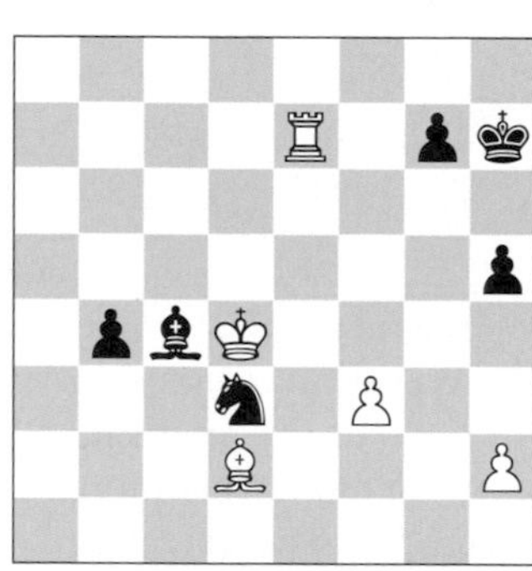

But since 53...♗b5 54.♖b7 ♗a6 55.♖b6 wins a piece and 53....♘b2 54.♗xb4 is hopeless, Karjakin resigned. ■

Stavanger Norway Chess 2021

				1	2	3	4	5	6	TOTAL
1	Magnus Carlsen	NOR	2855	*	3 1.5	3 1.5	1.5 1.5	3 0	1.5 3	19.5
2	Alireza Firouzja	FID	2754	0 1	*	3 0	3 1	1 3	3 3	18
3	Richard Rapport	HUN	2760	0 1	0 3	*	1 1	3 1.5	3 3	16.5
4	Ian Nepomniachtchi	RUS	2792	1 1	0 1.5	1.5 1.5	*	3 1	0 1.5	12
5	Sergey Karjakin	RUS	2758	0 3	1.5 0	0 1	0 1.5	*	1.5 1.5	10
6	Aryan Tari	NOR	2642	1 0	0 0	0 0	3 1	1 1	*	7

3 points for a win – when a game is drawn 1.5 for an Armageddon win and 1 for a loss.

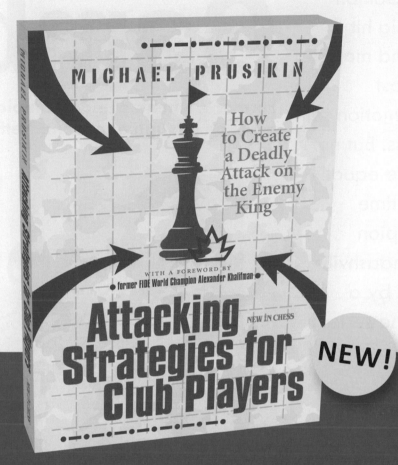

Nona's Gambit

The Queen's Gambit has been a big hit worldwide and many see it as a most welcome promotion for women's chess. But not all women are equally thrilled. Five-time World Champion Nona Gaprindashvili feels insulted by a comment in the series and has filed a lawsuit against Netflix, seeking $5 million in damages. **DYLAN LOEB MCCLAIN** looks at her case and weighs her chances.

Former Women's World Champion Gaprindashvili takes on a tough opponent: Netflix

After she had won the World Championship in Moscow in 1962, Nona Gaprindashvili received a hero's welcome on her return to Tbilisi.

The Queen's Gambit, the seven-part series about a fictional female chess prodigy named Beth Harmon, was a runaway hit on Netflix last year and sparked a global mini-surge of interest in the game. After the series aired, there was a wave of new memberships on internet chess sites and game makers and stores reported selling out of chess sets.

In September, Netflix, which produced *Queen's Gambit* and which said it was viewed by 62 million households, collected 11 Emmy Awards for the series in the annual prize-giving competition by the United States Academy of Television Arts & Sciences. The Emmys are for television what the Academy Awards, or Oscars, are for movies.

For all of the positive attention and reviews that *Queen's Gambit* garnered, it has also sparked something that Netflix almost certainly did not want: A lawsuit by Nona Gaprindashvili, the former Women's World Champion (1962-1978), accusing the streaming service of libel. The lawsuit was filed in late September in Federal District Court in Los Angeles, California.

Gaprindashvili's lawsuit is based on a throwaway line in the finale of the series in which Harmon plays, and wins, an elite tournament in Moscow, besting the World Champion in the last game. As the tournament begins, the announcer says of Harmon, 'The only unusual thing about her, really, is her sex, and even that's not unique in Russia. There's Nona Gaprindashvili, but she's the female world champion and has never faced men.' The camera then pans to show a young woman who looks strikingly like a young Gaprindashvili.

The lawsuit states that the comment that 'Gaprindashvili "has never faced men" is manifestly false, as well as being grossly sexist and belittling'.

'Degrading her accomplishments'
Indeed, at the time that the fictional tournament in the series takes place, 1968, Gaprindashvili had not only played against men, she had done so with some success, including winning the Hastings Challengers tournament in 1963/1964.

Later on in her career, she would do even better against men, tying for first at Lone Pine in 1977, and tying for second at Sandomierz in 1976 and Dortmund in 1978. After her performance at Lone Pine, though she had not satisfied all the requirements to become a grandmaster, she was awarded the title anyway by the International Chess Federation, becoming the first woman to achieve that distinction.

Gaprindashvili, who is 80 years old, is seeking at least $5 million in damages for 'impugning her professional standing' and 'degrading her accomplishments before an audience of millions'.

Gaprindashvili's lawsuit also notes that she is Georgian, not Russian, and that stating she was Russian, knowing that 'Georgians had suffered under Russian domination when part of the Soviet Union', was 'piling an additional insult to injury'.

'This is my entire life that has been crossed out, as though it is not important', she told *The New York Times*. 'They were trying to do this fictional character who was blazing the trail for other women, when in reality I had already blazed the trail and inspired generations. That's the irony.'

In the legal filing, Gaprindashvili said that she had reached out to Netflix to ask the company to apologize and issue a retraction, but that Netflix did not respond.

In reply to the lawsuit, Netflix told *The New York Times* and *NBC News*, among others, 'Netflix has only the utmost respect for Ms. Gaprindashvili and her illustrious career, but we believe this claim has no merit and will vigorously defend the case.'

Not by the book
In the 1983 book *The Queen's Gambit* by Walter Tevis on which the series is based, Gaprindashvili was among the spectators at the tournament, just as in the series. But, in the book, Tevis wrote, 'There was Nona Gaprindashvili, not up to the level of this tournament, but a player who had met all these Russian Grandmasters many times before.'

In its statement responding to the lawsuit, Netflix did not explain or mention why the text in Tevis's book had been changed for the series.

Eugene Volokh, a law professor at the University of California, Los Angeles, who specializes in issues dealing with the First Amendment to the United States Constitution, which includes libel, said that Gaprindashvili faces an uphill fight in trying to win her case. There are several legal paths that Gaprindashvili's lawyers could pursue, but they each have significant obstacles – just proving that what was said about her is false is, by itself, not enough.

Gaprindashvili was the first woman ever to be granted the Grandmaster title by FIDE

Nona Gaprindashvili

1941: May 3, born in Zugdidi, Georgia (Soviet Union)
1962: Beats Bykova 9-2 to become 5th Women's World Champion
1963/64: Wins Hastings Challengers
1964: Wins Soviet Women's Championship
1965: Defends world title against Kushnir, 10-6
1969: Defends world title against Kushnir: 12-7
1972: Defends world title against Kushnir: 12-11
1975: Defends world title against Alexandria: 9-4
1977: Ties for 1st in Lone Pine, first woman to score an IGM norm
1978: Loses world title to Chiburdanidze, 6½-8½
1978: Ties for 2nd in Dortmund
1978: Awarded International Grandmaster title by FIDE
1985: Wins Soviet Women's Championship for the 5th time
1986: Scores 10/10 at Dubai Olympiad

In her career Nona Gaprindashvili beat several male GMs, including Bojan Kurajica, Alexander Beliavsky, Anatoly Lein, Wolfgang Uhlmann, Ulf Andersson, Roman Dzindzichashvili, Ian Rogers, Maxim Dlugy and Zurab Azmaiparashvili.

The most difficult route is to prove defamation, because the statement has to be one that seriously attacks a person's character and makes people think negatively about that person as, for example, saying that someone is a serial killer who is not. Minimizing what Gaprindashvili accomplished is not likely to change people's opinion of her, even if they believe what was said to be true, according to professor Volokh.

An easier case is to show that Gaprindashvili was painted in a 'false light', meaning that the way that she was described is 'offensive' to a 'reasonable person'. As the quotes suggest, these terms are both legal and technical.

While the series understates Gaprindashvili's accomplishments, the question is whether it does so substantially. It correctly credits her with having been Women's World Champion, which arguably was her greatest claim to fame at the time. Beyond that, professor Volokh said, if she had rather limited success against the very top players, then it might be difficult to prove that the statement impugned her professional standing.

As an example, he pointed to a tournament in Reykjavik in 1964 in which Gaprindashvili competed and which is cited in the lawsuit. She finished in a tie for eighth in the tournament and, against the top three players – Mikhail Tal, Svetozar Gligoric and Fridrik Olafsson – she scored a half point.

Professor Volokh said, 'The United States legal system recognizes the defence of substantial truth. While she would have beaten 99.9 percent of chess players handily, the overall gist of the statement is that she wasn't among the very elite players.' That is implied even in what Tevis wrote about her.

For the case to go to trial, Gaprindashvili's lawyers have to first convince a judge that Netflix substantially understates her accomplishments. A judge, particularly an American one, might not see the understatement as being sufficiently significant. The judge would have to find that the statement is 'materially different' from the truth, professor Volokh said, and that Netflix knew that or probably knew that.

As for whether or not it was insulting to refer to Gaprindashvili as Russian instead of Georgian, professor Volokh, who was himself born in Kiev, Ukraine, said it was common practice at the time to conflate the various nationalities in the Soviet Union under the rubric of Russian. That detail is not sufficient for a defamation case.

Gaprindashvili told *The New York Times*, 'Not many things can damage me emotionally. But this was surprising to me – and humiliating'

'On balance, it is going to be difficult to persuade an American court that what Netflix did was malicious', said professor Volokh.

Nonetheless, Gaprindashvili told *The New York Times*, 'Not many things can damage me emotionally. But this was surprising to me – and humiliating.'

The interest of chess players

Zurab Azmaiparashvili, who is the president of the European Chess Union, is a friend of Gaprindashvili and, like her, from Georgia, was reluctant to be overly critical of Netflix. In a text message, he said that, as the head of the ECU, he will always support the interest of chess players and that the streaming service should not have made the error.

But, he added, 'What *Queen's Gambit* and Netflix did for the popularization of our lovely game is invaluable, and we should respect this.'

In addition to the legal obstacles for Gaprindashvili, there are also at least one or two errors in her lawsuit, which, while they may not hurt her case, are at least a bit embarrassing. The most glaring one comes in paragraph 7, when it says that by 1968 she had faced 59 men in competition, including 10 grandmasters of that era. Among them: Viswanathan Anand, the future world champion, who would not be born for another year. (They did play in 1988, however. The game ended in a draw.) ■

BORIS DOLMATOVSKY

Representing the Soviet Union, Georgian stars Nona Gaprindashvili, Nana Alexandria, Maya Chiburdanidze and Nana Ioseliani dominated women's chess for decades.

What is chessable?

Chessable is a comprehensive and social learning website that offers interactive video chess courses on all aspects of the game, from the opening to the endgame. Chessable also offers interactive versions of classic chess books built on top of its unique MoveTrainer® software.

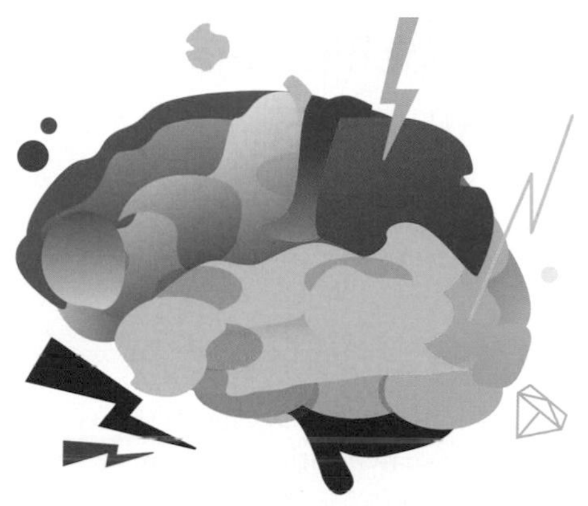

Science based technology

MoveTrainer® taps into the science of learning

Science can help us understand how chess learning happens. Instead of learning on your own, you have powerful allies: educators, psychologists and neuroscientists. We use the science they produce to make learning chess easier, fun and efficient! Chessable is at the forefront of chess education.

Spaced Repetition & Scheduling

Spaced repetition theory in a nutshell means: you learn best when you review your knowledge in increasing time increments rather than regularly. At Chessable, we provide a scheduling mechanism that prompts you to review what you've learned in an efficient way. Get the chess move right, and you won't see it for a while. Get it wrong, and we know it needs some work so you will soon be tested again.

What Chessable users say

NM Han Schut

“I had prepared a lesson for my 8-year-old student about pawn endings (key squares and opposition). To my surprise he solved every endgame perfectly and immediately. I was intrigued and asked him which coach had taught him to play these endgames so well. His answer surprised me. He had learned to play these endgames by practicing ‘100 Endgames You Must Know’ by Jesus de la Villa on Chessable, by himself.”

chessable

Magnus Carlsen teaches chess

The rook and the pawn in the endgame

A golden rule in the endgame is that the rook belongs behind the passed pawn. Magnus Carlsen shows you how fascinating it can be when the rook is on the 'wrong' side.

I like playing endgames. When I was little, I used to lose points in the endgame but then I learned, and eventually I've become the one who gains half points, whether that be drawn games won or sometimes even lost games drawn. One of my favourite themes in the endgame is when the rook is on the wrong side of the passed pawn – somehow that has always fascinated me. The main reason for that is the game that I played against the Czech grandmaster Zbynek Hracek in the German Bundesliga in 2007.

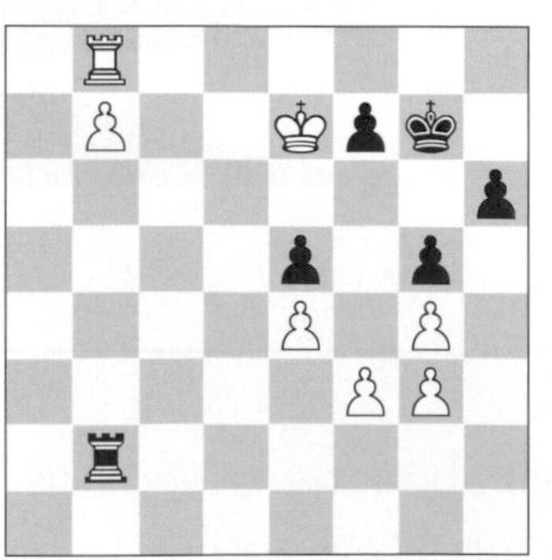

position after 58...♖b2

If you were to switch around the position of the rooks here – with the white rook on b2, and the black rook on b8 – the position would be an easy win for White: the black rook is completely immobile, and we can march over with the king, ♔e7-d7-c7. But in the position where the rooks are in the game, this is not possible because then the white king will be checked. Something more clever is needed, and I really like the idea that happened in the game.

'The nice thing about having a rook in front of the pawn is that your opponent's rook can never move away from that particular file'

Here I played:

59.♔d6

Obviously Black now needs to protect the e5-pawn, otherwise my cluster of pawns – e4, f3, g3 and g4 – will become pretty much mobile. So he protected it with the king:

59...♔f6

It should be noted that if he protects with 59...f6, I will simply play 60.♖e8 ♖xb7 61.♖e7+ ♖xe7 62.♔xe7 with an easily winning pawn ending.

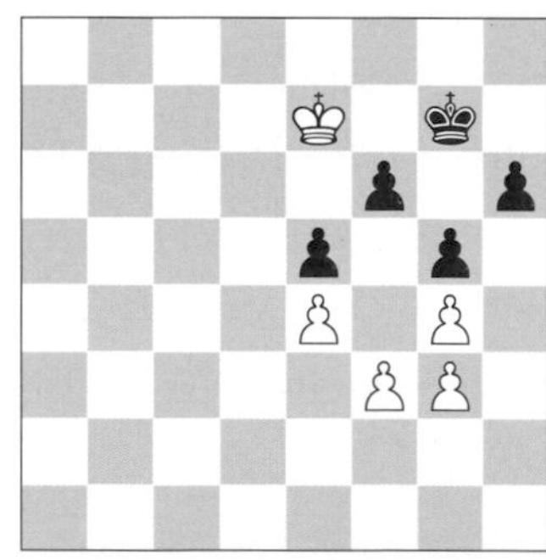

ANALYSIS DIAGRAM

For instance, 62...♔g6 63.♔f8 and there's nothing to do but push the h-pawn: 63...h5 64.gxh5+ ♔xh5 65.g4+ ♔h4 (if the king moves backwards with 65...♔g6 I just go 66.♔g8 which just forces his king away again, and 66...♔h6 67.♔f7 and I grab his pawn. So he has to go forward) 66.♔f7 ♔g3 67.♔xf6 ♔xf3

'Even in simple endgames it is often possible to play for mate – and that is one of the fascinating things about endgames'

ANALYSIS DIAGRAM

and once again he's not in time, and it is important just to play 68.♔f5! rather than capturing any of the pawns. Now, wherever he goes, I capture the pawn the same way the black king goes.
Therefore he played 59...♔f6 instead, which is his only chance. And now quite a bit of imagination is required to win the game.
Obviously, 60.♖h8 ♖xb7 61.♖xh6+ ♔g7 is not enough because I need to move my rook and he protects e5, and my extra pawn will be meaningless. So instead, already a long time ago, I had found this idea, but I needed to verify whether it actually worked. Here I played:

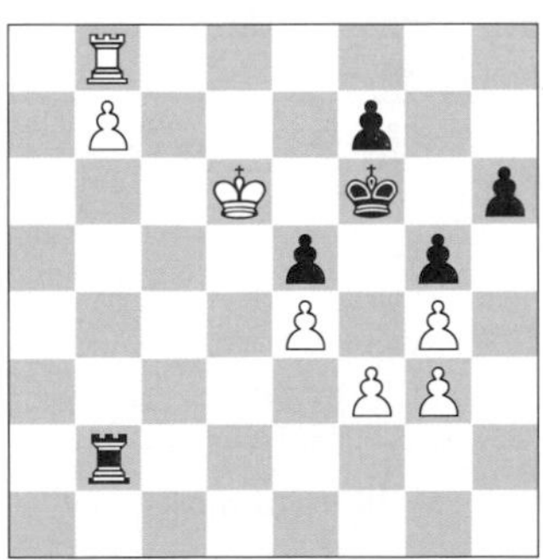

60.f4!
I remember one of my teammates, Peter Svidler, told me after the game that he didn't know what I was doing, whether I was trying to lose the game... Then, when he saw my idea, he calmed down. My opponent has no choice now but to take twice:
60...exf4 61.gxf4 gxf4
And now comes the point of my idea with

62.♖g8!
Now if 62...♖xb7, 63.e5 is checkmate!

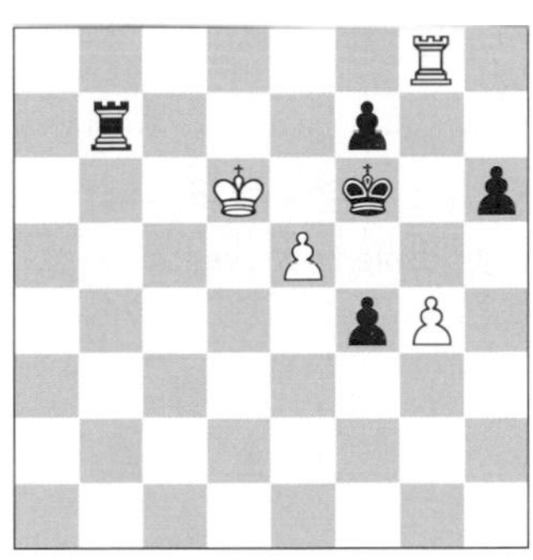

He has only one option:
62...♖b6+ 63.♔c7 ♖xb7+ 64.♔xb7 f3

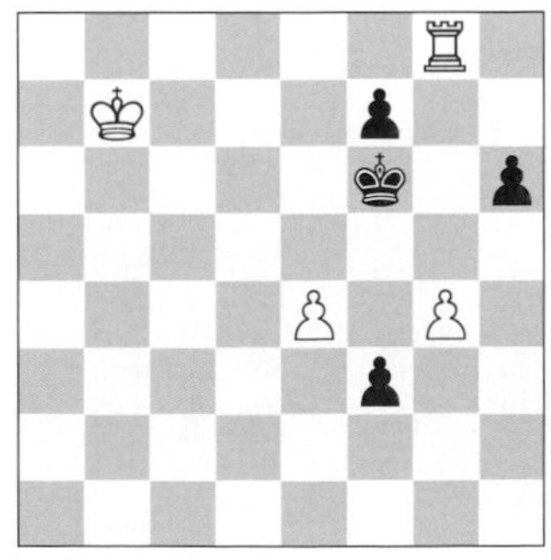

There are a couple of ways for White to win here – but by far the most elegant was the way that I chose, which is the same idea again with:
65.♔c6! ♔e5
If he advances with 65...f2 66.♔d6 f1♕, once again 67.e5 is checkmate.
66.♖e8+ ♔f4 67.♔d5 f6 68.♖f8

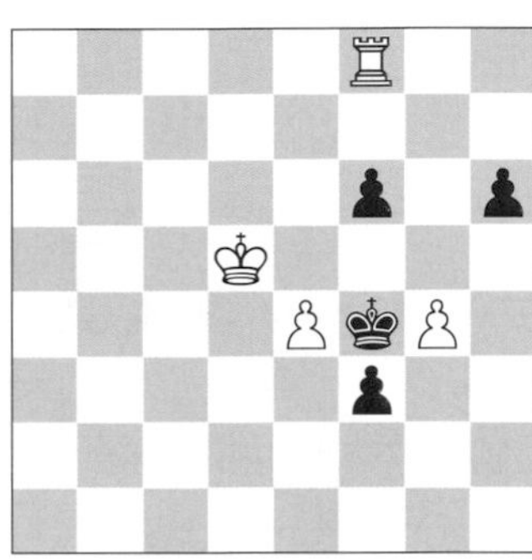

And Black resigned, he is completely lost.

I guess it is quite a bit better to have the rook behind the passed pawn than in front of it, but this game goes to show that there are many resources. Even in simple endgames it is often possible to play for mate – and that is one of the fascinating things about endgames.

Every time I have had the possibility since to get the rook in front of the pawn, I am always looking for some theme like this. And the nice thing about having a rook in front of the pawn is that your opponent's rook can never move away from that particular file, as the rook will move away and the pawn will promote. It decreases your options, but it also decreases your opponent's options. Remember to always look for checkmates even in the endgame! ■

(This column is co-produced with Magnus Carlsen's 'Magnus Trainer' app. Download on Google Play, App Store, or visit playmagnus.com to read more lessons)

Find the best move in the positions below

Solutions on page 91

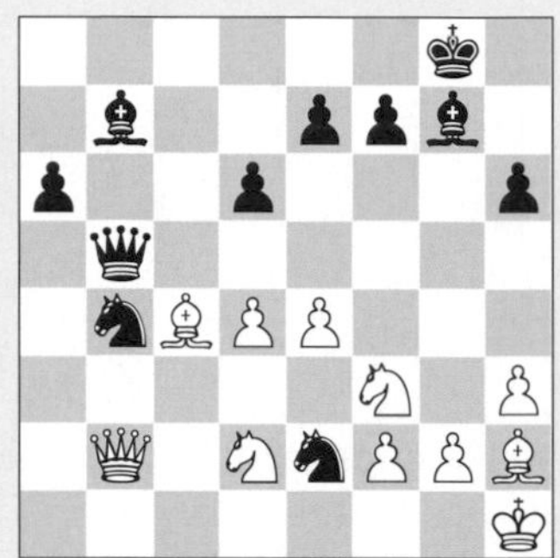
1. Black to move

2. White to move

3. Black to move

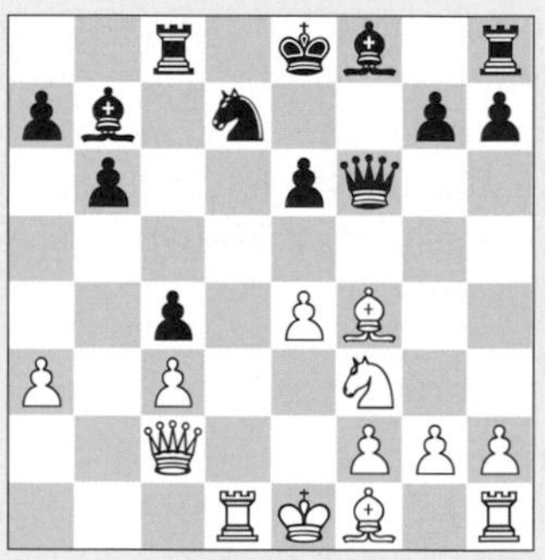
4. White to move

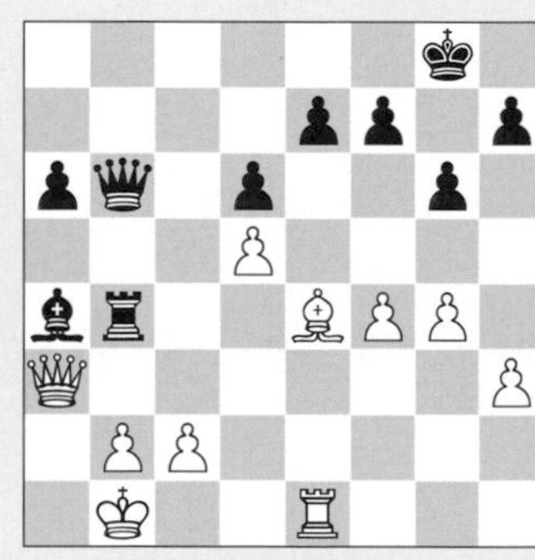
5. Black to move

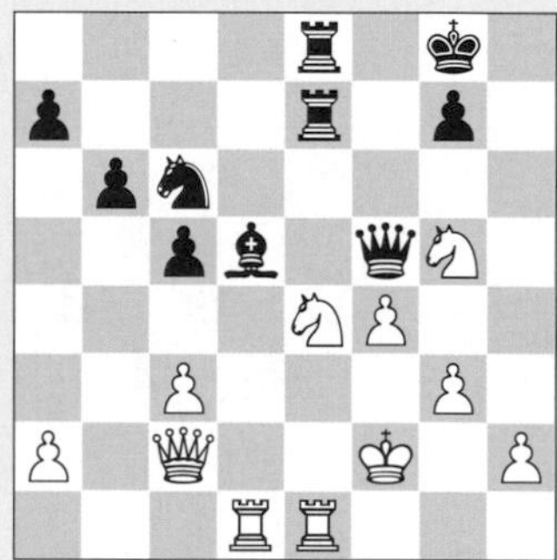
6. White to move

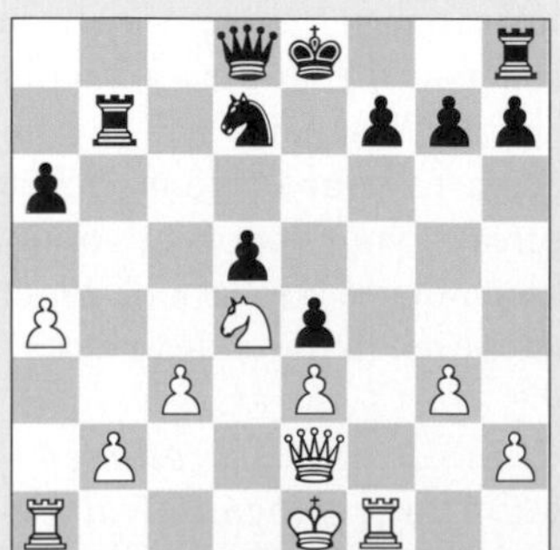
7. White to move

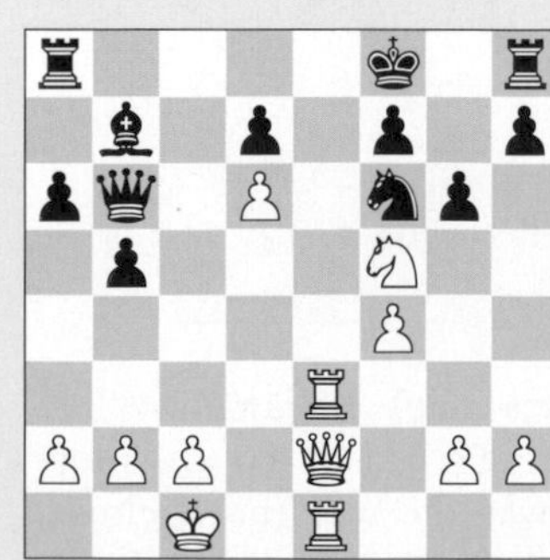
8. White to move

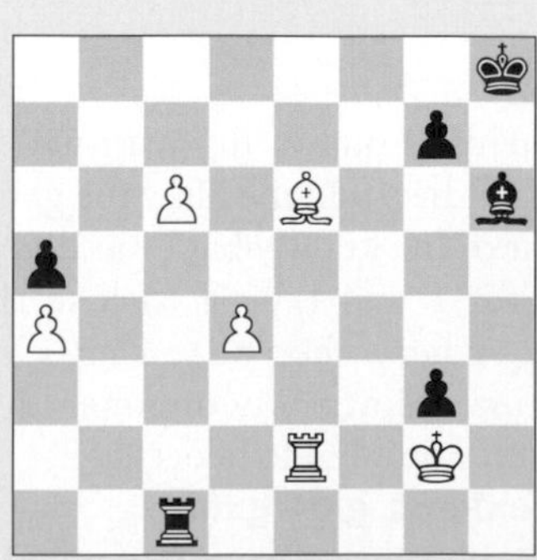
9. White to move

Judit Polgar

Beauty is a Feast

A special feature of this year's Global Chess Festival in Budapest was the Chess Artistry Competition, which attracted entries from all around the world. **JUDIT POLGAR**, a devoted fan of study solving since she was six, presents the winner and explains how her passion for studies helped her as a chess player.

In my permanent attempt to diversify the activities at my 'Judit Polgar's Global Chess Festival', I organized a Chess Artistry Competition for the 8th edition of the Festival, which was held in Budapest (and online) on October 9. The competition was in memory of Pal Benko (1928-2019), a good friend and trainer of mine, who was a great and active composer himself.

I was touched by the fact that most of the world-class composers took part, and I would like to address my special thanks to the team helping me to carry out this project. John Nunn, a composer and three-time Solving World Champion himself, was the judge of the competition. Harold van der Heijden, who has the biggest collection of chess studies (around 90,000!), took care of checking anticipations (in other words, whether similar studies had been submitted before), and Peter Gyarmati was the competition's director. Last, but not least, I am grateful to Vladimir Kramnik for joining me in the patronage of the competition.

My passion for problem-solving was ignited when I was six years old. I felt attracted to studies resembling practical games, with natural piece arrangements and play. Incidentally, my taste has not changed over the years!

I was especially fascinated by the tactical solutions in certain studies and the alternation of unexpected defensive moves and new attacking resources. I knew that if I did not see the solution, it just meant that I would have to work harder... Honing this aspect is useful for practical games, of course, but the difference is that in practice there is not always a solution. My favourite composers used to be Troitzky, Réti, Benko and Kasparian. Benko composed many beautiful studies that were really hard to solve. I remember how proud Pal was when he showed them to Kasparov or Kramnik, who also found them very challenging.

I will never cease to be amazed by the fact that players rated under, say, 2000, can create studies that force strong grandmasters to struggle when searching for the solution. Being a study composer requires different qualities from playing well. On the other hand, I remember with pleasure that I composed a few studies myself, inspired by games I had played.

When I was six years old, I felt attracted to studies resembling practical games, with natural piece arrangements and play

Calculating power and imagination

The moment has come to mention the reasons why solving studies can be useful for the tournament player. First of all, this habit develops your calculating power and imagination. It helps you to be persistent when searching for hidden resources in apparently simple positions. Not least, it develops a feel for unexpected defensive resources, no matter which side is supposed to win or draw. If it says 'White to win' you can be sure that White needs to sidestep several variations that include an unexpected save for Black.

Judit Polgar commissioned the artist Marya Yugina to make a painting of the winning study that will be presented to its composer Sergiy Didukh as a special prize.

The latter situation is nicely illustrated in the next study, which won the Chess Artistry Competition.

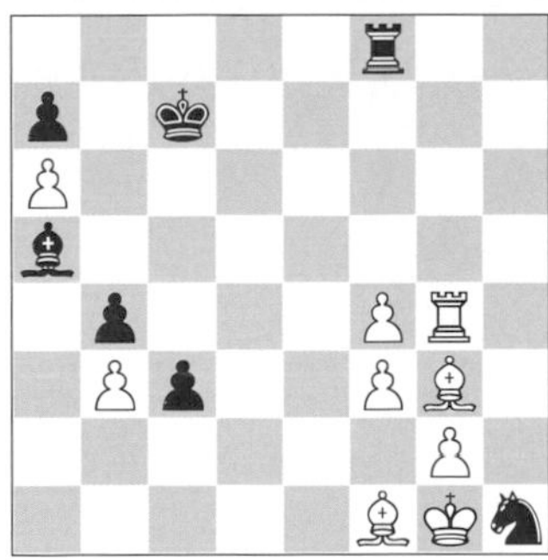

Sergiy Didukh
Chess Artistry Competition 2021
1st prize
White to play and win

The initial position is a bit congested and may seem unnatural, due to the errant knight. Things will improve after the introductory moves.
White has a material advantage, but needs to deal with the dangerous pawn on c3. Since the knight is doomed and the kingside pawns are potentially dangerous, it would in principle suffice to play f4-f5 and meet ...c1♕ with ♖c4+. However, this should be done with care, since Black has unexpected defensive resources...

1.♗h2!

This does not waste time, since with the bishop no longer under attack, f4-f5+ will gain the tempo back.
The natural question is whether 1.♔xh1 would not be a simpler way to threaten f4-f5+. Experienced solvers know that a good study would not start with such a natural move, especially if it is a piece capture. However, proving this move wrong is not trivial. Amazingly, Black can save the game in two thematic echo-lines: 1...♖h8+ (but not 1...c2? 2.f5+ ♔b6 3.♖c4, winning)

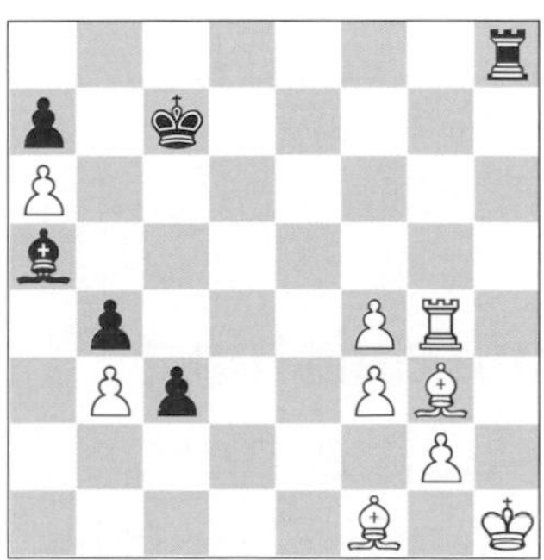

ANALYSIS DIAGRAM

2.♔g1 (the consequences of 2.♗h2 are easier to foresee: 2...c2 3.f5+ ♖xh2+ 4.♔xh2 c1♕ 5.♖c4+ ♔b6! – this is the leitmotif of Black's defence; the king uses the complex network created by the white and black pieces to strive for stalemate – 6.♖xc1 stalemate!) 2...♗b6+ 3.♗f2 ♗xf2+ 4.♔xf2 c2 5.f5.

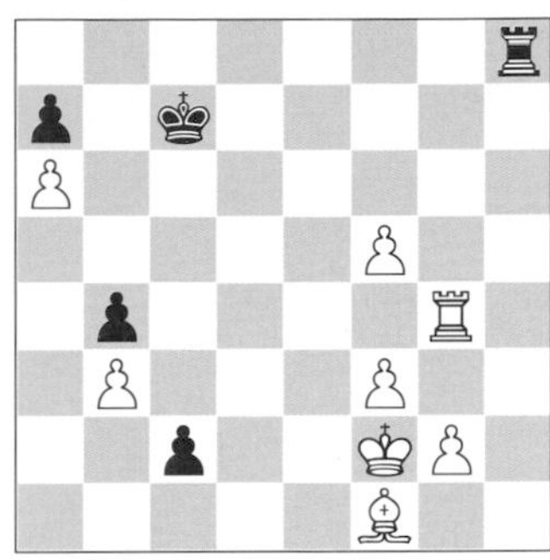

ANALYSIS DIAGRAM

Since square a5 is available, it may seem that Black can no longer play for stalemate... 5...♖a8!! (and yet he can! 5...c1♕? 6.♖c4+ ♕xc4 7.♗xc4 and White wins at leisure) 6.♖c4+ ♔b8 7.♖xb4+ (this does not change anything) 7...♔c7 8.♖c4+ ♔b8. Any neutral White move would run into ...c1♕, forcing the stalemate, as would 9.♖xc2.

1...♘g3!

Black needs to get rid of the knight in order to keep his saving ideas alive. The last move threatens ...♗b6 mate, so the answer is forced.

2.♗xg3 ♗b6+

Due to the threat of f4-f5+, Black has to fight against the bishop on g3.

3.♔h1 ♖h8+ 4.♗h2 c2 5.f5+

After the introductory moves, White finally clears the fourth rank for his rook, preparing to stop the advancing pawn.

5...♖xh2+ 6.♔xh2

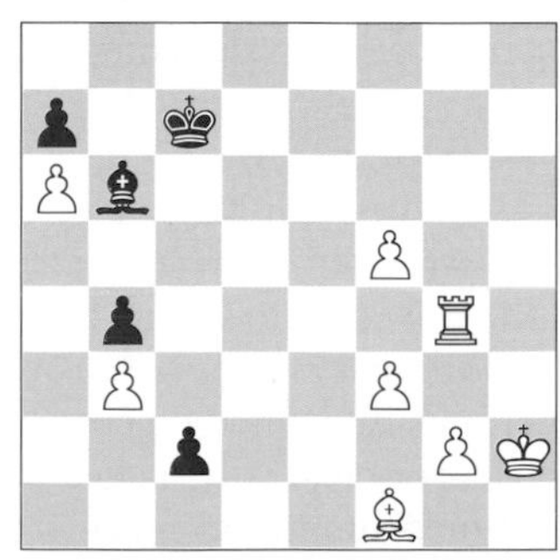

Is there still hope for Black? Less experienced solvers might think that the solution ends here. In practical games, one could simply resign at this point.
Solving studies develops the never-give-up attitude, which can help us to discover unexpected saving chances.
6...♗a5!!

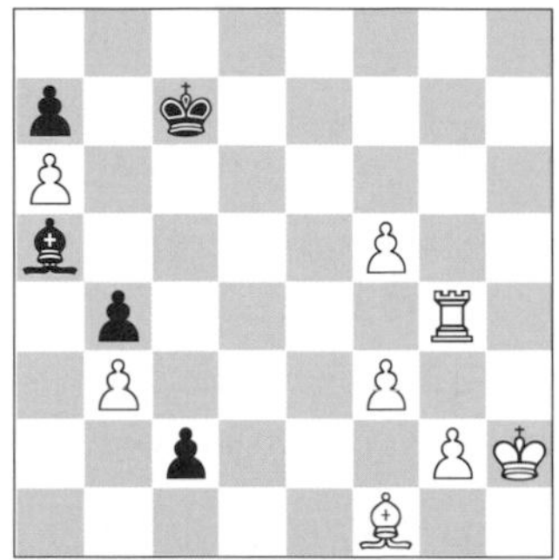

This fantastic move is similar to 5...♖a8!! in the comments to the first move. Sadly, White now throws in his last trump.
7.♗b5!!
The bishops' dialogue in this phase is impressive. White uses the available tempo for making the b5-square available to the black king at the end of the thematic variation.
In the event of 7.♖c4+ ♔b6, White cannot avoid stalemating Black, for instance 8.♗e2 c1♕ 9.♖xc1.
7...c1♕ 8.♖c4+ ♔b6 9.♖xc1
1-0.

When seeing such studies, with all these unexpected saves in the sub-lines, I cannot help thinking of a video game in which the hero has a clearly desired trajectory, but finds an incredible number of hidden traps on the way. To a certain extent, this is what a practical game is about, too.

Cross-fertilization

Solving studies can help players to become stronger... But conversely, over-the-board games can inspire study composers, too! Through the decades and maybe centuries, composers occasionally picked up a tactical or geometrical motif from a practical game, polished it and removed all the impurities to distil it into a perfect study.

Here is a recent case:

NEW IN CHESS

Daniil Dubov's inspired attacking play inspired a perfect study.

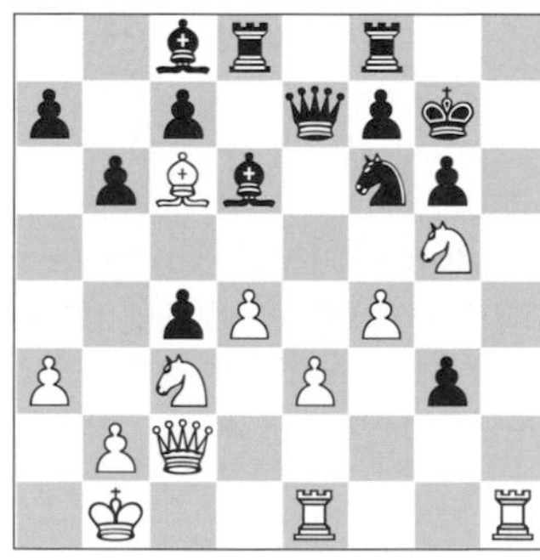

Daniil Dubov - Rasmus Svane
Batumi 2019
position after 19...♔g7

It is astonishing that such a fierce middlegame battle inspired a study with very few pieces

Black's king is exposed, but the threat ...♖h8 forces White to act resolutely:
20.♘d5! ♘xd5 21.♖h7+ ♔g8 22.♖xf7 ♖xf7 23.♕xg6+ ♔f8 24.♕h6+ ♖g7 25.♗xd5 ♔e8 26.♕h5+ ♔d7 27.♕h3+ ♔e8 28.♕h5+ ♔d7 29.♗e6+

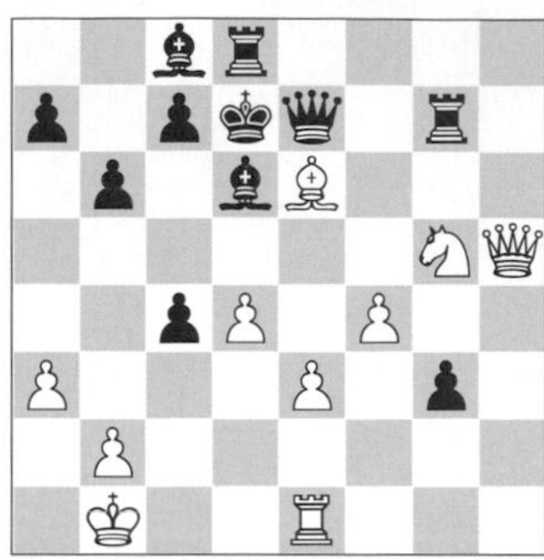

29...♔c6
As it turns out, 29...♕xe6 was the lesser evil, but Black did not believe that White could have more than a perpetual.
30.♕f3+ ♔b5 31.♗xc4+ ♔a5 32.♕d5+! ♗c5 33.b4+! ♔a4 34.♕g2 ♗xb4 35.♕c6+ ♔xa3

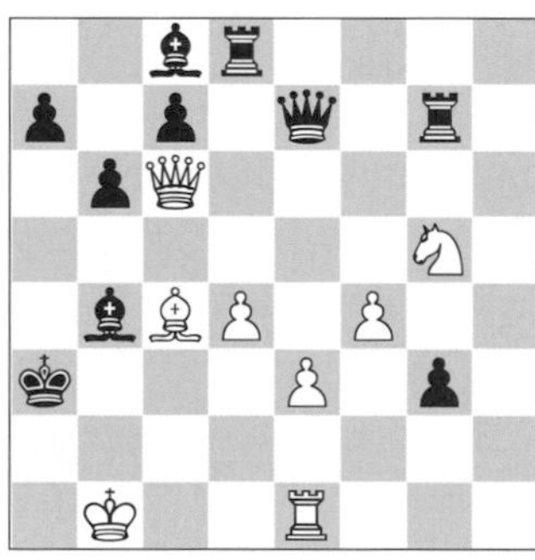

White has played a few only moves on the way to reach a winning position. But... is White winning at all? It looks more as if he will need to work miracles to avoid losing!
36.♗b3!! Here it is – the miraculous move that inspired the creation of the study below. White threatens ♕a4 mate. **36...♗d7** 36...♔xb3 cuts the finishing sequence by one move.
37.♕c1+ ♔xb3 38.♕c2+ ♔a3 39.♕a2 Mate.

It is easy to understand that study composers use such ideas from practical endgames as a source of inspiration. However, it is astonishing that such a fierce middlegame battle actually inspired a study with very few pieces.

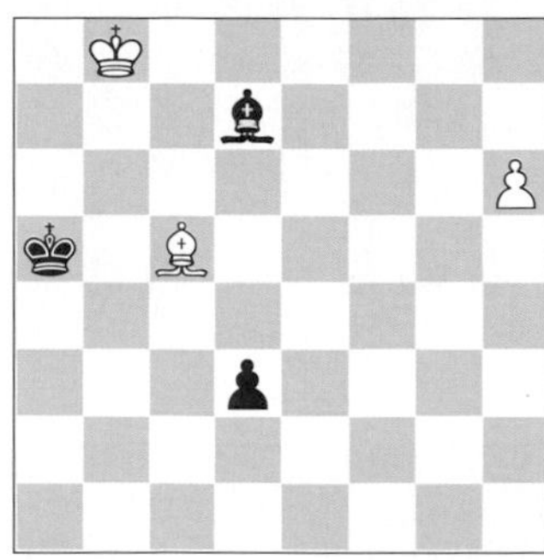

Steffen Nielsen/Martin Minski
Chess Artistry Competition 2021
7th prize
White to play and win

If this position arrived in a practical game, nobody would be surprised if a draw was agreed. However, there are hidden resources for White.

1.h7!

1.♗e3? ♗f5 leads to an obvious draw.

1...d2 2.h8♕ d1♕

Both pawns have queened, but White can use his right to move to present the enemy king with serious problems.

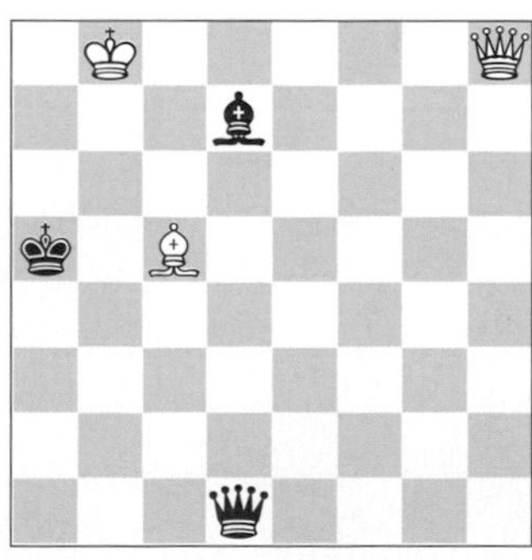

3.♕c3+! 3.♕b2? is parried by 3...♕e1 or 3...♕g4.

3...♔a6 3...♔b5 loses the queen to 4.♕b4+ ♔c6 5.♕b6+ ♔d5 6.♕d6+.

When solving studies, it is important to search for the weaker side's hidden resources

4.♕b2!

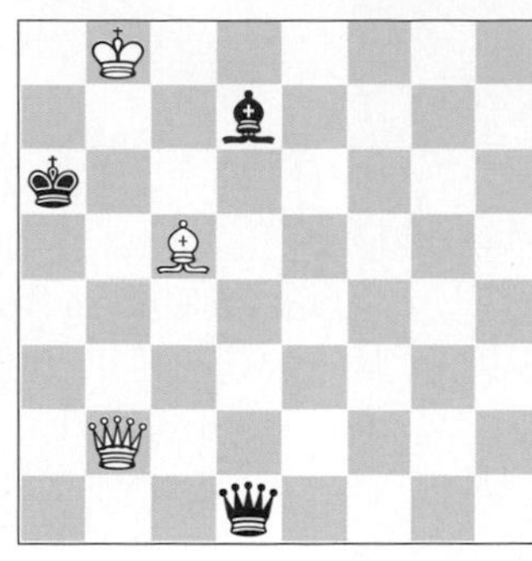

As the attack advances, we can see the same kind of subtle moves as Dubov's in the final phase, just before 36.♗b3!!. The last move threatens 5.♕b6, mate.

In studies, the battle typically consists of an alternation of concrete tactical moves and quiet captures.

4...♗b5 5.♕f6+

The start of a manoeuvre designed to improve the queen's placement with tempo, in order to generate new threats.

5...♔a5 6.♕c3+ ♔a6

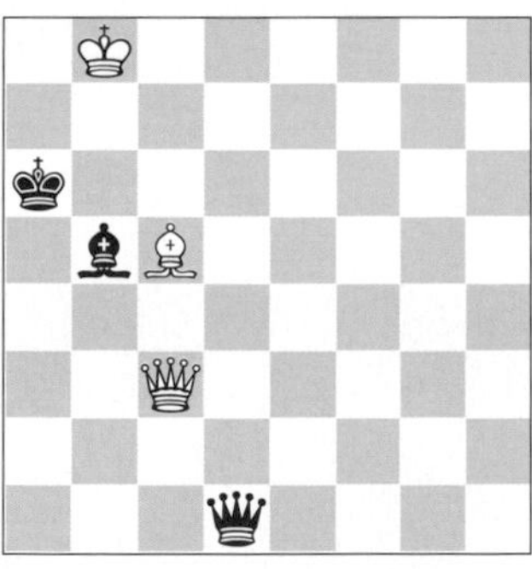

7.♗d4!

Another subtle move, preventing ...♕d8 (check or mate) and threatening 8.♕c5, with decisive threats.

7...♕b1

The only defence.

Here are two variations leading to mate after natural moves: 7...♗d3 8.♕c6+ ♔a5 9.♗c3, mate, and 7...♕d3 8.♕a1+ ♗a4 9.♕xa4, mate. After the last move, Black seems to be safe, partly because he threatens a discovered check.

8.♗b6!!

And finally Dubov's move, defending the b-file and creating a familiar pattern. The immediate threat is ♕a5, mate.

8...♔xb6 8...♕a2 leads to a similar end as in Dubov's game: 9.♕c8+! ♔xb6 10.♕c7+ ♔a6 11.♕a7, mate.

9.♕c7+ ♔a6 10.♕a7 Mate.

It is remarkable how this study imitated several aspects of the complicated Dubov game with a minimum of pieces on the board. The similarity goes beyond the final trick, referring to the previous phase, and there are surprising attacking moves, too.

Conclusions

■ You should aim to solve studies on a regular basis. This habit usually develops several skills that could be useful during a game.

■ When solving studies, it is important to search for the weaker side's hidden resources, so as to better understand what the winning line is.

■ When playing complicated games, be ready to use patterns highlighted in studies in pure and economical form. ■

Thomas Willemze

Club players, test your decision-making skills!

What would you play?

The most important technique to defend against an attack on your castled king is to open up the centre. This clears the path for your pieces to defend or to develop a counterattack. But what should you do and how should you defend if your king is uncastled?

Opening up the position is much less appealing when your own king is stuck in the middle. As a result these positions require different defensive techniques.

Exercises

This summer, at the Biel Open in Switzerland, Fareed Ahmed (1907) played a very convincing game against Siegfried Kipper (1724), until he lost the right to castle and had to defend his slightly exposed king. I selected four exercises in which you can experience the complexity of this task and demonstrate your own defensive skills.

Exercise 1

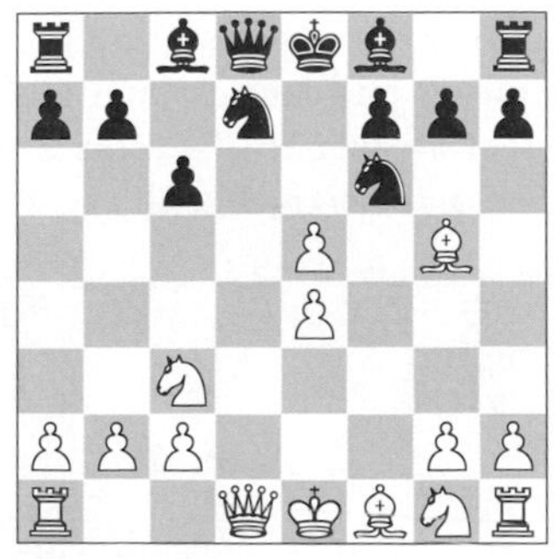

position after 7.dxe5

White's attempt to open up the position in his favour looks appealing, but is completely neutralized by Black's next move. Can you find it?

Exercise 2

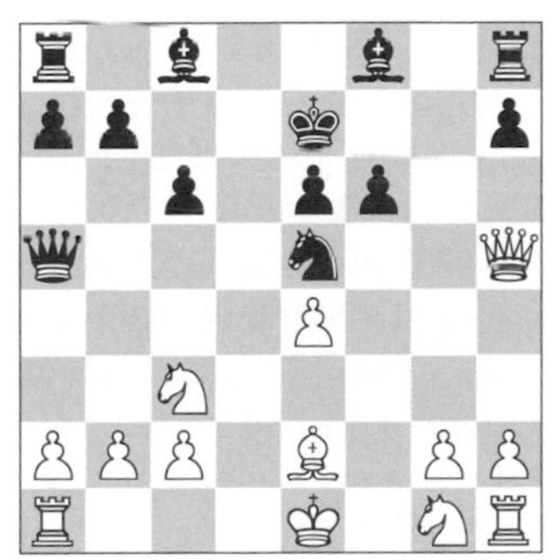

position after 12.♗e2

Black has lost the right to castle and has to come up with a plan. What would you play? **12...♗d7** to develop the bishop, **12...♕b6** to unpin the knight, or **12...♘c4** to trade the queens?

Exercise 3

position after 15.♖d3

Black has been provoked into winning an exchange with **15...♘f4**, attacking both the white queen and the rook on d3. Should he take the bait?

Exercise 4

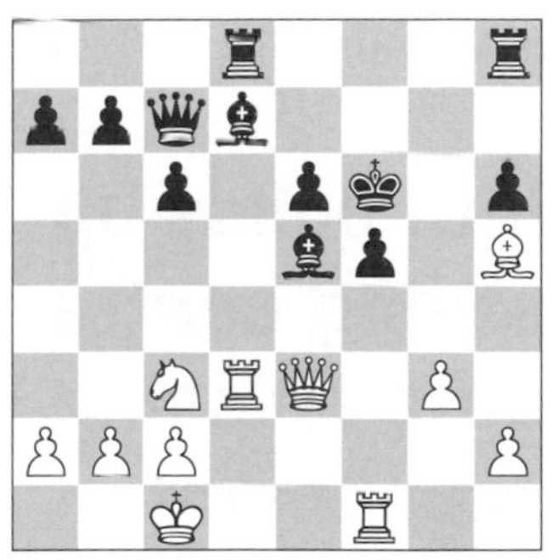

position after 26.♖f1

Black is under severe pressure. What should he do? Trade bishops with **26...♗e8**, or relocate the king with **26...♔g7**?

I hope you enjoyed these exercises and were able to keep your king safe. You can find the full analysis of this game below.

Opening up the position is much less appealing when your own king is stuck in the middle

Siegfried Kipper (1724)
Fareed Ahmed (1907)
Biel 2021
Queen's Pawn Opening, Richter-Veresov Attack

1.d4 ♘f6 2.♘c3 d5 3.♗g5 ♘bd7 4.f3

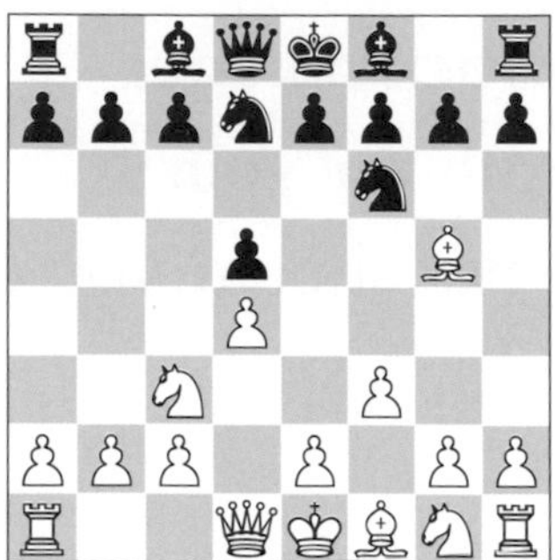

White aims to build up a strong centre before finishing his development. This is not without risk, because well-coordinated pieces are required to support his centre and cover the vulnerable dark squares that are about to arise.

White builds up a strong centre before finishing his development

4...c6! 5.e4 There was already no way back for White. Black will get a powerful initiative after both 5.e3 e5! and 5.♕d2 b5!.

5...dxe4 6.fxe4

6...e5! Black undermines the white centre before his opponent finds the time to consolidate it with his pieces.

7.dxe5

White had probably missed his opponent's next move. Supporting the centre with 7.♘f3 was the slightly better choice, even though Black is clearly on top after 7...h6! 8.♗e3 ♕c7, followed by 9...♗b4.

7...♕a5! This was the tactical justification for Black's last move and the right answer to **Exercise 1**. The e5-pawn is pinned and unable to capture the knight.

8.♗xf6 This is a highly committing move with so many vulnerable dark squares around, but White probably wanted to prevent his opponent from installing a stable knight on e5.

8...gxf6 9.e6 This looks like the most practical try, even though White will hardly get any compensation for the pawn that he sheds.

9...fxe6 10.♗c4

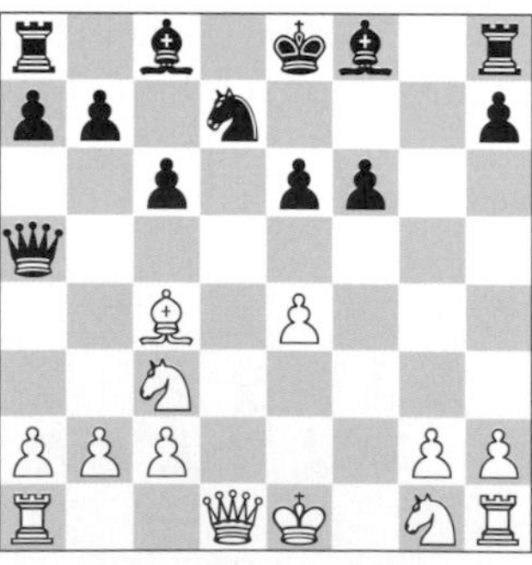

10...♘e5

This is indeed a beautiful square for the knight, but it allows White to upset the coordination in Black's camp with 11.♕h5+.

There are many strong moves for Black in this position, the best one being 10...♗a3!.

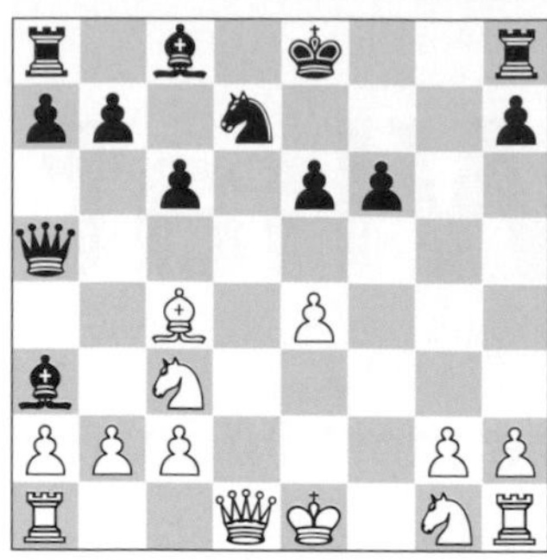

ANALYSIS DIAGRAM

The aim of this move is to undermine the defence of the white knight. It is a very typical tactic in the ♕a5-Scandinavian, and therefore also a recurring theme in my latest book *The Scandinavian for Club Players*. White can avoid losing material with 11.♕c1, but will end up in a very dubious endgame after 11...♕xc3+ 12.bxc3 ♗xc1 13.♖xc1 ♔e7.

11.♕h5+ ♔e7 12.♗e2 White is just in time to protect his queen and parry the discovered attack 12...♘d3+.

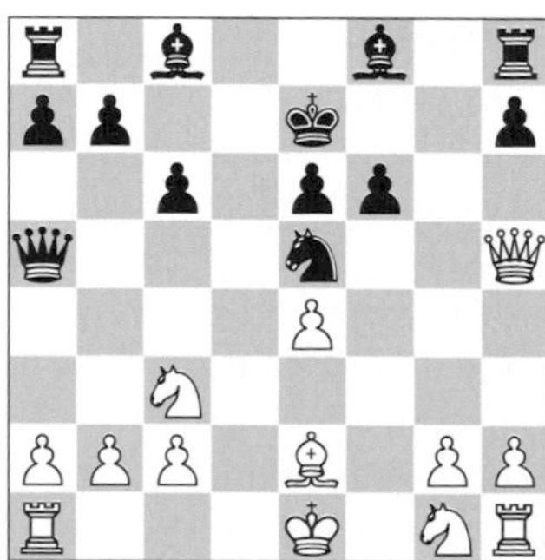

12...♗d7 This move spoils the last remnant of Black's advantage, since he allows his opponent to coordinate his pieces and launch an attack. The correct answer to **Exercise 2** was to pursue a queen trade with 12...♕b6!.

ANALYSIS DIAGRAM

White is clearly suffering on the dark squares and will not really be able to prevent 13.0-0-0 ♕e3+! 14.♔b1 ♕h6!, after which the queens will be traded and Black will have a very pleasant endgame that he will be happy to play.
Note that trading queens immediately with 12...♘c4 is impossible, since the black knight would be trapped after 13.♕xa5 ♘xa5 14.b4!.

13.0-0-0

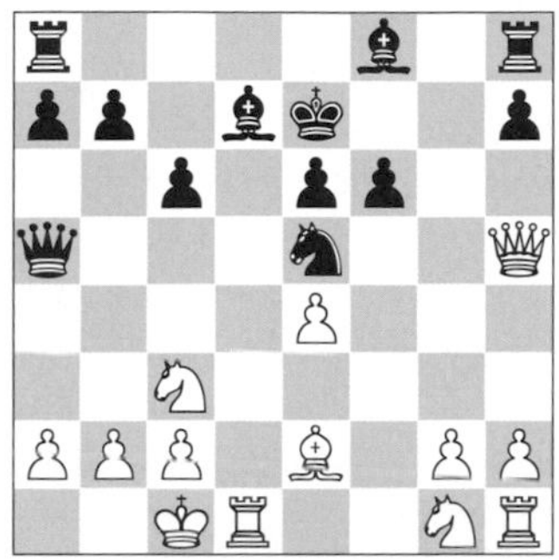

13...♕b6

Black is too late for manoeuvring his queen to h6. 13...♖d8, followed by ...♗e8 and ...♘g6, was the only way to keep the game level. Black has to expel the annoying queen and keep the e5-square under control at all cost.

14.♘f3

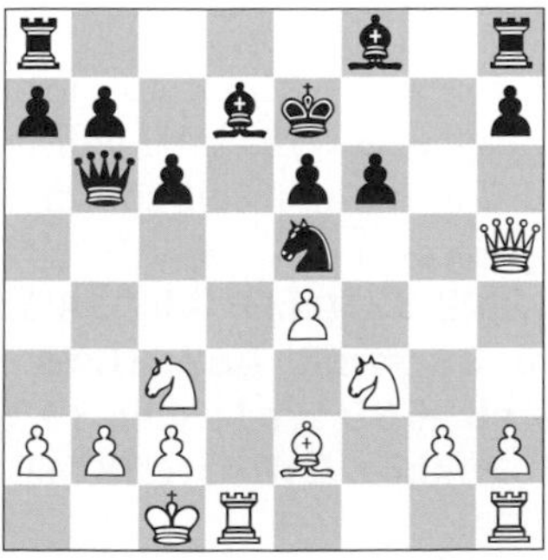

Black can no longer maintain his knight and is in serious trouble, since this knight (and the e4-pawn) were responsible for keeping his king safe.

14...♘g6

14...♕e3+ 15.♔b1 ♕h6 is no longer possible, because the white queen is defended after 16.♘xe5!.

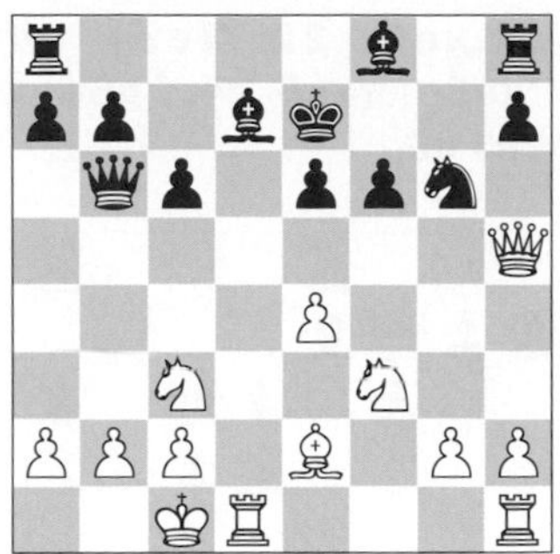

15.♖d3

White prepares 16.♖hd1 to prevent 15...♕e3+, but in doing so allows 15...♘f4, with a double attack on his queen and rook. White must be very certain or avoid this forced move and pick one of the many simple and strong alternatives available. My favourite would be 15.♔b1! to eliminate all the checks and hope for the following beautiful line: 15...♘f4 16.♘e5! ♘xh5 (16...fxe5 17.♕xe5 ♘g6 18.♕d6+ regains the piece with interest)

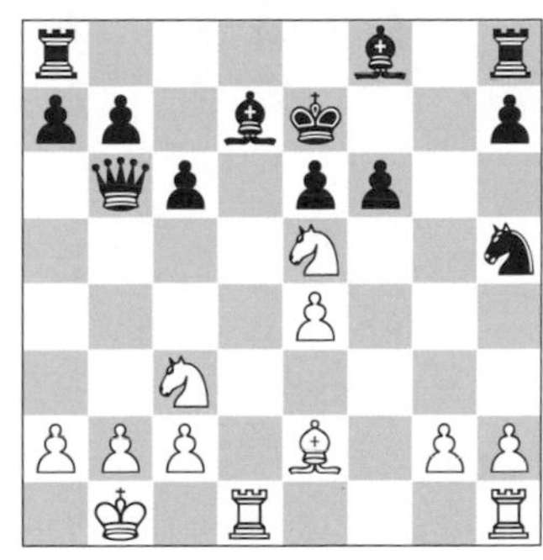

ANALYSIS DIAGRAM

17.♖xd7+! ♔e8 18.♗xh5, mate.

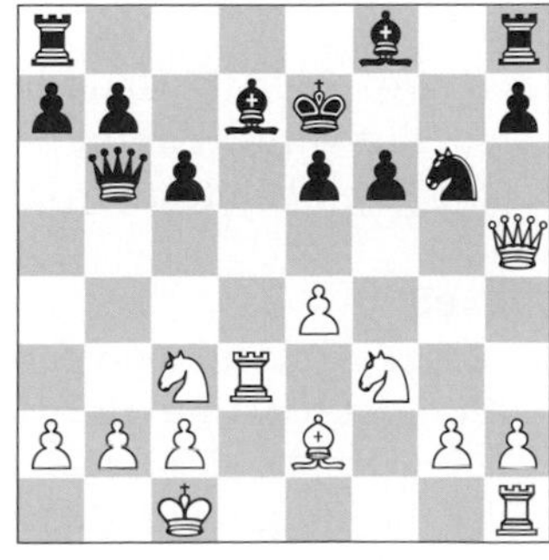

15...♖d8

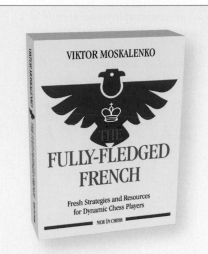

Exercise 3 was an important moment in the game. Black is desperately in

need of counterplay and should not hesitate to enter the complications with 15...♘f4!. The critical position arises after 16.♖xd7+! ♔xd7 17.♕f7+ ♔c8 18.♕xf6 ♘xe2+ 19.♘xe2.

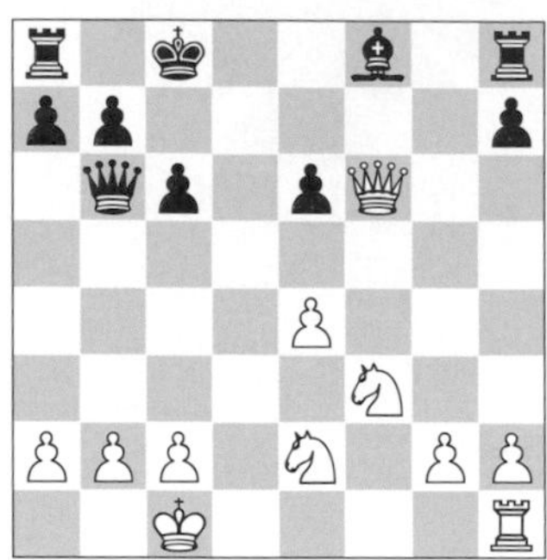

ANALYSIS DIAGRAM

White had probably foreseen this position, but might have missed the tricky 19...♕d8!, preparing 20.♕xh8?? ♗h6+!. 20.♕xe6+! gives White ample compensation for the exchange, but Black is not without chances either.

16.e5!

Well played! Putting your opponent under constant pressure is the most effective way to prevent counterplay.

Putting your opponent under constant pressure is the most effective way to prevent counterplay

16...♗g7 17.g3 f5 18.♕g5+ ♔f7 19.♖hd1 ♕c7 20.♕d2 ♔e7 21.♕e3

21...♘xe5 22.♕c5+ ♔f7 23.♘xe5+ ♗xe5 24.♗h5+ ♔f6 25.♕e3 h6

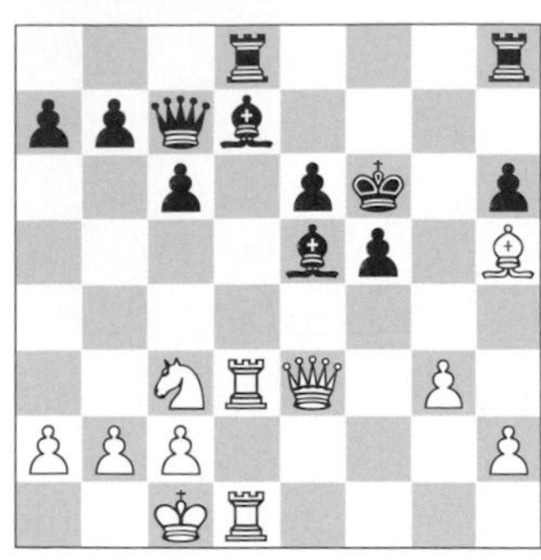

26.♖f1

This move gives Black unexpected chances for survival. White should have opened up the position and crowned his smooth attack with 26.♘e4+! fxe4 27.♖f1+ ♔g7 28.♖f7+ ♔g8 29.♕xe4, followed by 30.♕g6.

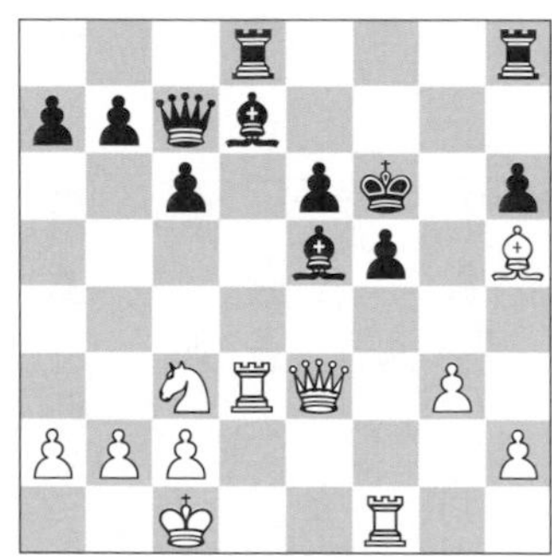

26...♗e8

It seems logical to trade this bishop, but it was more important to keep the white knight at a distance. 26...♔g7!, to unpin the f-pawn, was therefore the right answer to **Exercise 4**.

27.♗xe8

27.♘e4+! ♔g7 28.♘c5 would have activated the white knight with tempo and given White an irresistible attack.

27...♖dxe8

Black misses a golden opportunity to fight himself back into the game with 27...♖xd3!. The idea is to either eliminate the knight with 28.cxd3 ♗xc3!, or trade queens after 28.♘e4+ ♔e7! 29.cxd3 ♕b6!. White can only relocate one piece at a time, which means that Black will always be able to regain his piece one move later and level the game.

28.♘e4+ ♔e7 29.♕c5+ ♔f7

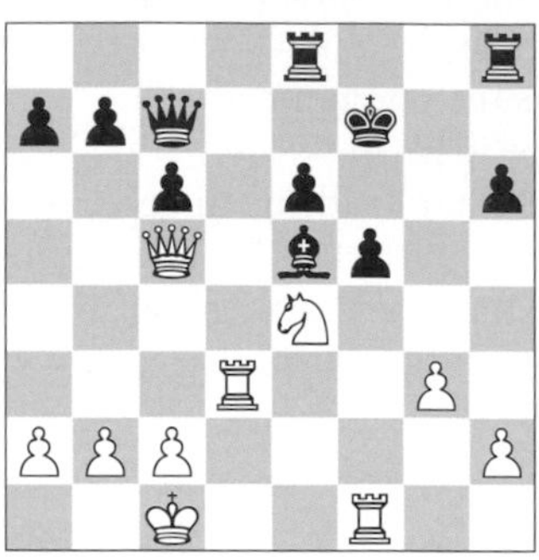

30.g4 The only road to an advantage was to trade the last minor pieces with 30.♘d6!+ ♗xd6 31.♖xd6, before opening up the position with g3-g4.

30...♔g6 30...♗f4+! 31.♘d2 ♖hf8! was very difficult to find for a human being, but it was Black's last chance to stay in the game.

31.♘d6! ♗xd6 32.♖xd6

Black is stuck without any form of counterplay and his king will be no match for White's well-coordinated major pieces.

32...♖hf8 33.gxf5+ ♔h7 34.♖xe6 ♖xe6 35.♕xf8 ♖e7 36.f6 ♖f7 37.♕e8 b6 38.♕e4+ ♔h8 39.♕g6 c5 40.♕xh6+ ♖h7 41.♕f8 Mate.

Conclusion

Black started the game really well, but allowed an annoying check and was unsuccessful in defending his uncastled king. This game taught us how controlling critical squares, trading off hostile attackers, and seeking counterplay would have been valuable tools to keep his king safe. ■

from page 80

MAXIMize your Tactics Solutions

1. Salinas-Kabanov
Titled Tuesday 2021

32...♘d3! The best White can obtain now is two minor pieces for the queen. He preferred to go down in style: **33.♕xb5 ♘xf2** Mate.

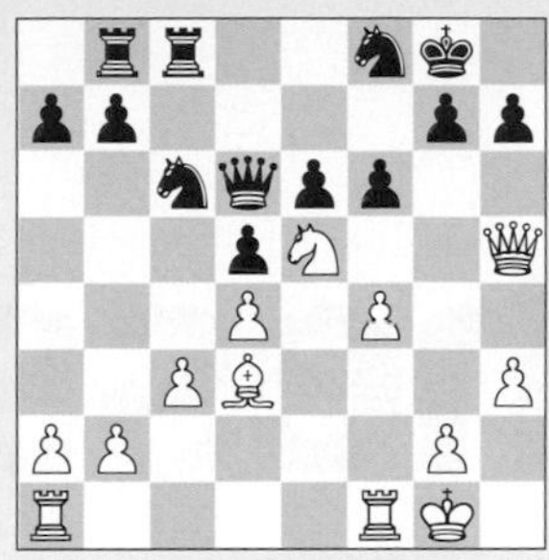

2. Krysa-Kabanov
Titled Tuesday 2021

The h7-pawn is protected and the check on f7 is harmless? Not exactly true: **18.♗xh7+!** Black resigned in view of 18...♘xh7 19.♕f7+ ♔h8 20.♘g6 mate.

3. Riehle-Rasulov
Leon Blitz chess.com 2021

A neat little fork reveals that the white queen is overloaded: **15...♘e5! 16.dxe5 ♗xc4 17.♕xc4 ♕d1** Mate.

4. Guseva-Solozhenkina
Cheboksary 2021

14.♖xd7! ♔xd7 15.♗g5 Both queen retreats to f7 and g6 lose to 16.♘e5+. Black's last-ditch attempt was **15...♗xe4**, hoping for 16.♕xe4? ♕xc3+, but after **16.♕d1+ ♗d6 17.♗xf6** White converted easily.

5. Chandran-Andriasyan
Philadelphia 2021

27...♖xe4! 28.♖xe4 ♕g1+ 29.♔a2 ♗xc2 White resigned. He can save his king but the rook will be lost anyway: 30.♕e3 ♕b1+ 31.♔a3 ♗xe4.

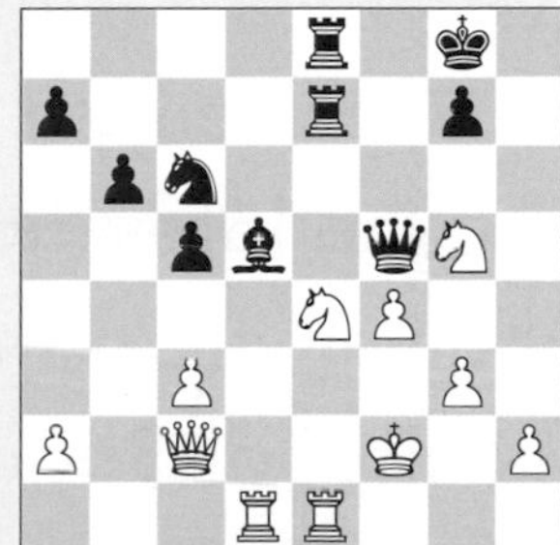

6. Obregon-Tsaruk
Titled Tuesday 2021

29.♖xd5 ♕xd5 30.♘f6+ gxf6 31.♕g6+ ♔f8? 32.♘h7+! ♖xh7 33.♖xe8 mate was the game, but 31...♔h8 forced a perpetual. Correct was **29.♘f6+! ♕xf6 30.♕h7+ ♔f8 31.♕h8+ ♗g8 32.♘h7+**, winning the queen.

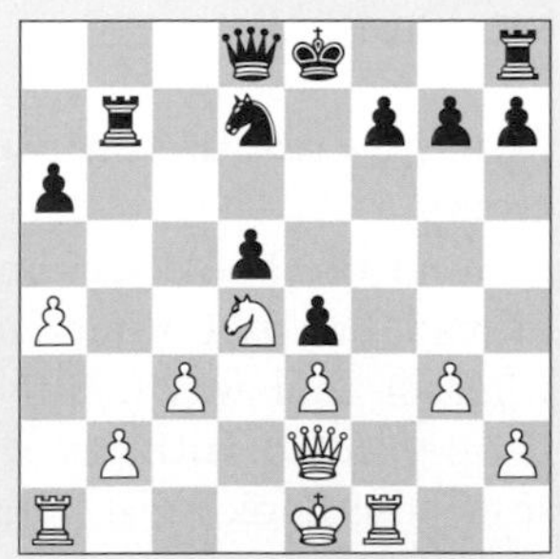

7. Aronian-Carlsen
San Fermin Masters 2021

Even the big guys sometimes muff. In the game Black took over after 23.♘f5 0-0 24.0-0-0 ♘e5. Instead, **23.♖xf7! ♔xf7 24.♕h5+ ♔f6** (24...g6 25.♕xd5+; 24...♔f8 25.♘e6+) **25.♕f5+ ♔e7 26.♘c6+** was winning.

8. Aldokhin-Srihari
Titled Tuesday 2021

White won after 21.♖e7 gxf5 22.♕e5 ♖g8? 23.♕xf6 ♗d5 24.♖e8+! but 22...♔g7 23.♕xf5 ♕xd6 would have saved Black. The rook dropped one square short of brilliancy: **21.♖e8+! ♖xe8** 21...♘xe8 22.♕e7+ ♔g8 23.♕xe8+. **22.♕e7+! ♖xe7 23.dxe7+ ♔e8 24.♘g7** Mate.

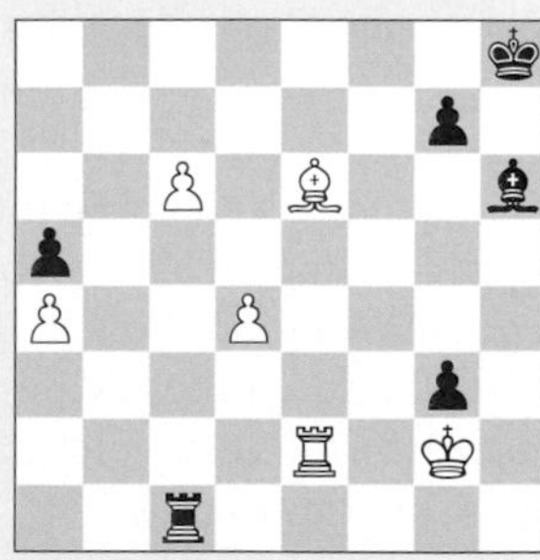

9. Murashova-Galliamova
Cheboksary 2021

43.♗f5! Mate is threatened, and 43...♔g8 44.♗g6 provides no defence at all. **43...g6 44.♗c2** And now the passed pawn comes to the fore: **44...♗f4 45.c7! ♗xc7 46.♖e8+ ♔g7 47.♖e7+** Collecting the enemy bishop and protecting her own at the same time. Black resigned.

How to enjoy chess on your own

Chess is endless in its variety and diversity, and so are books on our game. MATTHEW SADLER looks at the latest harvest that includes an unusual memoir, a serious self-study guide, a reappraisal of Bogoljubov, and an explanation of Magnus's play.

A friend remarked recently to me, 'Aren't you afraid your life is getting a bit narrow?' I was taken aback and started – a little defensively – to list all the things I do... and saw the problem. After all, after giving up chess and going into IT, I took up chess again as a hobby, and then got into engine chess. I did take up shogi, and Chinese Chess, too... And to be honest, I love it because it's so similar to chess!

So I had to move on to the second line of defence and claim it wasn't a bad thing. But I thought about this conversation a few times in subsequent days, and therefore found it very interesting to receive Larry Kaufman's *Chess Board Options: A memoir of players, games and engines* (New In Chess) through the post.

Larry Kaufman may not be that well-known to European chess players but he's very well-known to shogi and computer enthusiasts! Born in 1947, he was one of America's best juniors in the mid-1960s. After graduating from MIT in Economics he became a stockbroker, starting a company called Chess Options. He achieved the IM title in 1980 and retired from the financial world in 1986 to focus on engine chess and shogi, in which he was one of the strongest Western players for many years, reaching the 5-Dan level (more or less the highest level you can achieve as an amateur).

Winning the World Senior Chess Championship in 2008 brought him the Grandmaster title, and he was a driving force behind the Komodo engine (rebranded to Komodo Dragon after chess.com took a stake in the project), which is nowadays the number 3 engine, behind Stockfish and Leela Zero. Lastly, Kaufman also knew the American chess player Diana Lanni very well, who many have suggested as the inspiration for *Queen's Gambit*'s heroine Beth Harmon (see New In Chess 2021/1 – ed.) so there's a little chapter on that, too! He obviously managed to pass on his love of games, as his son Raymond also became a chess IM and 5-Dan shogi player.

The book is organized broadly in chronological order. The first thirteen chapters describe encounters with great players such as Gligoric and Kortchnoi (Kaufman gave Viktor a quick lesson to teach him the moves of shogi!). After a couple of chapters on his business career and adventures in shogi and other games, there are five chapters of his own memorable games and those of his best students (including his son Raymond!), and the last eleven chapters have an engine chess theme, including related topics such as making Armageddon fair and reforming chess to make it less drawish.

Musings about computer chess

I found the book very interesting to read, but part of me did wonder whether that was mainly because it intersected with my obsessions so neatly! Looking at it objectively, some of the musings on computer chess, especially towards the end of the book, could have done with some

I found the book very interesting, but part of me did wonder whether that was mainly because it intersected with my obsessions so neatly!

more background and examples. Many of these topics are the subject of regular debate in engine chess forums but might not mean that much to 'normal' chess players!

A number of such topics are discussed in the chapter 'What is a won game?'. This is a big topic of debate in engine chess circles, as the starting position is drawn when played by two strong engines. The normal solution to ensure excitement with a fair proportion of decisive games has been to run matches using an opening book specifying unbalanced positions. The recent Top Chess Engine Championship (TCEC) Season 21 SuperFinal between Stockfish and Leela featured an opening book of 50 positions put together by Jeroen Noomen (a chess engine book expert) and myself. For example, positions like these:

1.e4 c5 2.♘f3 d6 3.d4 cxd4 4.♘xd4 ♘f6 5.♘c3 a6 6.h3 g6 7.♗e3 ♘c6 8.♕d2 ♗g7 9.0-0-0 0-0 10.g4 ♗d7

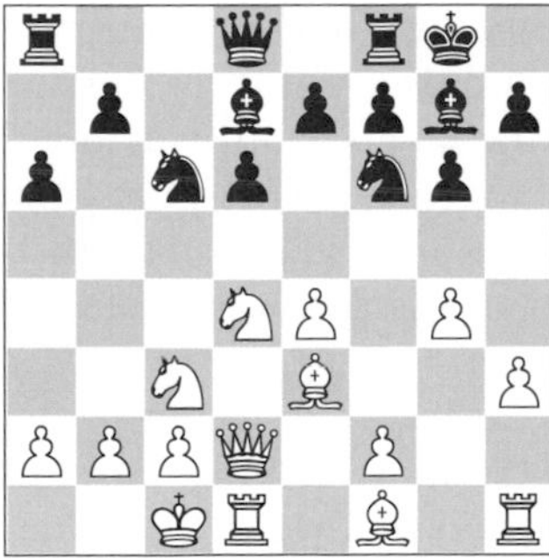

1.d4 d5 2.c4 c6 3.♘c3 ♘f6 4.♘f3 a6 5.c5 ♗g4

Nothing too extreme, but a helping hand! In the SuperFinal, Stockfish

Chess Board Options
Larry Kaufman
New In Chess, 2021
★★★☆☆

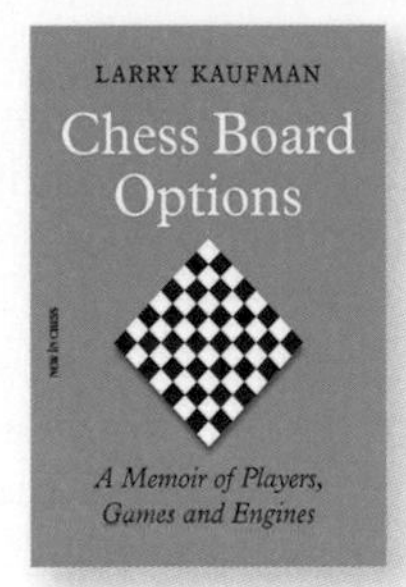

How to Study Chess on Your Own
Davorin Kuljasevic
New In Chess, 2021
★★★★★

won the first diagram as White and Leela won the second.

Kaufman discusses all sorts of ways in which to gauge the advantage required to achieve the win. For example, he ran a series of tests from a position in which White starts with two bishops against two knights. This led to 30% White wins and 70% draws – a good score for White but hardly decisive. This and other tests seemed to indicate that a clear positional advantage plus a tempo (White moves first) does not constitute a winning advantage. Funnily enough, the TCEC are currently running a monster bonus event in which viewers can submit openings for testing, and this was one of them:

Leela Zero
Stockfish
TCEC Season 21 – Viewer Submitted Opening Bonus (3.7)
31.08.2021

1.d4 d5 2.c3 c6 3.e4 dxe4 4.♕g4 ♘f6 5.♕xg7 ♖g8 6.♕h6 ♘bd7 7.♕h3 ♘f8 8.f3 exf3 9.♕xf3 ♕d5 10.♕xd5 ♘xd5 11.g3 h5 12.♗e2 h4 13.gxh4 ♘e6 14.h5 ♘ef4 15.♗f3 ♖d8 16.♔d2 ♖h8 17.♔c2 ♘xh5

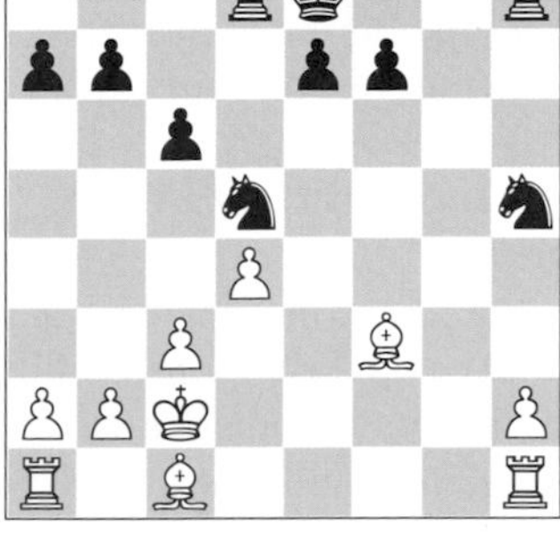

Both Leela and Stockfish held the draw as Black with consummate ease, which I hadn't necessarily expected!

As I said, an interesting book, but you'll get the most out of it if you have some background or interest in engine chess and shogi! 3 stars!

■ ■ ■

Davorin Kuljasevic is perhaps another unfamiliar name – certainly daunting to pronounce! – but the Croatian-born grandmaster now living and coaching in Bulgaria produced an earlier excellent book called *Beyond Material: Ignore the Face Value of Your Pieces and Discover the Importance of Time, Space and Psychology in Chess*, which was a finalist in the FIDE Book of the Year competition.

His newest book addresses a topic that I'm sure will resonate with many aspiring players: *How to Study Chess on Your Own* (New In Chess). I have to confess that I lack a certain empathy with the problems people have in studying chess, but that's entirely due to the way my chess career went. The bulk of my hard study was done as a child and as an aspiring young professional in the pre-computer age. As a child, spending time on something I loved seemed as natural as breathing, while studying – analysing (without any computer help!) was just an intrinsic part of my job as a chess professional. Once you've worked so intensively on a topic in your youth, studying in later life is never too painful. You never start from zero on anything – there are always some old notes, half-remembered thoughts and ideas, comments you once heard, to give you a flying start on your study path.

Much more difficult than expected

However, I remember that a friend of mine once took six months off from his job to try and complete his IM title (he was 2300 and had an IM norm already at the time, if memory serves me right) and struggled terribly with studying effectively. It surprised me, as I assumed that anyone used to the discipline of a job (getting up early, dragging yourself to the train station...) would automatically slot into a regular routine for chess, but it seemed much more difficult than expected. I think in the pre-computer age the main difficulty was that you never knew anything for certain, which meant that analysis of a complicated line was essentially a long-term project. Analyse the Najdorf Poisoned Pawn for two weeks and you would have advanced your understanding of the line, but still not be able to say anything definite about the objective assessment of the position. Revisit the same line in two months and you'd notice many tactical mistakes in your analysis, which might change your conception of the position completely. I mentioned this process to the then very young Dutch grandmaster Robin van Kampen and I could see he didn't find the idea too attractive! Nowadays, as Kuljasevic points out, the big problem is the reverse: there is so much help and information available, it's hard to know where to put the focus. And after all, life is getting busier and busier, free time is at a premium, you don't want to waste those precious few hours you have just for yourself and your chessboard!

This book is beautifully conceived and structured to help any aspiring player put together a good study plan. I'd say perhaps its only drawback is that you have to study 373 pages to be able to do that! It helps as well if you are a fan of tables, as Kuljasevic uses these quite extensively throughout the book to summarise his approach and the conclusions in the book. Kuljasevic starts with an examination of your study mindset, addressing the most common pitfalls and obstacles before moving on to fifteen study methods which he categorises according to relevance, intensity (how much effort will this cost you?) and long-term learning potential. Of the study methods mentioned I found watching YouTube speed chess videos to be an interesting one. When Natasha Regan and I interviewed Keith Arkell in *Chess for Life*, the English grandmaster mentioned this as a favourite method to hone his intuition – you see very clearly what a top player's instinctive thought is in a position when he is playing blitz! I have to say that my favourite training method for shogi is watching rapid games played by the strongest amateur players (probably between 2300 – IM strength in chess terms) on the main shogi site (81dojo.com). I find that trying to guess moves of players who are clearly but not stratospherically better than me to be a really rewarding and active way of studying, and I'm sure it would be the same in chess.

After this general introduction, Kuljasevic moves on to drawing up your own study plan, with two chapters: 'Identify your study priorities' and 'Choose the right resource for your study plan'. I think the second chapter in particular answers many of the questions that aspiring players typically ask: which books should I study for which topic? Appropriately enough, Kuljasevic also takes a look at digital resources and spends some time explaining useful functions in ChessBase for analysis and training.

The next few chapters examine how to analyse specific phases of the game: opening, middlegame and endgame, and then we round off with the most important product: drawing up your own study plan!

It's a serious book for serious people which I would recommend to anyone looking to achieve serious improvement in their game, or even for budding chess professionals looking for a way to structure their days working at chess. I'm going to give this one 5 stars, as I think it fills a gap in chess literature beautifully!

■ ■ ■

The Creative Power of Bogoljubov: Volume II by Grigory Bogdanovich (Elk and Ruby) is the second volume of a most welcome reappraisal of the life and games of one of the best – and least appreciated – players of the 1920s and 1930s.

You might compare Bogoljubov's fate to that of tennis players in the last ten years. How do you stand out from the crowd when facing that triumvirate of geniuses Federer, Nadal and Djokovic? In the same way, Bogoljubov had to contend with Alekhine, Capablanca and Lasker during the best years of his career!

Bogoljubov's play normally gets described in terms of what it wasn't: he didn't have Alekhine's

Nowadays, as Kuljasevic points out, the big problem is the reverse: there is so much help and information available, it's hard to know where to put the focus

The Creative Power of Bogoljubov
Volume II: Attack, Defense, Planning and More
Grigory Bogdanovich
Elk and Ruby, 2021
★★★★☆

overwhelming attacking flair or Capablanca's genius for smooth positional play. From a playing point of view, he was much closer to Lasker's practical approach, though he lacked Lasker's astonishing relentlessness. However, Bogoljubov's best games against the strongest players of his era show a player of the highest class, displaying a high level of mastery for the era in all areas of the game.

The book is organised thematically, which is a structure I like very much. We look first of all at his attacking play, then at his defensive play (Bogoljubov was an extremely tricky swindler!) and then at his strategical play, specifically his planning. Bogdanovich then examines Bogoljubov's contributions to opening theory – he had the reputation of being one of the best-prepared players of his era – and then his endgame play.

I like this book very much. The selection of games is very good and the organisation of material along thematic lines helps to highlight Bogoljubov's good moves and decisions in a way that might not be obvious normally. What did Bogoljubov's best play look like? Let me show you a really nice game which Bogoljubov played against Réti in Berlin in 1919. It isn't perfect but you can see how strong the white player is!

Bogoljubov's best games against the strongest players of his era show a player of the highest class, displaying a high level of mastery in all areas of the game

Efim Bogoljubov
Richard Réti
Berlin 1919
Queen's Pawn Opening

1.d4 ♘f6 2.♘f3 d6 3.♗f4
Bogoljubov liked to put the bishop to f4 against King's Indian systems. Later in the book Bogdanovich demonstrates Bogoljubov's game against Tarrasch at Carlsbad 1923 where he played 3.c4 g6 4.♘c3 ♗g7 5.e4 0-0 6.♗f4, which hasn't ever been played at the highest level even at blitz... It can only be a matter of time!

3...♘bd7 4.♘bd2 g6 5.e4 ♗g7 6.♗d3 0-0 7.h3 c6 8.0-0 ♕c7 9.♗h2 e5 10.c3 ♘h5

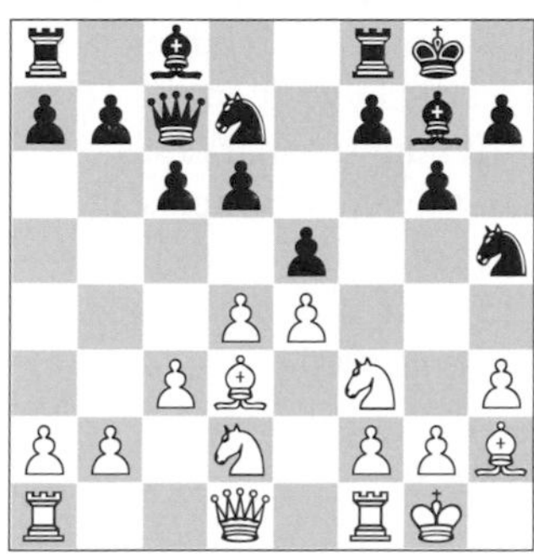

Black's setup is not particularly successful, as White's bishop on h2 combines nicely against Black's fragile d6- and e5-pawns, together with a knight on c4, the d4-pawn, the knight on f3 and the queen on d1. Bogoljubov's next move intends to secure the c4 outpost for his knight, and Réti fights immediately to prevent this.

11.a4 a6 12.♘c4 b5 13.axb5 cxb5 14.♘e3 ♘b6 15.g4
A really concrete move! It looks odd to weaken White's kingside dark squares and invite the knight on to the f4-square it has been eyeing since the tenth move. However, Bogoljubov is looking at a concrete goal: a weak pawn is created on f4, which can be targeted by a white knight from g2.

15...♘f4 16.♗xf4 exf4 17.♘g2 h5
Réti doesn't sit back and creates counterplay against White's exposed kingside. Again, Bogoljubov reacts concretely and aggressively, putting the pressure back on Black's own kingside structure.

18.gxh5 ♗h6 19.♘fh4 ♗xh3 20.♕f3 ♕c8 21.♘f5 21.hxg6 fails to 21...♗g4. **21...♗xf5 22.exf5 g5**

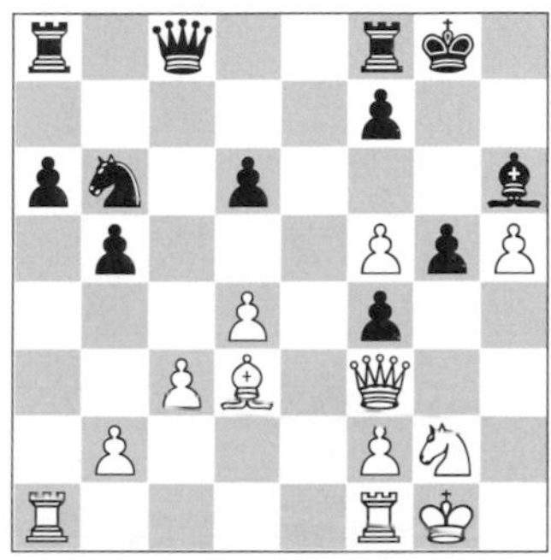

Black has defended the f4-pawn, but the kingside light squares are now extremely vulnerable once f5-f6 happens. This might have been played immediately but Bogoljubov prefers to bring the passive rook on f1 into play first.

23.♖fe1 ♘d7 24.♕d5 ♕b8
24...♘f6 25.♕xd6 ♗g7 was Black's best defence, when 26.h6 ♖d8 is just equal, as White cannot maintain the attack on the knight on f6 without allowing a repetition.

25.f6 Strong, but White had an even stronger idea!
25.♖e6 was immediately decisive: 25...fxe6 26.♕xe6+ ♖f7 27.♕xh6 ♕f8 28.♕xg5+ ♖g7 29.♕xf4 ♘f6 30.♕f3, with ♔f1 and ♘f4 to follow, is very strong for White, according to my engine, though I could imagine having some slight doubts if I was evaluating this from afar, due to White's doubled kingside pawns.

25...♘xf6 26.♕f5 ♕d8 27.f3
Perhaps not the very best idea – my engine likes the surprising 27.♗xb5, with the point 27...axb5 28.♖xa8 – but a really nice one!

27...♔g7 28.♔f2 Freeing the g-file and preparing the line-opening sacrifice ♘xf4. Perfect use of the now passive knight on g2? Well, Bogoljubov does even better in the game!
28...♕c8 28...♖h8 was best, freeing f8 for the king's escape already. The text runs into a stunning rejoinder!
29.♘h4

Turning the passive knight on g2 into a monster!
29...♖h8 29...gxh4 30.♖g1+. **30.♖e7 ♕xf5 31.♘xf5+ ♔g8 32.♖b7 ♗f8 33.h6 ♗xh6 34.♗xb5 ♗f8 35.♔g2 a5 36.c4** 1-0.
A lovely book! 4 stars!

■ ■ ■

The Magnus Method by Emmanuel Neiman (New In Chess) uses the games of a somewhat better-known player as a training course! Neiman identifies 11 facets of Magnus's play – for example 'Exchanges – Carlsen's main positional weapon', 'Attack – inviting everyone to the party' – and then extracts positions from Magnus's games to allow the user to test his own skill against Magnus. Perhaps the most striking part of this is that the games of a player aged just 30 could provide so much instructional material (and still have plenty left over, I'm sure). It's quite remarkable.
There are many lovely examples in the book. I very much liked this one, played by a 13-year old(!) Magnus against Nigel Short in 2004:

Magnus Carlsen
Nigel Short
Hoogeveen 2004

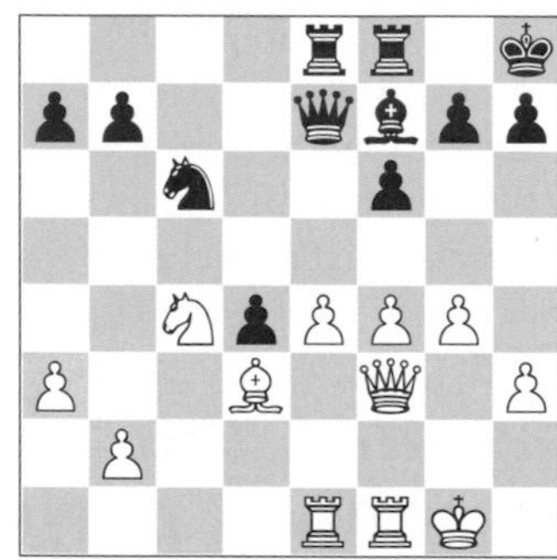

23.♘d2 Not a winning move by any means – the position is still balanced

The Magnus Method
Emmanuel Neiman
New In Chess, 2021
★★★☆☆

– but a lovely one nonetheless. The knight looked nice on c4 but was simply providing a target to the black pieces. It works particularly well as it offers White an additional resource against the plan Nigel had presumably prepared against quiet moves such as 23.♔h1.
23...g5 This logical move fights to give control of the e5-square to the c6-knight, but Magnus's last move has given him a new way to fight this.
24.♗b5 a6 25.♗xc6 bxc6 26.fxg5 fxg5 27.♕f6+
Offering the exchange of queens with a better endgame for White. Nigel offered the d-pawn but ended up exchanging the queens a move later on the same square but a pawn down!
27...♔g8 28.♕xd4 c5 29.♕f6 ♕xf6 30.♖xf6 And Magnus nursed his extra pawn to victory in 54 moves.
A useful and instructive book! 3 stars. ■

NEW IN CHESS bestsellers

Caruana explains the Ruy Lopez for club players

Fabiano Caruana takes you by the hand and lays out a complete and practical White repertoire for club players. He avoids complicated chaotic lines, but doesn't shy away from sharp battles. Caruana loves to find and use the tactics to punish Black for risky choices.

This one-volume and crystal-clear repertoire covers fifteen main variations, from the classical lines to the anti-Marshall (8.a4), and from the Schliemann (3...f5) to the Modern Steinitz.

The Singular Skills of the World's Strongest Chess Player Uncovered and Explained
Emmanuel Neiman

Why do Carlsen's opponents, the best players around, fail to see his moves coming? Moves that look self-evident? Emmanuel Neiman's findings will surprise, delight and educate players of all levels. He explains a key element in Carlsen's play: he doesn't play the 'absolute' best move, but often the move that gives him the better chances, offering his opponents the maximum amount of ways to go wrong.

Fundamental Tactics and Checkmates for Improvers
Peter Giannatos

The perfect first chess Workbook for adult improvers and other beginners. Coaches might find the book, with 738 exercises, very useful as well. The book features a complete set of fundamental tactics and checkmate patterns. Written by Peter Giannatos, founder and executive director of the Charlotte Chess Center & Scholastic Academy, in North Carolina.

Strategic Concepts, Typical Plans and Tactical Themes *Oscar de Prado*

De Prado revisits his favourite opening. He avoids long and complicated variations and explains straightforward plans, clear-cut strategies and standard manoeuvres. If you follow his lessons you are unlikely to face surprises and you will learn to make the right middlegame choices. The most efficient way to acquaint yourself with an opening that is easy to learn and hard to counter.

Start Playing an Unsidesteppable & Low Maintenance Response to 1.e4 and Simultaneously Improve Your Chess Technique
Thomas Willemze

"This is a real gem! It's almost as if each annotation specifies the key strategic elements that uphold the assessments and choice of plans. A repertoire apt for club players, offering lessons in strategy, plus antidotes to seemingly troublesome White tries."
GM Glenn Flear

A Skeptic's Guide to Getting Better at Chess
Willy Hendriks

"Willy Hendriks' book is terrific. It totally changed my view on the history of chess." – *GM Erwin l'Ami*

"Well researched, endlessly fascinating, always thought-provoking and sometimes extremely funny. If you want to improve your rating you'll find a lot of inspiring suggestions."
Richard James, British Chess News

Learn From the Greatest Players Ever
Joel Benjamin

GM Joel Benjamin presents the most instructive games of each of the seventeen World Champions. He describes both their historical significance and how they inspired his own development as a player. Magic names such as Kasparov, Capablanca, Alekhine, Botvinnik, Tal and Karpov, they're all there, up to current World Champion Magnus Carlsen. Benjamin explains, in words rather than in chess symbols, what is important for your own improvement.

A Manual for Modern-Day Club Players
Gerard Welling & Steve Giddins

Will dramatically boost your skills – without carrying the excess baggage that many of your opponents will be struggling with.

"Aimed at amateur players who don't have much time to study."
IM Gary Lane, Chess Moves Magazine

"A refreshing attempt at producing s chess manual with a difference." – *Sean Marsh, CHESS Magazine*

A Solid and Straightforward Chess Opening Repertoire for White
Christof Sielecki

Sielecki's repertoire with 1.d4 may be even easier to master than his 1.e4 recommendations.

"A repertoire that packs a punch."
Miguel Ararat, Florida Chess Magazine

"A host of interesting new and dangerous ideas."
John Upham, British Chess News

"As I think that I should keep my advice 'simple', I would say 'just get it'!" – *GM Glenn Flear*

Vital Lessons for Every Chess Player
Jesus de la Villa

"If you've never read an endgame book before, this is the one you should start with."
GM Matthew Sadler, former British Champion

"If you really have no patience for endgames, at least read *100 Endgames You Must Know*."
Gary Walters Chess

available at your local (chess)bookseller or at www.newinchess.com

Jan Timman

Two fighters

A substantial part of the entertainment in Norway Chess was provided by youngsters Alireza Firouzja (18) and Richard Rapport (25). **JAN TIMMAN** takes a closer look at the two newcomers in the world top-10 and the impressive chess they showed in Stavanger.

The Top-10 players in the FIDE Elo list rarely change. There is an almost unchanged contingent of top players that rarely fall under 2770. With this in mind, it is surprising that the recent Norway Chess tournament in Stavanger yielded two newcomers in the Top-10: Alireza Firouzja and Richard Rapport, both of whom played absolutely fantastically during much of the tournament.

The final standings in Stavanger were slightly clouded by the mandatory Armageddon games after a draw. Looking only at the purely classical games – and there's no reason not to – it will strike you that Carlsen and Firouzja won the tournament with 6½ out of 10, half a point ahead of Rapport. The other three players were far behind. The young heroes' results were achieved in very different ways. While Rapport played the first seven rounds as if there was no tomorrow, Firouzja only built up a head of steam in the second half of the tournament, winning his last four games.

When you think of it, Rapport's ascent to the world top was a very quiet affair. His play was mainly solid, with one outlier. At the end of last year, he won the 11th Danzhou tournament (which was played online due to the pandemic) half a point ahead of Ding Liren. I remember what Peter Leko told me seven years ago: he regarded his youthful compatriot as an attacker *pur sang*. Meanwhile, however, he has developed more into a Karpov than a Tal.

In the first round in Stavanger, Rapport defeated Aryan Tari in a model strategic game.

Aryan Tari
Richard Rapport
Stavanger 2021 (1)
French Defence, Winawer Variation

1.e4 e6 2.d4 d5 3.♘c3 ♗b4 4.exd5 exd5 5.♗d3 ♘e7 6.♘f3
The queen sortie 6.♕h5, originally played by Esteban Canal in 1926, was crucial.
6...♗g4 This is also what Capablanca and Nimzowitsch played.
7.h3 ♗h5 8.0-0 ♘bc6

9.♗e2
A passive retreat that promises nothing in the way of an opening plus. With 9.a3 White could have gone for an opening advantage, after which the play might become sharp if Black decided to castle queenside. After 9...♗xc3 10.bxc3 ♕d7 11.♖e1 0-0-0 an interesting position arises, with chances for both sides.
9...0-0 10.♘h4
A strategically inferior move. With 10.♖e1 ♖e8 11.♗d2 White could have preserved the balance.

10...♗xc3!
The strategic refutation. With the white d-pawn hanging, White must recapture on c3. Weaker than the text was 10...♗xe2, after which White maintains the balance with 11.♘xe2.
11.bxc3 ♗xe2 12.♕xe2 ♖e8 13.♕f3 ♕d7 14.♗d2 ♘a5
On its way to c4. The white knight is obviously badly placed, unable to prevent Black's strategic plans.
15.♖ae1 ♘c4 16.♗c1 a5!
A strong move with a dual purpose: Black wants to increase his queenside territory and possibly deploy his queen's rook via a6.
17.♕h5

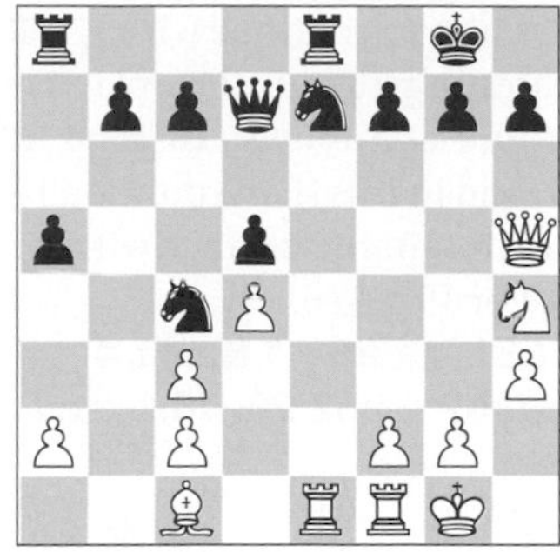

17...♖a6

Consistent, but the computer prefers 17...b5. The reason is clear: Black keeps his rooks connected for the moment, and starts exerting pressure on the queenside first. White has few useful moves: 18.♖e2 is met strongly by 18...♘g6, after which Black will play consistently for the thematic position with a strong knight against a weak bishop.

18.♘f3 g6 19.♕h4

19.♕g4 came into consideration, since Black cannot go for a queen swap in view of the pin along the e-file. After 19...♘f5 20.♘e5 ♘xe5 21.♖xe5 ♖xe5 22.dxe5 ♖e6 Black will be better, but White will hold.

19...f6

The alternative was 19...♘f5. After 20.♖xe8+ ♕xe8 21.♕f4 ♖c6 Black keeps a plus.

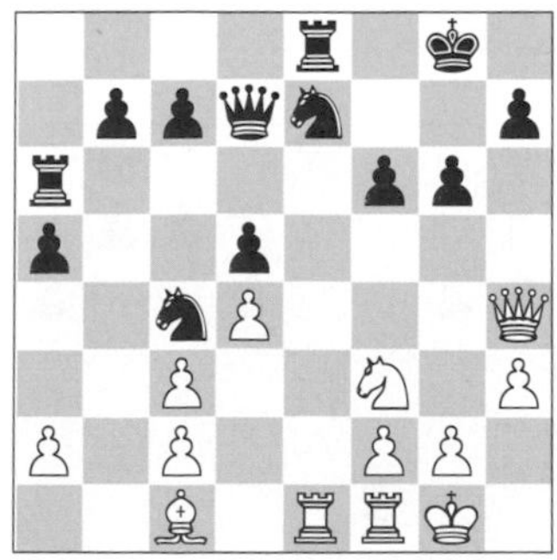

20.♖e2

Wasting a tempo, after which it's all downhill for White. 20.♘d2 was absolutely necessary, intending to swap on c4 to eliminate the strong black knight, with less of a plus for Black.

20...♘f5 21.♖xe8+ ♕xe8 22.♕f4 ♕d7 23.♖e1 g5!

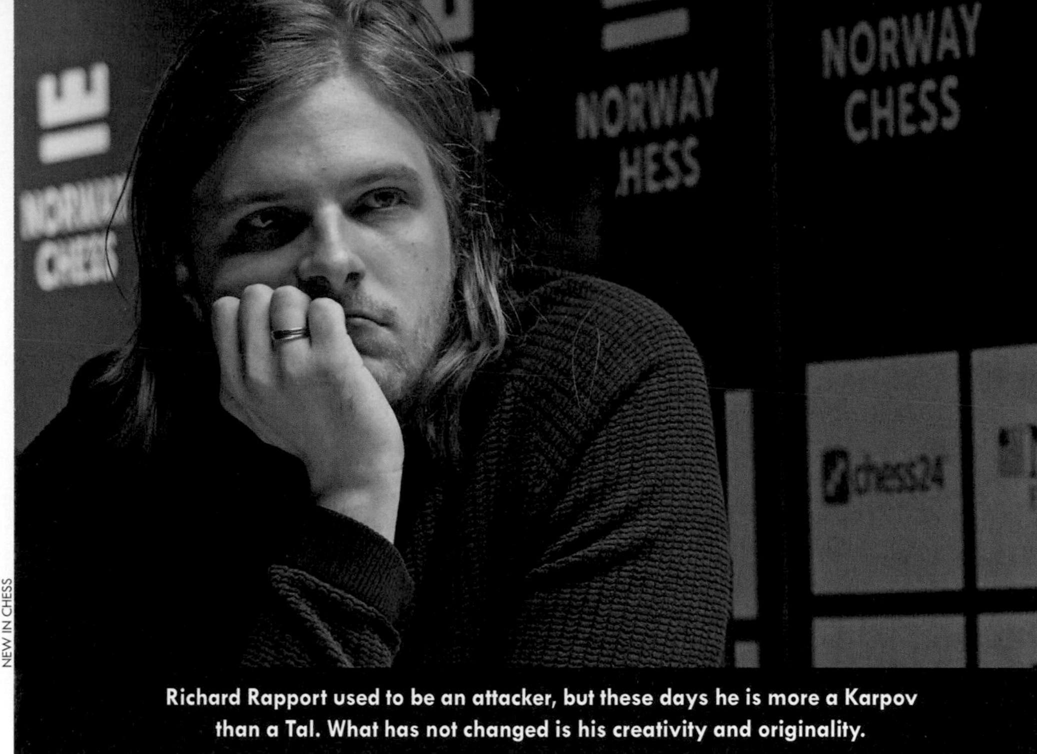

NEW IN CHESS

Richard Rapport used to be an attacker, but these days he is more a Karpov than a Tal. What has not changed is his creativity and originality.

Very strong, especially in combination with Black's next move.

24.♕g4 ♖e6

Taking control of the e-file.

25.h4 ♖xe1+ 26.♘xe1 ♕e6 27.♘d3 ♕e4

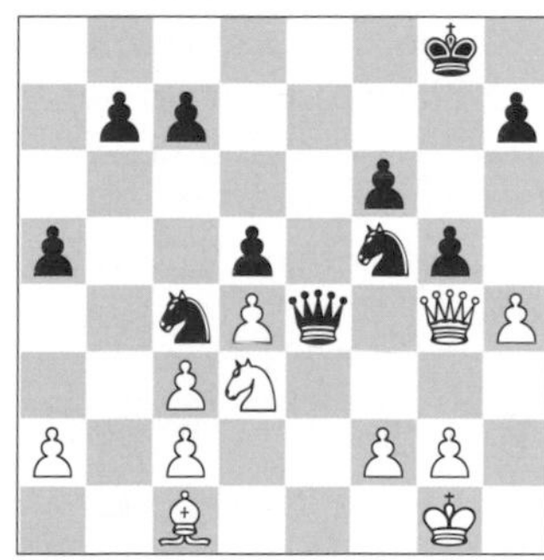

The strategic death blow.

28.♕xe4

White accepts his fate. With 28.♘f4 he might have sown some confusion, after which Black could have secured his winning advantage with the accurate 28...h6!.

Richard Rapport played the first seven rounds as if there was no tomorrow

28...dxe4 29.♘c5 ♘xh4 30.♘xb7 ♘f5 31.♘c5 ♘fd6

Everything fits. Black is in absolute control of the position.

32.g4 ♔f7 33.♔g2 ♔g6 34.a4 h5 35.gxh5+ ♔xh5 36.♔g3 f5

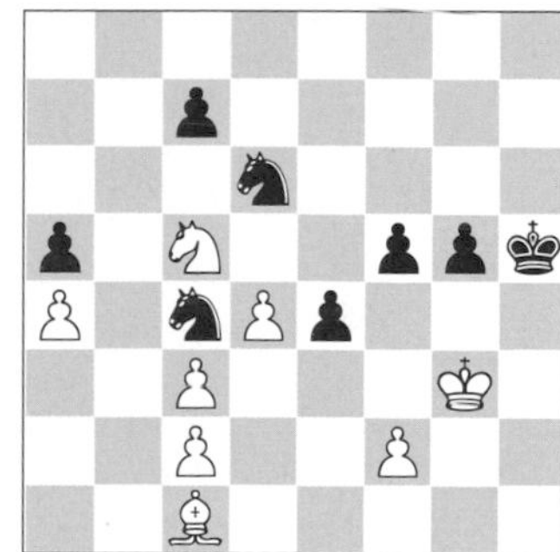

The material is still equal, but White is powerless in the face of the black pawn front.

37.♘e6 f4+ 38.♗xf4

Desperation. The piece sacrifice just prolongs the agony.

38...♘f5+ 39.♔h3 gxf4 40.♘xf4+ ♔h6 41.♘e6 ♘e7 42.♘xc7 ♔g5 43.♔g2 ♔g4 44.♔f1 ♔f3 45.♔e1 ♘c8 46.♘e6 ♘8b6 47.♘g5+ ♔f4 48.♘e6+ ♔g4 49.♘c5 ♔f3 50.♘b3 ♘xa4 51.d5 ♘ab6 52.d6 a4 53.♘d4+ ♔f4 54.♘b5 ♘xd6 55.♘xd6 a3

White resigned.

Tenacity

After quiet draws against Sergey Karjakin and Magnus Carlsen, Rapport bested Alireza Firouzja in Round 4 (for notes to this game, see the tournament report in this issue). In Round 5, he drew against Ian Nepomniachtchi, but in Rounds 6 and 7 he struck again, against Tari and Karjakin. In the latter game especially, he showed his tenacity in an endgame in which, for a long time, he had only a minimal advantage.

Richard Rapport
Sergey Karjakin
Stavanger 2021 (7)
Nimzo-Indian Defence, Three Knights Variation

1.d4 ♘f6 2.c4 e6 3.♘c3 ♗b4 4.♘f3 0-0 5.♕c2 d5 6.♗g5 h6 7.♗xf6 ♕xf6 8.a3 ♗xc3+ 9.♕xc3 dxc4 10.♕xc4

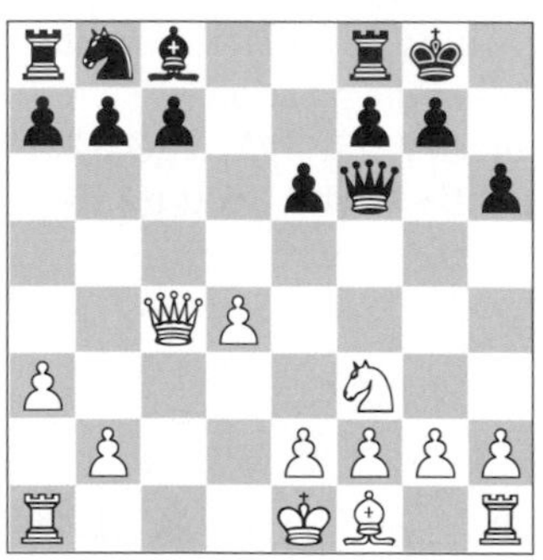

10...c6
The alternative 10...♘c6, as Gelfand had played against Abdusattorov in the Tolstoy Memorial three days earlier, was probably slightly better. After 11.♖d1 ♖e8 12.♕c3 e5 13.d5 ♘b8 14.e3 ♗g4 15.♗e2 ♘d7 Black had no opening problems. An interesting question is whether Karjakin knew this game. He was probably following his own preparation.
11.g3 ♘d7 12.♗h3!
This is how White prevents the freeing advance ...e6-e5.
12...c5
The best freeing attempt.
13.dxc5

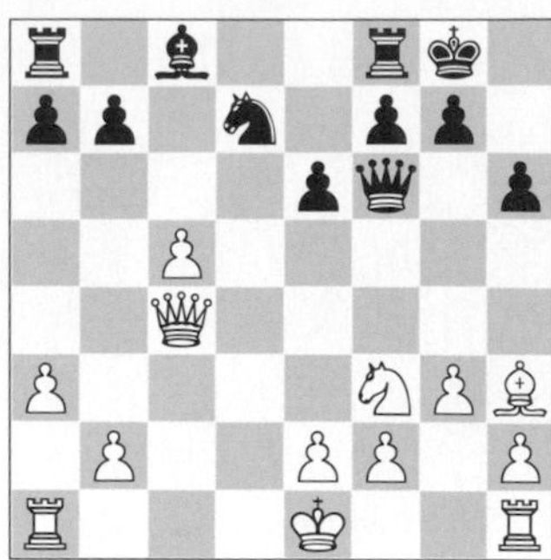

13...b6!
Undoubtedly still prepared. After 13...♕xb2 14.0-0 b6 15.♗g2! Black would be in trouble. A possible continuation is: 15...bxc5 (not 15...♘xc5 in view of 16.♘d4, and White wins material) 16.♖fb1 ♕f6 17.♘d4! ♖b8 18.♖xb8 ♘xb8 19.♕xc5, and White has a large positional plus.
14.c6 ♕xb2
Now it's OK!
15.0-0 ♘c5 16.♘d4
Covering the e-pawn. The alternative was the pawn sacrifice 16.♕b4, forcing Black to be accurate. After 16...♕xe2 17.♗g2 ♗a6 18.♖fe1 ♕c2 19.♖ac1 ♕a2! 20.♘e5 f6! White has nothing better than 21.♖a1, forcing repetition.

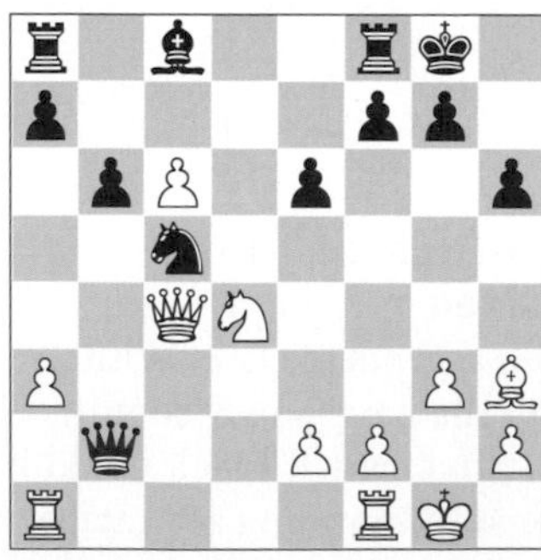

16...♖d8 A natural move, but 16...e5 was probably stronger, since 17.♘f5 allows him to continue with 17...♔h7, threatening 18...g6. The play could continue as follows: 18.♕h4 ♕d2 19.f4, and in this sharp position Black can maintain the balance with either 19...e4 or 19...♗e6.
17.e3! ♗a6 18.♕b4 ♘d3 19.♕xb2 ♘xb2 20.♖fb1 ♘a4

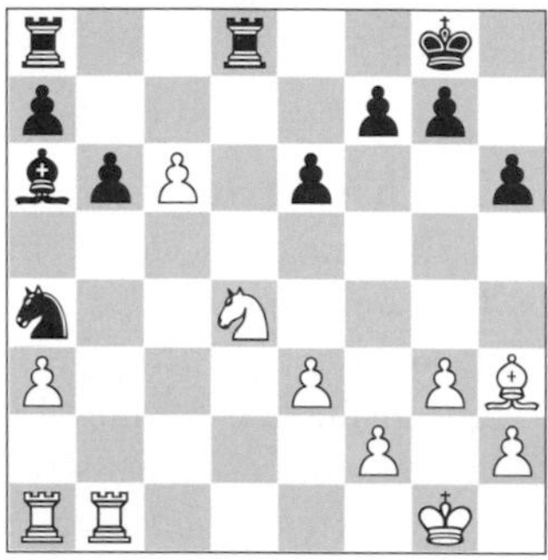

21.f4 The computer prefers 21.c7, winning an exchange by force. Rapport probably thought that the position after 21...♖d7 22.♗g2 ♖c8 23.♗c6 ♖xd4 24.exd4 ♘c3 25.♖b4 ♖xc7 wasn't clearly winning, and it's true that in this structure, the chances of a draw are considerable.
21...♘c3
Not a very effective manoeuvre. The knight was OK on a4. 21...♖ac8 looked like a better defence. A possible continuation was: 22.♗g2 g5 23.♖b4 ♘c5, and it will be hard to breach Black's defences.

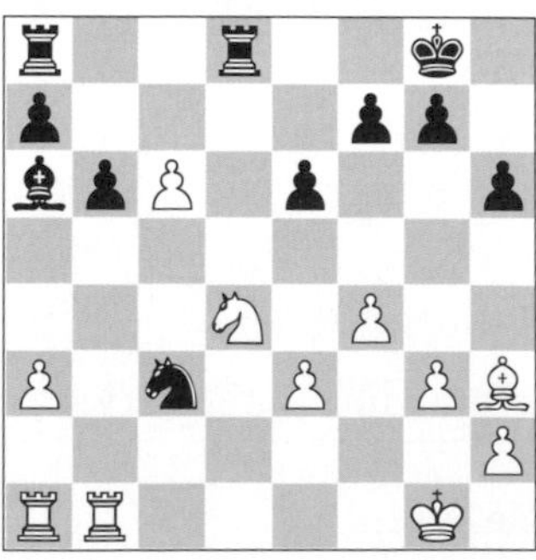

22.♖b2
22.♖c1 was probably stronger, but the consequences of liquidating with 22...♖xd4 23.exd4 ♘e2+ 24.♔f2 ♘xc1 25.♖xc1 were not easy to assess. Black must defend carefully with 25...♖e8 (since the obvious 25...♔f8

Rapport showed his tenacity in an endgame in which, for a long time, he had only a minimal advantage

loses after 26.c7 ♔e7 27.♗f1 ♗b7 28.♗g2). Nor does the careful rook move offer much hope, since White has 26.f5!. After 26...♗c8 27.fxe6 fxe6 28.♔e3 White will be able to reinforce his position at his leisure. I think he is winning.

22...♘d5 23.♔f2 ♘c7 24.♖d1
24.♗g2, taking control of square d5, would have been better.

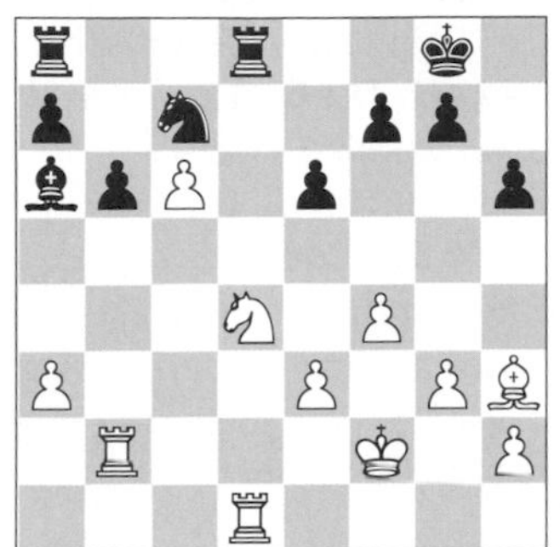

24...♖d6
Black fails to grab his chance. With 24...♖d5! 25.♗g2 ♖a5 he could have activated his rook, which would make it even harder for White to break through the black defences.

25.♖bd2 ♖ad8 26.♔e1 ♗c4 27.e4 f6 28.♗g2 e5 29.fxe5 fxe5 30.♘f3 ♖xd2 31.♖xd2 ♖xd2 32.♔xd2 ♗b5 33.♘xe5 ♔f8 34.h4 ♔e7 35.♘g6+ ♔d6 36.e5+ ♔c5 37.♘e7

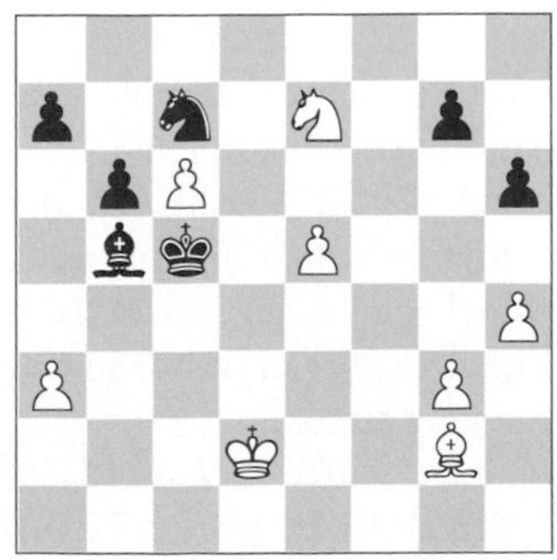

White has managed to hang on to his c-pawn, but it remains difficult to convert his advantage.

37...♔d4 38.♘c8 ♔xe5 39.♘xa7 ♔d6 An understandable move in time-trouble, but objectively wrong. After 39...♗a6 Black would still have had good drawing chances.

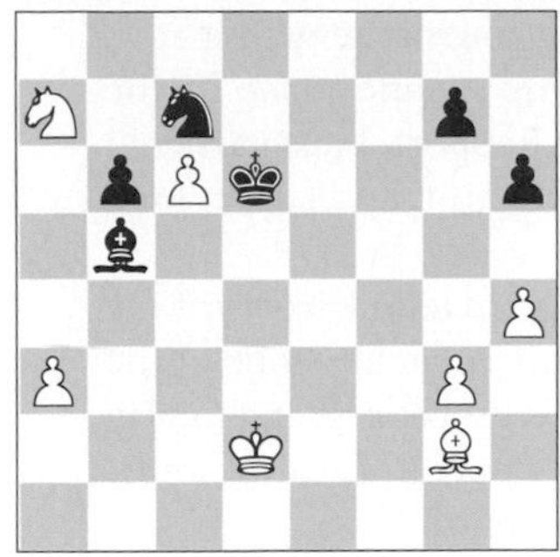

40.♘c8+ With 40.♘xb5+ ♘xb5 41.a4 White could have secured the win, but this was hard to calculate over the board, since it looks as if White has nothing special after 41...♘d4.

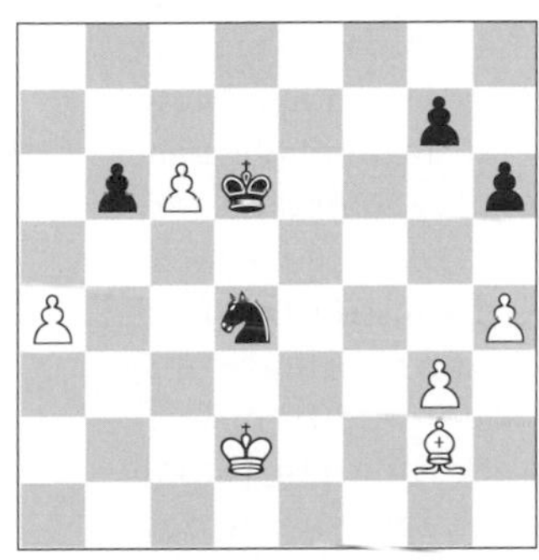

ANALYSIS DIAGRAM

But White plays 42.h5!, an extremely important move in the upcoming pawn ending. After 42...♘xc6 43.♗xc6 ♔xc6 44.♔c3! White is winning, e.g.: 44...♔c5 45.♔b3 ♔d6 46.♔b4 ♔c7 47.♔c3 ♔c6 48.♔c4 ♔d6 49.♔b5 ♔c7 50.♔a6 ♔c6 51.g4 ♔c7 52.♔a7 ♔c6 53.♔b8, and everything is clear. With the king having penetrated the enemy lines, it will arrive decisively on f7 after the swap of the queenside pawns.

40...♔c5 41.♘e7 ♘e6 42.♔c3 ♔d6 43.♔b4

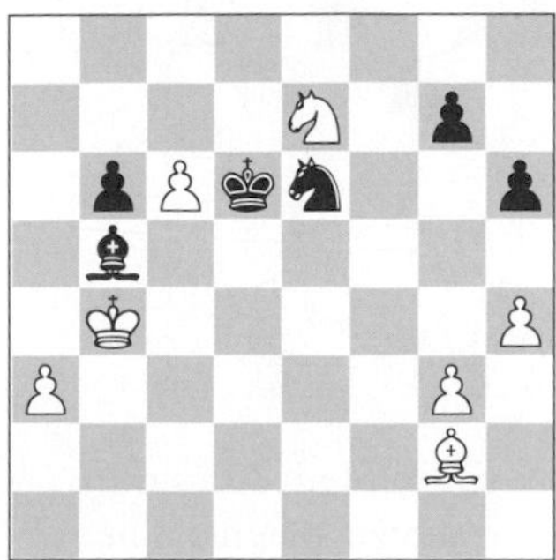

Celeb 64

John Henderson

Dmitri Shostakovich

Soviet composer and pianist Dmitri Shostakovich thrived under the favour of Stalin. It made him both a controversial figure within the world of classical music whilst at the same time being lauded as one of the major composers of the 20th century.
Shostakovich also played chess, a youthful pursuit that became a passion following a chance encounter with one of the all-time greats of the game, as was revealed by an *Izvestia* journalist, who had spotted several neatly clipped newspaper chess problems sitting on the composer's desk. Shostakovich told him he followed all the major tournaments and matches, and so he was thrilled that as a 14-year-old he had the privilege of playing a game with Alexander Alekhine in the lobby of a Leningrad cinema.
Some have questioned the validity of this story – including Boris Spassky – but the timeline is plausible. And Shostakovich himself often retold the story, pointing out that he did not know who had thrashed him... until the future Champion introduced himself to the young cinema pianist after their game!
Many of the greatest Soviet writers and musicians were obsessive players – and whether she knew this or not, Dutch director Marleen Gorris linked Shostakovich and chess in yet another cinematic connection, using his Waltz No. 2 from Jazz Suite No. 2 prominently in her Nabokov-inspired chess movie, *The Luzhin Defence*. ■

43...♗a6 Up to this point, the 'Minister of Defence' has lived up to his name, despite his slip-up on move 39. But here he should have gone 43...♘d4! to prevent the knight check on f5. After 44.♘c8+ ♔c7 45.♘a7 ♗a6 46.a4 g5 White no longer has realistic winning chances.

44.♘f5+ ♔e5 45.♗h3!

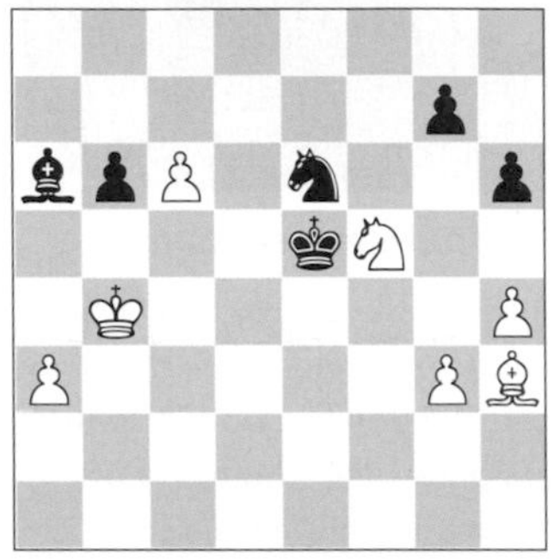

Karjakin must have underestimated this covering move. White keeps his c-pawn, after which the win is relatively easy.

45...h5 46.♘e3 ♘c7 47.♗g2 g6 48.a4 ♔d4 49.♘c2+ ♔e5 50.♔c3 ♔d6 Or 50...♗c8 51.♘e3, and wins. **51.♗e4 ♗e2 52.♘d4 ♔e5 53.♗xg6 ♘d5+ 54.♔d2 ♗g4 55.♘b5 ♘e7 56.♗e8 ♗f3 57.c7 ♗g4 58.♗f7 ♘c6 59.♗xh5** Black resigned.

Disillusion and dejection

Rapport now was on 5½ out of 7, a phenomenal score. He had suddenly catapulted to sixth place in the world rankings. But then fate struck. In the final three rounds he lost against two of his rivals and slipped behind them – an enormous disillusion that really depressed him. As a result, he felt incapable of annotating one of his magnificent victories for our magazine.

I can understand his dejection very well, because something similar happened to me four decades ago. In the fifth Interpolis tournament in Tilburg in 1981, I was leading with six points after eight rounds. If I managed to hold my own in the final three rounds, I would have won my third big tournament in a row, cementing my second place in the Elo list. Like Rapport, I just garnered a meagre half point. I was upset for a long time.

But Rapport needn't worry. Like Jan-Krzysztof Duda, he is one of the players who is probably going to play an important part in future Candidates tournaments.

High expectations

The same thing applies to Firouzja, of course, who is seven years younger than Rapport. Many people even regard him as Carlsen's inevitable challenger. I have the feeling that Firouzja is sometimes weighed down by these high expectations. He was slow to build up steam in Stavanger, anyway, struggling to find his form. In the first half, he scored 50%, and then he allowed himself to be tricked by Carlsen. In the final stage of the tournament, he never dropped the ball, though, beating Ian Nepomniachtchi in an impressive manoeuvring game.

Alireza Firouzja
Ian Nepomniachtchi
Stavanger 2021 (7)
Italian Game, Giuoco Pianissimo

1.e4 e5 2.♘f3 ♘c6 3.♗c4 ♘f6 4.d3 ♗c5 5.c3 d6 6.0-0 0-0 7.♖e1 a5

The alternative is 7...a6. Interestingly, top players like Aronian and Giri alternate between these two moves.

8.h3 ♗a7 9.a4 h6 10.♘bd2

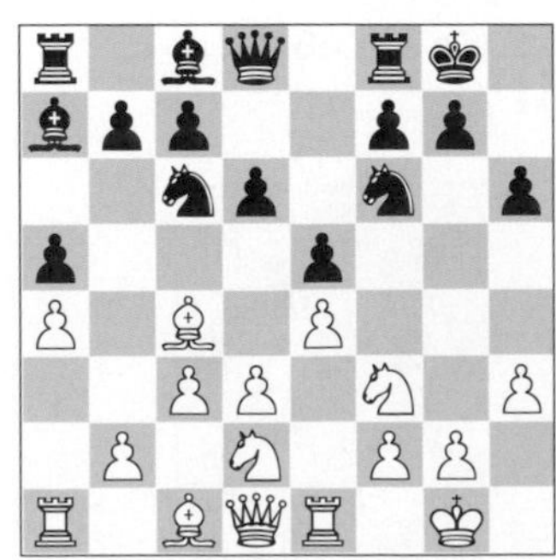

10...♗e6 A principled decision. Black accepts doubled pawns. The

I have the feeling that Firouzja is sometimes weighed down by these high expectations

alternative 10...♖e8 was insufficient for equality. After 11.♘f1 ♗e6 12.♗b5! White has the initiative.

11.♗xe6 fxe6 12.♘c4 ♘h5 13.♗e3 ♗xe3 14.♖xe3

The most ambitious way to recapture.

14...♘f4 15.♘cd2

A somewhat passive move, enabling Black to take the initiative. A good move was 15.♔h2, preparing 16.g3 to chase back the strong black knight.

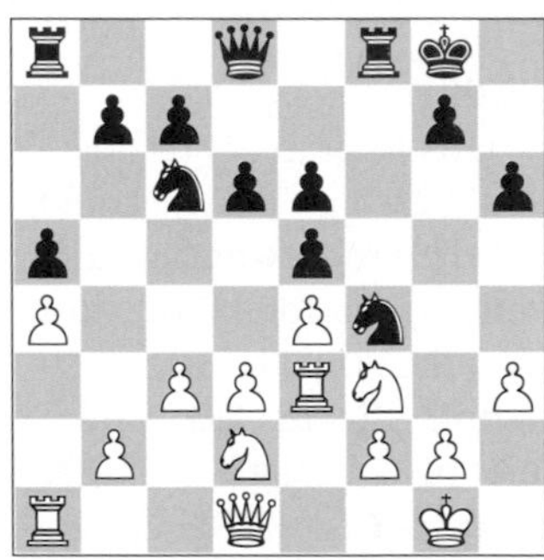

15...♕f6

Black fails to take advantage. With 15...d5 he could have increased his influence in the centre considerably. White seems to be able to exert pressure with 16.exd5 exd5 17.♕b3, but then 17...♖f7! will be a strong reply, after which White cannot take any black pawn, e.g. 18.♕xb7 ♖f6 19.♕b3 ♖g6 20.♘e1 ♕h4, and Black has a strong attack.

16.♘h2 ♔h8 17.♕f1 ♖f7 18.♘df3 ♖af8 19.g3 ♘h5 20.♖d1 ♕e7 21.♔g2 ♕e8

Black's queen manoeuvre is not very impressive. He wants to transfer his queen's knight to e7, attacking the white a-pawn *en route*. But concentrating the black troops on the kingside isn't very wise, since it will allow White to break through in the centre.

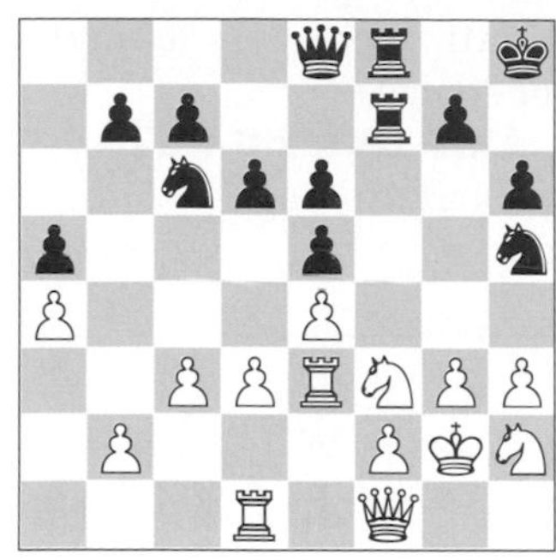

22.♖d2! A strong little move. White vacates square d1 for the queen.

22...♘e7

Consistent. But the passive 22...♘f6 would have been better, anticipating the advance of the white d-pawn.

23.♕d1 ♘g6 24.d4!

The correct moment to take the initiative. Black has no threats on the kingside.

24...exd4 25.cxd4 ♘f6 26.♕c2

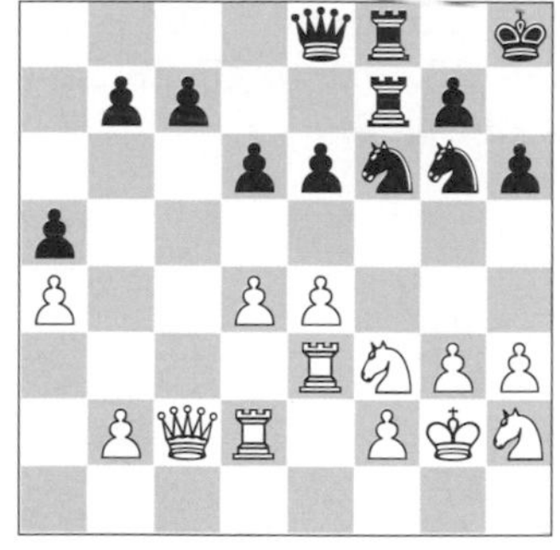

26...e5

The black position was hard to handle, and the text doesn't solve anything. A better defence was 26...♘e7, awaiting further actions from White.

27.dxe5 dxe5 28.♖c3 c6 29.♖d6

With his solid structure and excellent piece coordination White is holding all the trumps.

29...♖d7

A rook swap won't relieve the pressure. A more tenacious defence was 29...♔h7. The more pieces on the board, the better your chances of counterplay.

30.♖cd3 ♖ff7 31.♘f1 ♖xd6 32.♖xd6 ♖d7 33.♖xd7 ♕xd7 34.♘1d2 ♘h5

A demonstration of powerlessness.

LENNART OOTES

Alireza Firouzja has to live up to high expectations. Many even see him as Magnus Carlsen's inevitable future challenger.

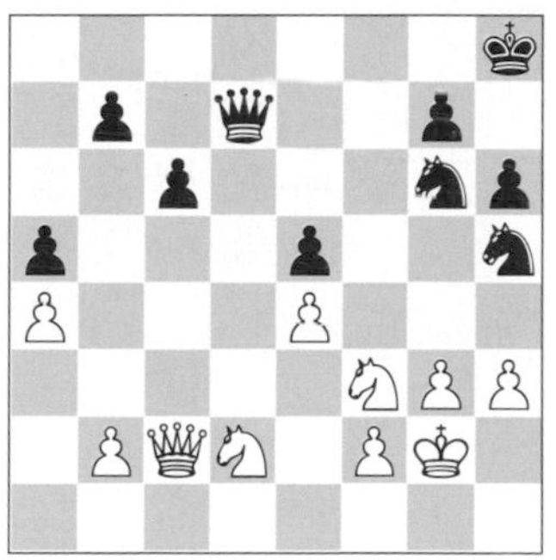

35.♔h2! Preventing a knight check on f4. **35...♘f6 36.♕c3 ♕c7 37.♔g2**

Quietly preparing for further action. Black is bound hand and foot.

37...c5 This pawn move messes it up even more for Black strategically. He should have hung back and waited with 37...♕d8.

38.♕d3 ♘e7 39.♘c4 ♘c6 40.♕d6!

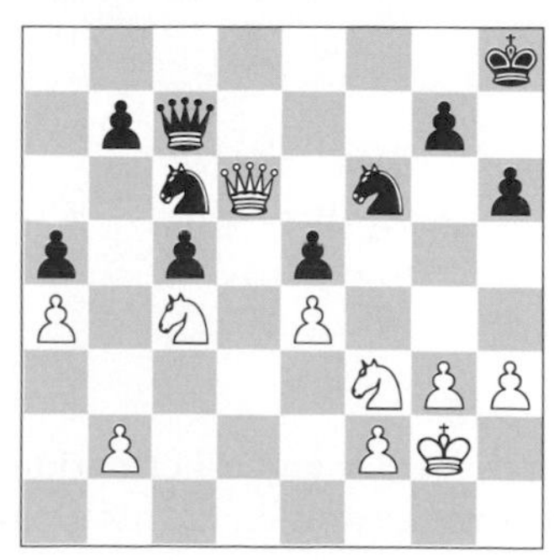

The best way. After the queen swap the weak black pawns would fall one by one.

40...♕d7 40...♕xd6 41.♘xd6 b6 42.♘d2 was also completely hopeless.

41.♘fxe5 ♘xe5 42.♕xe5 ♕xa4 43.♕xc5 ♕c2 44.e5 ♘g8 45.♕d5 ♕b3 46.e6 b5

The issue briefly seems to be in doubt, as there is only one road leading to the win.

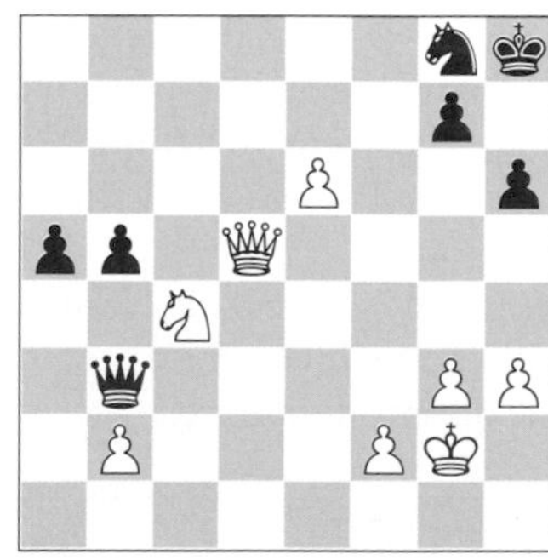

47.♕a8! The death blow, which Firouzja must have seen coming from a long way off. White is threatening to queen his e-pawn.

47...♔h7 48.♕e4+ ♔h8 49.♘xa5 ♕xb2 50.e7 ♘xe7 51.♕xe7 b4 52.♕e8+ ♔h7 53.♕e4+ ♔h8 54.♕d5 ♕a3 55.♘b3 ♕a4 56.♘d4 ♕e8 57.♕b7

Black resigned.

Firouzja's victory over Karjakin in the next round was of a lesser calibre, but still convincing enough.

Sergey Karjakin
Alireza Firouzja
Stavanger 2021 (8)
Sicilian Defence: Najdorf Variation

1.e4 c5 2.♘f3 d6 3.d4 cxd4 4.♘xd4 ♘f6 5.♘c3 a6 6.h3 e5 7.♘f3 ♗e7 8.g4

An old move from as long back as the game Khalikian-Anastasian from the 1983 Armenian Junior Championship. Earlier this year, Giri tried it against Vachier-Lagrave, going on to win after many adventures. I think the text is not suitable to get an opening advantage.

8...h6

This was also Anastasian's reaction. It is a good idea to prevent the further advance of the g-pawn. Vachier-Lagrave went for the alternative 8...0-0. This gives White more starting-points.

9.♖g1 ♕c7 Here 9...b5 came into consideration, intending to get active on the queenside at once.

10.♘h4

Both of them lost two games and drew less than half of them. With such fighters, Armageddon rules will no longer be needed!

The start of a laborious plan. White would have been better off going for 10.g5 hxg5 11.♘xg5. The knight is strong on g5. A possible continuation would be 11...♘c6 12.♗c4 ♘d8 13.♗b3 ♘e6, and the chances are roughly equal.

10...g6

Keeping the knight away from f5.

11.♘g2 ♗e6 12.♘e3 ♘bd7 13.h4 ♕c6 14.♕f3 ♘c5 15.♗g2 ♘a4

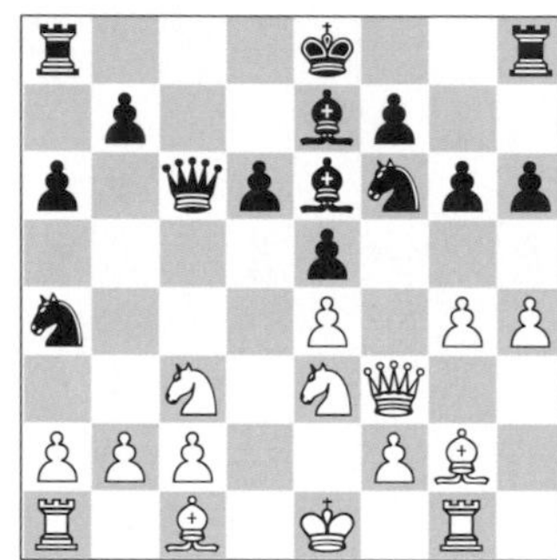

16.♘ed5?

The wrong knight! 16.♘cd5 was called for. After 16...♗xd5 17.exd5 ♕c5 18.♕e2 ♘d7 19.♖h1 White will just manage to hold, but Black will still have the initiative.

16...♘xc3

17.♘xf6+

There's hardly any other option. If White recaptures on c3, his g-pawn will fall. White is completely wrong-footed.

17...♗xf6 18.♕xf6 ♔d7

Simple and winning.

19.g5

19...♘xe4

Even stronger was 19...♕c4, only going 20...♘xe4 to meet 20.♗f3. The white position collapses like a house of cards.

20.♕f3 d5 21.♕d1 ♕b6 22.♗e3 ♕xb2 23.♗xe4 ♕b4+ 24.c3 ♕xe4 25.♖b1 hxg5 26.♖b4 d4 27.cxd4 ♔e8!

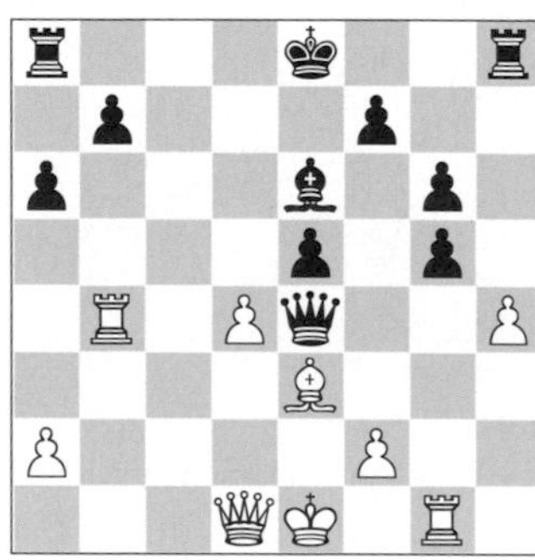

The most convincing way to the win.

28.hxg5 ♖h3 29.♔d2 ♗f5 30.♕b3 ♖c8 31.♖c1 ♖xc1 32.♔xc1 ♖h1+ 33.♔d2 b5 34.d5 ♕f3

White resigned.

Equally impressive was Firouzja's win against Rapport in the final round, which you find annotated elsewhere in this issue. What strikes one in Firouzja's and Rapport's scores is that both of them lost two games and drew less than half of them. With such fighters, Armageddon rules will no longer be needed! ■

by Han Schut

They are The Champions

CAMEROON
Population: 27 million
Active rated players: 48

FM Victor Ebosse Kingue is the 2021 champion of Cameroon. The championship was held over two weekends in August, with four rounds in Yaoundé and four rounds in Douala. The champion won his first four games, including a victory over his nemesis IM Marius Amba. With two draws and two wins in the second weekend, Victor clinched his fifth national title with an impressive score of 7 out of 8.

After studying law and running a trading company for 12 years, Caissa was calling, and Victor decided to switch to his life-long passion: chess. Currently, he teaches five classes at the international school Lycée Dominique Savio in Douala.

Last year he founded the Douala Chess Academy with his friend, Bertrand Mbouck, the CEO of Dangote Cameroon. During Covid, most classes were conducted online, but Victor plans to open in a physical location soon. One of his students is Cameroon's U-18 national champion, Whilema Ndjock.

Victor represented his country in two Chess Olympiads, Tromsø (2014) and Batumi (2018). His first Olympiad was quite memorable. It was the first time Victor travelled outside his country and he was still unrated. In the first round, he was paired against IM Suhrob Khamdamov from Tajikistan. Victor built up a winning attack but was unable to deliver the final blow and ended up losing. After the game, Tajikistan's first-board player, GM Farrukh Amonatov, analysed the game with him and showed him how he could have won. Victor was impressed by the kindness of the 'chess family' at the Chess Olympiad.

Victor shows his fighting spirit in the following game fragment and overcomes his opponent, who is rated 250 points higher. Playing with the black pieces, he does not shy away from investing material to get access to the white king and eventually outplays his opponent in the endgame.

VICTOR EBOSSE KINGUE
Cameroon

Yannick Berthelot (2292)
Victor Ebosse Kingue (2043)
Tunesia 2017

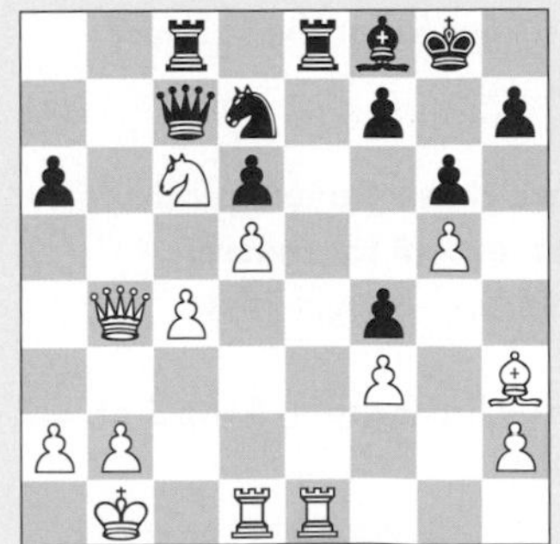

position after 22.♖he1

22...♖b8 Offering an exchange for control of the b-file. **23.♘xb8 ♖xb8 24.♕a4 ♕b6 25.♕b3 ♕c7 26.♕a4 ♕b6** Draw? **27.♖d2** No draw! **27...♘e5 28.♗g2 ♘d3 29.♖ee2 ♘c5 30.♕d1 ♗g7 31.♖c2 ♘a4** All Black's pieces have joined the attack. **32.♕e1? ♗e5?** Black wants to avoid a rook trade after ♖e8+, but could have played 32...♗xb2, making square g7 available to the king. **33.♖xe5 dxe5 34.♕xe5 ♘xb2 35.c5 ♘c4+ 36.cxb6 ♘xe5 37.♖e2 ♖xb6+ 38.♔c2 ♘c4 39.♖e8+ ♔g7 40.♔d3 ♘e3 41.♗h3 ♘xd5 42.♔e4 ♘c3+ 43.♔xf4 ♘xa2 44.♖e7 ♘b4 45.♖a7 ♘c6 46.♖d7 a5 47.♗e6 ♘e5 48.♔xe5 ♖xe6+ 49.♔f4 ♖a6 50.♖d3 a4 51.♖a3 ♔f8 52.h4 ♔e7 53.♔e5 ♖a5+** 0-1.

Victor is Vice-President of the national chess federation FECADE (Fédération Camerounaise des Echecs). In this role, he is working hard to develop the game by attracting more corporate sponsorship and expanding the chess-in-the-schools program. He believes that more schools will add chess to their curriculum once other schools see the positive academic impact of the chess programme at the prestigious international school Lycée Français Dominique Savio. Using the 'Teach-the-Teacher' concept, Victor plans to educate schoolteachers on how to give chess lessons and organize a chess programme in their schools. The best players of the various schools will then be asked to join his Douala Chess Academy, and Victor will nurture the talent of these players directly himself. ■

In **They are The Champions** we pay tribute to national champions across the globe. For suggestions please write to editors@newinchess.com.

David Smerdon

PEAK RATING: **2532**

DATE OF BIRTH: **September 17, 1984**

PLACE OF BIRTH: **Brisbane, Australia**

PLACE OF RESIDENCE: **Brisbane, Australia**

What is your favourite city?
Amsterdam.

What was the last great meal you had?
With my wife at a Korean BBQ joint. It was pretty great, perhaps because I didn't have to clean up after babies for a change.

What drink brings a smile to your face?
Caipirinhas. They remind me of my days backpacking in South America.

Which book would you give to a friend?
Either an accessible introduction to the sort of economics I do, like *Poor Economics* (Banerjee and Duflo) and *Thinking, Fast and Slow* (Kahneman), or else *Africa* by Richard Dowden.

What book is on your bedside table?
The Making of the Fittest by Sean B. Carroll, and *Gone Tomorrow* by Lee Child.

What is your all-time favourite movie?
The Matrix.

And your favourite TV series?
Boston Legal.

Do you have a favourite actor?
Pilou Asbæk.

And a favourite actress?
I like stand-up comedy a lot, and a few of my favourites right now are Katherine Ryan, Aisling Bea, Michelle Wolf and Nikki Glaser.

What music are you listening to?
A Different Kind of Human, by AURORA.

Is there a work of art that moves you?
Not really. I come from a family of artists (painters), but I never caught that bug. A 'psychic' once told me I was the reincarnated soul of Vincent Van Gogh.

What is your earliest chess memory?
When I was five, I used to set up boards in different rooms and move through the house playing games against myself.

Who is your favourite chess player?
Tony Miles. He had a deep psychological awareness of his opponents, which is probably why he was such a fantastic swindler.

Is there a chess book that had a profound influence on you?
Van Perlo's Endgame Tactics. This was the first endgame book I could happily read cover to cover.

What was your best result ever?
My 2012/13 season for Guildford in the 4NCL was quite something; as our manager put it, I scored '8½ points out of 9 lost positions'.

What was the most exciting chess game you ever saw?
Smerdon-Carlsen, Baku 2016. Well, it was the most exciting for me.

What is your favourite square?
Dam Square.

What are chess players particularly good at (except for chess)?
The Dunning-Kruger effect.

Facebook, Instagram, Snapchat, or?
LinkedIn.

How many friends do you have on Facebook?
1900 and shrinking.

Who do you follow on Twitter?
Academics with a sense of humour.

What is your life motto?
Don't be boring.

When were you happiest?
Teaching children in Huaycán, Peru, in 2011.

When was the last time you cried?
I have a faulty tear duct in one eye; I cry every day.

Which three people would you like to invite for dinner?
Slavoj Zizek, Abdulrazak Gurnah and Jeffrey Sachs.

What is the best piece of advice you were ever given?
Block out time in your schedule to relax and think.

What would people be surprised to know about you?
I enjoy my job more than playing chess.

What is your greatest fear?
Irrelevance.

And your greatest regret?
Not playing 21.♗xh7+.

If you could change one thing in the chess world, what would it be?
Developing African chess.

What is the best thing that was ever said about chess?
'A bad position does not discourage me [...] Everybody gets into a bad position once in a while, so that's not a reason at all to simply lose them.' – Tony Miles